W9-CCI-050

DATE DUE

Measuring Up

Measuring Up

Educational Assessment Challenges and Practices for Psychology

Edited by
**Dana S. Dunn,
Chandra M. Mehrotra,
and Jane S. Halonen**

American Psychological Association • Washington, DC

150. 71

M 484

First Printing April 2004
Second Printing November 2005

Published by
American Psychological Association
750 First Street, NE
Washington, DC 20002
www.apa.org

To order
APA Order Department
P.O. Box 92984
Washington, DC 20090-2984
Tel: (800) 374-2721; Direct: (202) 336-5510
Fax: (202) 336-5502; TDD/TTY: (202) 336-6123
Online: www.apa.org/books/
E-mail: order@apa.org

In the U.K., Europe, Africa, and the Middle East, copies may be ordered from
American Psychological Association
3 Henrietta Street
Covent Garden, London
WC2E 8LU England

Typeset in Goudy by Stephen McDougal, Mechanicsville, MD

Printer: United Book Press, Inc., Baltimore, MD
Cover Designer: Mercury Publishing, Rockville, MD
Technical/Production Editor: Rosemary Moulton

The opinions and statements published are the responsibility of the authors, and such opinions and statements do not necessarily represent the policies of the American Psychological Association.

Library of Congress Cataloging-in-Publication Data

Measuring up : educational assessment challenges and practices for psychology / edited by Dana S. Dunn, Chandra M. Mehrotra, and Jane S. Halonen.
   p. cm.
  Includes bibliographical references and indexes.
  ISBN 1-59147-108-7 (alk. paper)
  1. Psychology—Study and teaching—Evaluation. I. Dunn, Dana. II. Mehrotra, Chandra. III. Halonen, Jane S.

  BF77.M385 2004
  150'.71—dc22   2004004235

British Library Cataloguing-in-Publication Data
A CIP record is available from the British Library.

Printed in the United States of America

To the participants in the Psychology Partnerships Project,
All-Stars all

CONTENTS

CONTRIBUTORS

William E. Addison, Eastern Illinois University, Charleston

Virginia Andreoli Mathie, James Madison University, Harrisonburg, VA

Kevin J. Apple, James Madison University, Harrisonburg, VA

Kenneth E. Barron, James Madison University, Harrisonburg, VA

Ronan S. Bernas, Eastern Illinois University, Charleston

Theodore N. Bosack, Providence College, Providence, RI

Caridad F. Brito, Eastern Illinois University, Charleston

Shirley P. Clay, Northeast Texas Community College, Mt. Pleasant

Nancy J. Cooledge, Mansfield University, Mansfield, PA

Francis W. Craig, Mansfield University, Mansfield, PA

Patrick J. Devine, Kennesaw State University, Kennesaw, GA

Donna Killian Duffy, Middlesex Community College, Lowell, MA

Dana S. Dunn, Moravian College, Bethlehem, PA

Michael Firment, Kennesaw State University, Kennesaw, GA

George D. Goedel, Northern Kentucky University, Highland Heights

Jane S. Halonen, University of West Florida, Pensacola

Diane F. Halpern, Berger Institute for Work, Family and Children, Claremont McKenna College, Claremont, CA; American Psychological Association, Washington, DC

Peter A. Keller, Mansfield University, Mansfield, PA

Margaret H. Launius, Mansfield University, Mansfield, PA

Brian T. Loher, Mansfield University, Mansfield, PA

Maureen A. McCarthy, Austin Peay State University, Clarksville, TN; American Psychological Association, Washington, DC

Rob McEntarffer, Lincoln Southeast High School, Lincoln, NE

Thomas V. McGovern, Arizona State University West, Phoenix

Chandra M. Mehrotra, College of St. Scholastica, Duluth, MN

Paul Nelson, American Psychological Association, Washington, DC

Randall E. Osborne, Southwest Texas State University, San Marcos
Retta E. Poe, Western Kentucky University, Bowling Green
Thomas P. Pusateri, Florida Atlantic University, Boca Raton
Monica Reis-Bergan, James Madison University, Harrisonburg, VA
Anupama Sharma, Eastern Illinois University, Charleston
Robert J. Sternberg, Yale University, New Haven, CT
Michael L. Stoloff, James Madison University, Harrisonburg, VA
Donna Sundre, James Madison University, Harrisonburg, VA
Walter F. Wagor, Indiana University East, Richmond
Kenneth A. Weaver, Emporia State University, Emporia, KS
Valerie Whittlesey, Kennesaw State University, Kennesaw, GA

FOREWORD

VIRGINIA ANDREOLI MATHIE

It is truly an honor to write the foreword for this extraordinary and innovative book showcasing best practices in assessment in psychology education. The book is a timely and invaluable resource for all psychology teachers and administrators as they respond to the growing demands to incorporate assessment into the culture of higher education.

There are many factors driving the assessment movement. Parents and state legislatures, facing increasing costs for higher education, demand evidence that their investments are paying off in tangible desirable outcomes. With the baccalaureate degree serving as the entry-level degree for many jobs in today's marketplace, employers want evidence that college graduates do indeed have the knowledge and skills the educational institutions claim their students have acquired. The ethnic, racial, cultural, and age diversity of college students is growing, and the life experiences, values, learning styles, college preparedness, and goals students bring to their educational endeavors vary widely.

Assessment is a vital tool in helping institutions determine if they are meeting the academic needs of all of these students and preparing them to be successful in tomorrow's marketplace and society. As an increasing number of students at four-year colleges and universities acquire some of their college credits from community colleges, certificate programs, distance learning programs, for-profit education institutions, and corporate universities, the ability to assess student competencies is a critical element in ensuring high quality across a variety of educational venues. Accrediting agencies also contribute to assessment pressures by requiring institutions to establish educational goals and objectives, assess student competencies to determine if the institutions have met their objectives, and use assessment data to improve the educational experience.

Psychology is responding to these demands. Indeed, as pointed out in the final chapter of this book, psychology has been on the forefront of the assessment movement, with psychologists producing some of the early seminal books, chapters, and articles on educational assessment. It is evident that there is a cadre of psychology educators who value assessment, possess the skills to do assessment effectively, and are dedicated to implementing assessment activities in their programs. What has been lacking, however, are examples of successful and practical models for integrating assessment into all aspects of psychology education from high school through graduate school. Now, with the publication of this unique book, psychology educators finally have these models.

The impetus for this volume, *Measuring Up: Educational Assessment Challenges and Practices for Psychology*, was the first national conference on assessment issues in psychology, held in September 2002. The conference was conceived at the *National Forum on Psychology Partnerships* held in June 1999. The forum was the centerpiece of the *Psychology Partnerships Project: Academic Partnerships to Meet the Teaching and Learning Needs of the 21st Century* (P3), an initiative sponsored by the American Psychological Association's Board of Educational Affairs and Education Directorate. P3 brought together psychology teachers from high schools, community colleges, four-year colleges and universities, and graduate programs to address critical issues in psychology education. One of these issues was assessment in psychology education. I chaired P3 and had the privilege of working with the dedicated and visionary group of teachers who planned and implemented the conference and spearheaded the production of this book.

It is gratifying to see this extraordinary final product—a book that is truly unique in its scope and invaluable as a resource for psychology educators in all academic settings. The authors, leaders in psychology education and assessment, have written a book that contains thoughtful discussions of assessment issues as well as practical guidelines and successful models that teachers and administrators can use to formulate and guide their own assessment plans. In this one volume the reader will find innovative strategies for assessment at every level, from assessing student learning and competencies to assessing psychology courses (both traditional and distance learning courses), programs, and departments, using a variety of techniques, including self-assessment, authentic assessment, student and administrative portfolios, and departmental self-studies. Congratulations to all contributors to this volume for writing a book that teachers and administrators will want to keep close at hand for regular consultation.

PREFACE

Assessment fever has swept through higher education. Psychologists—teachers, researchers, and administrators—have long been concerned with what and how well students are learning, retaining, and applying disciplinary information; however, growing national concerns about educational accountability encourage greater scrutiny of what we strive to accomplish in the psychology classroom, regardless of the specific academic context. As this book attests, the concern about assessing psychology education is broad and deep, involving teachers at the high school, two-year college, and four-year college and university levels.

The problem for psychology education is obvious: Few available resources tackle assessment by outlining concrete practices. Educators and administrators want access to effective research on teaching and learning that can be applied in the classroom or shared with the public. This book fills the current void in assessing outcomes, measuring achievement, and promoting quality instruction in psychology. It does so for several compelling reasons. First, there are no current books examining student assessment in psychology education. Yet student assessment is a nascent, lively topic in educational circles, so a resource like this one is long overdue. Second, the discipline of psychology has not yet formally endorsed recognized competencies and outcomes that are widely available or publicly accepted. This volume is a first step toward doing so. Third, disparate assessment articles are available in the psychological literature but are not readily available in a single source like this one. This book is a moveable feast of assessment options, great and small.

Psychology educators and administrators at all levels—high school, two-year institutions, undergraduate college and university departments, and graduate programs—will find much to use here. They will be interested in the book because of its practical application to what they do each day, notably the thoughtful balance between assessing teaching and assessing student learning. Novice teachers and graduate students with teaching opportunities will find practical tools and techniques for course development, classroom management, and assessing student performance and knowledge. Seasoned professionals can rely on this book for retooling their efforts in the classroom as well as the conference room. The chapters in this book may be of interest to colleagues from other disciplines, who may find compelling comparisons and potential solutions for their respective assessment challenges.

Educational enterprises, especially new ones, are inevitably based on the good work of many committed individuals. This book is no different. Our forays into assessment would not have been possible without the responsible, thoughtful, and energetic efforts of our authors. We are also grateful for the collective and sustained efforts of our fellow Assessment All-Stars: Theodore N. Bosack (Providence College), Shirley P. Clay (Northeast Texas Community College), G. William Hill IV (Kennesaw State University), Maureen A. McCarthy (Austin Peay State University and the American Psychological Association [APA]), Rob McEntarffer (Lincoln Southeast High School), Robbye Nesmith (Navarro College), Kenneth A. Weaver (Emporia State University), and Kristin Whitlock (Davis County School District). Their enthusiasm for and hard work toward various assessment initiatives over the past several years is inspiring. Finally, we thank our colleagues at APA, especially Lansing Hays and Kristine Enderle, who guided the book skillfully through the production process.

On behalf of our authors, we hope this book will help teachers and administrators validate their efforts while ultimately improving how students learn about and contribute to the discipline of psychology.

I

OVERVIEW OF ASSESSMENT CHALLENGES AND PRACTICES

AN INTRODUCTION TO ASSESSMENT CHALLENGES AND PRACTICES FOR PSYCHOLOGY

DANA S. DUNN, CHANDRA M. MEHROTRA, AND JANE S. HALONEN

A variety of external constituencies are challenging psychology teachers and administrators to present solid evidence that instruction is both effective and demonstrative. The constituencies involved vary, including parents, employers, and local, state, and national accrediting boards. Whatever their interest, all parties recognize the need for convenient, interpretable, and comprehensive assessment of student learning (e.g., O'Neil, 1992; Schneider & Schoenberg, 1998). These calls for accountability mean that designing, adapting, and using appropriate assessment methods and tools are now a paramount concern for educators (Maki, 2001). Beyond these external pressures, most teachers have an intrinsic and genuine interest in producing clear evidence of student learning. Just as we want to measure student outcomes, as teachers, we want to "measure up," as well.

Assessment—the measurement and evaluation of learning—should encourage student competence (Mentkowski et al., 2000); highlight standards for student performance ("benchmarks") teachers can use to demonstrate learning (e.g., Astin, 1993; Banta, Lund, Black, & Oblander, 1996); enable administrators to track student achievement and gauge quality of in-

3

struction; and provide future directions for relevant research and application. Although proposals for identifying a set of educational standards for psychology exist (e.g., Allen, Noel, Deegan, Halpen, & Crawford, 2000; Graham, 1998; Halpern et al., 1993; Sheehan & Granrud, 1995; see also, Benjamin, 2001), as yet no shared agreement regarding what to do with them does. Left to their own devices, many teachers and administrators rely on traditional, often questionable, objective tests without ensuring that these measures are linked with what students really learn, or with the outcomes they are expected to achieve (Shavelson & Huang, 2003).

To address this important need, we sought contributions from nationally recognized practitioners of educational assessment. They present current scholarship on and encourage future research efforts toward effective, efficient, and useful assessment in psychology education at secondary and post-secondary levels. Drawing upon their experience they offer guidance and practical techniques for introducing meaningful, authentic assessments for psychology classrooms, curricula, and programs. Our contributors' chapters are organized into four sections: key issues in assessment, departmental models, a collection of specific "best practices" in assessment, and a commentary on the progress of assessment in psychology education.

KEY ISSUES IN ASSESSMENT

The first section of this book identifies the key issues in educational assessment in psychology. Diane F. Halpern (chap. 1) summarizes the calls for evidence and makes the case that assessment is neither a luxury nor a burden. She explains why demonstrating learning as an educational outcome only recently became a concern in and outside the academic community. Previously, authentic learning was simply *assumed* to occur and concrete proof was neither wanted nor sought after. Things have changed dramatically, however, and Halpern reminds us that psychology educators have the tools and training to do assessment; we need only commit ourselves to the task. She reviews guidelines for quality assessment practices that can help teachers and administrators think about and set up effective assessment practices at their institutions. As readers will learn, the skills teachers believe our students are learning are precisely the ones we should be assessing. Halpern also identifies a variety of measurement issues and concrete tools for teachers of psychology to consider.

MODELS FOR DEPARTMENTAL ASSESSMENT AND PROGRAM EVALUATION

The decision to implement educational assessment in any teaching institution involves many choices and participants. Ideally, serious efforts at assessment should begin at the departmental level. Effective programs and departments, as well as experienced administrators, recommend beginning assessment by examining what efforts are already in place.

Michael L. Stoloff, Kevin J. Apple, Kenneth E. Barron, Monica Reis-Bergan, and Donna Sundre, all of James Madison University (JMU, chap. 2), describe their department's focus on issues of content, curriculum, and outcomes. Their institution has a well-established culture of assessment and their department relies on the evaluation of student learning and performance as an organizing theme for the psychology program. Stoloff and colleagues discuss seven goals that guide assessment activities and accompanying measures in all areas of the department. A strength of the JMU approach is the ready acceptance of assessment by students, teachers, and administrators; indeed, the psychology faculty find that collecting and interpreting assessment data is a natural extension of their accustomed roles as academic psychologists and educators.

Michael Firment, Patrick J. Devine, and Valerie Whittlesey of Kennesaw State University (chap. 3) describe another approach to assessing an undergraduate program that serves a large number of both traditional and nontraditional students. They present useful matrices to illustrate how the focus and the methods of their assessment program have changed over time. They illustrate how assessment can directly benefit program and curricular development and increase student satisfaction and retention by presenting in detail (a) how they designed and used advising surveys by involving faculty and students; (b) how they used the results to create an advisement center, a careers in psychology course, and a coordinator of assessment position; and (c) how they documented the impact of these changes in increased student satisfaction and enrollment. Readers will find Kennesaw's advisement survey to be very helpful at their own institutions.

Besides evaluating students, of course, psychology teachers must also conduct periodic reviews of their programs. Should an existing program be continued? How might it be improved? Thomas P. Pusateri, Retta E. Poe, William E. Addison, and George D. Goedel (chap. 4) provide a helpful structure for conceiving and executing a quality departmental self-study report. Beyond providing a detailed explanation regarding how to conduct an internal survey, Pusateri and colleagues present valuable advice on selecting, inviting, and hosting an external reviewer or reviewing team to conduct a program review. The suggestions found in this chapter make the idea of conducting a self-study or hosting an external review much less daunting. Departments and their chairpersons, too, will benefit from the clear suggestions on how to effectively discuss report results with administrators in order to implement recommendations.

The final contribution in this section is by Kenneth A. Weaver (chap. 5), who is concerned with helping the administrative leaders of programs, departments, or schools document what they do well while reflecting on the accountability issues inherent in their positions. Weaver advocates that academic leaders, notably department chairs, should create their own "administrative portfolios," a written description of an individual's administrative activities coupled with solid evidence of his or her effectiveness. This novel alternative to teacher or student portfolios (see Keller and colleagues, (chap. 10, this volume) gives department chairs or other administrators an opportunity to reflect on accomplishments, to address key constituents (e.g., provosts, deans, departmental colleagues) about their work, and to develop direction for the next stage in their administrative careers.

BEST PRACTICES IN ASSESSMENT

Quality assessments can be implemented in a variety of ways in psychology education. Some forms of assessment are occasional, others continue throughout a student's education. This section of "best practices" offers an array of possibilities that readers can choose, use, and modify according to their own campus customs, departmental standards, or specific course needs. A clear advantage of these best practices is that some will appeal to individual instructors, others to whole departments or programs.

This section opens with an obvious assessment problem in psychology: Robert J. Sternberg (chap. 6) asks how assessment tools can be used to illustrate successful intelligence among students? He explains why the kinds of learning and thinking that are typically rewarded in the classroom (very often at the introductory level) do not necessarily reflect what students actually need to know in order to succeed in the discipline. Using clear examples and a compelling theory of successful intelligence, Sternberg explains how instructors at all levels can use different types of instruction and accompanying assessment methods in any class in order to capitalize on the strengths of all students. Introducing straightforward changes to our teaching and testing can expose students to assessments calling upon memory-based as well as analytical, creative, practical, and synthesized items. Sternberg suggests how teachers can adopt new assessments, provide evidence for the effectiveness of the successful intelligence model, and anticipate potential objections for various quarters.

Assessment works best when it is ongoing and when the course objectives have been explicitly stated. With clear objectives, instructors can establish fair standards and criteria for student performance and conduct formative assessment to facilitate students' progress toward achieving the desired objectives. Randall E. Osborne and Walter F. Wagor (chap. 7) present an integrative model they have developed to conduct formative assessment. The model's five steps include defining objectives, deciding assessment methods, describing assessment goals to students, discovering students' progress and providing feedback, and determining what instructional changes need to be made. The authors provide useful examples from introductory psychology courses to illustrate the model and these procedures.

Besides demonstrating the acquisition of knowledge, assessment strategies can also be used to help students develop scientific inquiry skills in psychology. Theodore N. Bosack, Maureen A. McCarthy, Jane S. Halonen, and Shirley P. Clay (chap. 8) describe how authentic assessment can be used in concert with the rubric for scientific reasoning they developed previously (Halonen et al., 2003). This rubric, which identifies disciplinary domains and skill areas, can be used in a variety of ways in psychology education. Bosack and his colleagues present three practical applications of the rubric at different levels of psychology education. They also present suggestions for scoring the authentic assessments derived from the rubric. Readers will find the rubric to be readily applicable for both teaching and class assessment, a constructive way for students and teachers to monitor the development of theoretical and practical reasoning about the science of psychology.

One aspect of the Halonen et al. (2003) rubric advocates that assessment is not limited to teachers tracking student learning—students themselves can assess their own learning. As Dana S. Dunn, Rob McEntarffer, and Jane S. Halonen (chap. 9) argue, assessment is very much about "doing," especially when students are provided with guidance and insight into self-assessment. Using the rubric for assessing scientific reasoning (Halonen et al., 2003; Bosack et al., chap. 8, this volume), these authors discuss how self-regulatory and self-reflective practices vary at different points of students' intellectual development in psychology. Dunn and colleagues describe how students' self-assessment changes from basic through professional levels of development. The chief benefit of self-assessment, of course, is that students become responsible for their own learning.

One of the more popular pedagogical innovations in the past decade, the student portfolio, turns out to be a very effective method for assessing a variety of learning outcomes. Peter A. Keller, Francis W. Craig, Margaret H. Launius, Brian T. Loher, and Nancy J. Cooledge (chap. 10) describe how the development of a comprehensive portfolio of student learning in psychology is helpful in improving their department's program and major. The portfolios represent a venue for students to present examples of their best work in psychology—from major declaration up to graduation—and for teachers to assess the quality and depth of the lessons learned. Keller and colleagues describe how the portfolio exercise came into being and why it is now a seamless and valued aspect of pedagogy in their department.

The next best practice deals with one of the more practical matters of psychology education—demonstrating student learning through comprehensive examinations. Caridad F. Brito, Anupama Sharma, and Ronan S. Bernas (chap. 11) discuss the pros and cons of developing a local or department-generated comprehensive exam. Although several national comprehensive tests exist, creating one tailored to a single department's orientation has decided benefits for the students who must take it and the teachers who must use scores on it to evaluate and improve instruction. Brito and colleagues do a fine job of outlining the process of creating a local comprehensive exam, assessing its reliability and validity, and then linking results to departmental learning goals and the psychology curriculum.

Nontraditional approaches to psychology education must also be open to assessment. One of the newest and increasingly popular innovations is distance learning, where technology carries the instructor, course materials, and fellow classmates "virtually" to students. Chandra M. Mehrotra, Kenneth A. Weaver, and Paul Nelson (chap. 12) describe the issues and expectations concerning the remote assessment of courses and student learning therein. As the authors demonstrate, distance learning in psychology has distinct advantages for learners, a reality that encourages faculty and administrators to incorporate meaningful assessments in the creation and maintenance of these courses.

The last chapter in this section emphasizes that best practices in assessment are by no means limited to either student or teacher-centered venues. Donna Killian Duffy's chapter (chap. 13) examines the role service learning can play by educating students as they participate in community settings. Her particular interest centers on resilience as a generative topic for students to study in abnormal psychology. Duffy describes assessment challenges and benefits in creating a "permeable classroom," one where students actively apply course material out and about in a community settings ad with the people who inhabit them. She reports that students are enthusiastic when they can work closely with clients in the community and then share their experiences with classmates. Duffy outlines the authentic assessment in her course, illustrating how community service and the theme of resilience can lead to authentic learning.

ASSESSING ASSESSMENT IN PSYCHOLOGY

Assessment is as much about looking forward as it is looking back over what has been learned. In this book's final chapter, we invited Thomas V. McGovern to offer thoughtful comments on the origins of the assessment movement in higher education and a look back at the precursors to assessment in psychology education. McGovern also comments on the contributions in this book, the challenges they highlight, and the future directions our authors pose. He concludes by considering a postdisciplinary, liberal arts future for the discipline of psychology and its assessment orientation.

PROSPECTS FOR ASSESSMENT IN PSYCHOLOGY EDUCATION

As the messages, models, and practices presented in this book testify, the prospects for meaningful assessment at all levels of psychology education are excellent. At the outset of the assessment movement, many educators reported feeling bullied by top-down assessment initiatives that felt like so much busy work, yet another unwelcome "add-on" to already packed academic lives (Hutchings, 1990). However, many in the psychology education community have willingly responded to the call to provide evidence to substantiate our claims of pedagogical and disciplinary excellence. The educators' enthusiasm, creativity, and rigor demonstrate a productive, scholarly response to the call of assessment and accountability. The contributions in this book suggest that psychology appropriately embraces leadership in the area of educational assessment. We believe that this book offers a trove of tools and techniques for making assessment an integral and welcome part of psychology education at all types of institutions. We and our contributors look forward to working with other educators from psychology and other disciplines to promote models and practices that will serve the learner and the teacher more effectively in the future. All of us can, should, indeed must, continue to "measure up" in our classrooms, departments, and educational institutions.

REFERENCES

Allen, M. J., Noel, R., Deegan, J., Halpern, D., & Crawford, C. (2000). *Goals and objectives for the undergraduate major: Recommendations from a meeting of the California State University psychology faculty.* Retrieved January 21, 2002, from http://www.lemoune.edu/OTRP/otrpresources/otrp_outcomes.html

Astin, A. W. (1993). *Assessment for excellence: The philosophy and practice of assessment and evaluation in higher education.* New York: Macmillan.

Banta, T. W., Lund, J. P., Black, K. E., & Oblander, F. W. (1996). *Assessment in practice: Putting principles to work on college campuses.* San Francisco: Jossey-Bass.

Benjamin, L. T. Jr. (2001). American psychology's struggles with its curriculum: Should a thousand flowers bloom? *American Psychologist, 56,* 735–742.

Graham, S. E. (1998). Developing student outcomes for the psychology major: An assessment-as-learning framework. *Current Directions in Psychological Science, 7,* 165–170.

Halonen, J. S., Bosack, T., Clay, S., & McCarthy, M. (with Dunn, D. S., Hill IV, G. W., McEntarffer, R., Mehrotra, C., Nesmith, R., Weaver, K., & Whitlock, K.). (2003). A rubric for authentically learning, teaching, and assessing scientific reasoning in psychology. *Teaching of Psychology, 30,* 196–208.

Halpern, D. F., Appleby, D. C., Beers, S. E., Cowan, C. L., Furedy, J. J., Halonen, J. S., et al. (1993). Targeting outcomes: Covering your assessment concerns and needs. In T. V. McGovern (Ed.), *Handbook for enhancing undergraduate education in psychology* (pp. 23–46). Washington, DC: American Psychological Association.

Hutchings, P. (1990, June 30). *Assessment and the way we work.* Closing plenary, 5th American Association of Higher Education Conference on Assessment, Washington, DC.

Maki, P. L. (2001). From standardized tests to alternative methods: Some current resources on methods to assess learning in general education. *Change, 33*(2), 29–31.

Mentkowski, M., Rogers, G., Doherty, A., Loacker, G., Hart, J. R., Richards, W., et al. (2000). *Learning that lasts: Integrating learning, development, and performance in college and beyond.* San Francisco: Jossey-Bass.

O'Neil, J. (1992). Putting performance assessment to the test. *Educational Leadership, 49*(8) 14–19.

Schneider, C. G., & Schoenberg, R. (1998). *The academy in transition: Contemporary understandings of liberal education.* Washington, DC: American Association of Colleges and Universities.

Shavelson, R. J., & Huang, L. (January/February 2003). Responding responsibly to the frenzy to assess learning in higher education. *Change, 35*, 1.

Sheehan, E. P., & Granrud, C. E. (1995). Assessment of student outcomes: Evaluating an undergraduate program. *Journal of Instructional Psychology, 22*, 366–372.

1

OUTCOMES ASSESSMENT 101

DIANE F. HALPERN

Is your department doing a good job of educating its students? How do you know? These two questions are at the heart of student outcomes assessment and, by extension, of discussions about educational quality. It is a good bet that the overwhelming majority of readers responded to my first question with an enthusiastic nod. I make this bet on the basis of the responses I have received to this question when I posed it to groups of faculty at the approximately 40 presentations I have made on this topic over the last two decades. My second question is most often answered with a few anecdotes about stellar graduates and some indignation that I would even ask for evidence of learning from college and university faculty. Tales of former students whose post-graduation lives would make any office of alumni affairs proud are rarely followed with data about more typical alumni and virtually never with anecdotes about those who are an embarrassment to their alma mater or students who never made it to graduation. Every college and university has a list of outstanding alumni of whom they are rightfully proud, but few consider that their most outstanding alumni are hardly representative of the vast majority of current or former students.

Although most faculty and campus administrators believe that they are doing a good or excellent job of educating their students, we are clearly in the minority with this belief as higher education has been the focus of considerable criticism over the past two decades as multiple Blue Ribbon Panels have examined the health of our nation's colleges (e.g., Boyer Commission, 1998; National Commission on Excellence in Education, 1983; Secretary's Commission on Achieving Necessary Skills, 2000). For the most part, their conclusions are scathing; they have not minced words in decrying the quality of undergraduate education. Private industry, prospective students and their families, faculty and administrators, the military, and state agencies have joined the various task forces created to examine the status of higher education and have begun to demand evidence that the large and growing amount of public money spent on higher education is producing educated adults.

A number of factors have come together to create a climate for assessment. Perhaps the most persuasive reason for embarking on a nationwide effort to assess outcomes in higher education comes from concern over the crisis in human capital. North American students routinely rank below those from other parts of the industrialized world in academic areas such as scientific knowledge, mathematical problem solving, and general literacy (National Center for Education Statistics, 2000). Economists and politicians have argued that the poor performance of North American students indicates a threat to our ability to remain a world leader in science and technology. Individuals and agencies that share this concern believe that the information gained from outcomes assessment will provide direction for our efforts to keep America's work force strong and competitive (and cooperative) as we enter the 21st century. If these noble and, I believe, logical reasons for assessing student learning are not convincing, *every* accrediting agency in the United States requires that we examine educational outcomes (Council for Higher Education Accreditation, 2002).

STUDENT OUTCOMES ASSESSMENT: A PRETEST

Given that this book is about the assessment of learning, it is only logical to begin with a pretest against which we can assess later learning. Readers will be glad to know that this is a one-question test that is obviously not entirely serious in its intent.

Outcomes Assessment is

(a) more work than it's worth;
(b) a plot to get rid of faculty without going through standard personnel procedures for retention, promotion, and tenure;
(c) unneeded because we already test students in all of their classes;
(d) a sneaky way to give departments less money (I'm not sure how—but there will be less money); or
(e) a communist plot (where are the communists when we need a scapegoat?).

These are, of course, meant to be humorous alternatives, but they are a sample of the responses that faculty and administrators commonly raise when they learn that they are now being expected to provide evidence that the students in their classes and in their majors are learning.

The assessment of student outcomes has become one of the most controversial topics in higher education. Some faculty in colleges and universities that have collective bargaining have turned to their union representatives for clarity as to how they should be responding to this new mandate. For the most part, unions have focused on the workload implications of requiring faculty to go beyond grades earned in individual classes when assessing and reporting student learning. I think that it is safe to say that student outcomes assessment generates strong emotions, although these emotions are often not data based.

TRADITIONAL INDICATORS OF EDUCATIONAL QUALITY

How does the general public make decisions about the educational quality of any college or university? This is an important question because millions of students enroll in higher education in the United States every year, and, if we broaden our question to include students in all countries, many times that number make such decisions. How are prospective students and their parents making important decisions about where to apply and where to attend after the acceptances are received? On the basis of annual sales of U.S. News and World Report and other similar publications, large numbers of prospective students rely on the college and university rankings that are announced with all the hype of a new-model car (Arnone, 2003). The colleges and universities that make it into these rankings are often unwilling participants in a game that I have named "the tyranny of the rankings." How do the staff at U.S. News and World Report and other publications that make huge sums of money by arranging colleges and universities on a single dimension labeled "quality" decide who is best, who is second best, and who is out?

Many ranking systems use a weighted combination of seven categories (or some similar list): (a) the opinions of college administrators (hardly an unbiased source of data); (b) student retention rates (which are important, but highly correlated with characteristics of entering students—variables such as the educational level of their parents, for example); (c) faculty resources, which includes faculty salaries (as a faculty member, I tend to favor this category because it should keep salaries high); (d) selectivity of the school, usually indexed by the Scholastic Aptitude Test (SAT) scores of entering students; (e) financial resources (richer is better in case you had any doubt—a large endowment will garner a higher rank than a small endowment); (f) alumni giving measured in percentage of alumni who donate money to their alma mater (richer is better here, too); and (g) graduation rates (certainly important, but also highly correlated with characteristics of incoming students).

Can you think about something really important that is missing from this popular index of educational quality? How about student learning? There are no indicators of whether students actually learn anything while they are at the college or university. Faculty and administrators often respond to these rankings from both sides of their mouths. Publicly, they protest that these rankings have little merit and that a multidimensional construct like educational quality cannot be captured with a single rank order, but they also respond that, if there are rankings that influence how prospective students select schools, they want their institution to be near the top. The result of these systems of ranking is that colleges are competing fiercely for students with high SAT scores because SAT scores count in the rankings and they tend to ignore other indicators of student potential, such as an unusual talent in music, art, or science.

If we care about something, we measure it, and when we have to report our measures for public scrutiny, we care even more. This maxim has empirical support. A recent study found that educational systems with external exams have more indicators of enhanced learning than those without external exams (Bishop, 2000). Given the variables that are assessed in the rankings game, it should not be surprising to learn that colleges and universities are not paying much attention to whether, what, or how well students learn after their admission. In any educational system, outputs are highly correlated with inputs, so the students who enter college with high SAT scores will also graduate with high scores on standardized measures, and any "value added" learning that occurred during their undergraduate years is not likely to be captured with the rankings system. No wonder there is so much hostility and confusion over the assessment of educational quality.

DEFINING TERMS

Part of the commotion about assessing student educational outcomes is due to differences in the way these terms are used and the many possible uses and abuses of outcomes assessment data. Student outcomes assessment is a term that conveys multiple meanings to those engaged in the debate about quality in higher education. Student outcomes assessment refers to a wide range of activities that involve gathering and examining data for the purpose of improving teaching and learning (Halpern, 1988; Halpern et al., 1993). Of course, if you have bad data or make faulty inferences from good data, you end up with an outcome that is not likely to have the desired effect of improving teaching and learning. When done well, however, outcomes assessment has the potential to enhance student growth, foster faculty development, and accomplish real educational objectives.

PRACTICING WHAT WE PREACH AND TEACH

Virtually every program of study in psychology includes a course or courses on research methods (Perlman & McCann, 1999). The scientific bases of our discipline have become a mantra as we teach our students how to determine whether an intervention has been effective. We expect our students to know that they need quality data to decide, for example, whether a particular form of psychotherapy alleviated depression or whether abusive parents caused psychological harm to their children. Research methods form the backbone of the social and physical sciences. It would seem hypocritical if we did not apply the same basic principles that we teach in our classrooms to determine the effectiveness of our teaching. I think of teaching and learning as a continuum and not two distinct processes because it is difficult to conceptualize teaching in a situation in which no one learns. (If I taught something and no one learned, can we call what I did teaching?) To link teaching and learning, one needs some evidence or assessment of learning that can then be used to direct the teaching process so that it becomes a continuous cycle of teaching, learning, and assessment. Despite the difficulties associated with changing the way we think about the teaching–learning cycle, many of the players in higher education have come to realize that "without tests, we flunk" (Doyle, 1991, p. 1).

As Denis Philip Doyle (1991) so eloquently said in an editorial in the *Washington Post*:

> Modern organizational theory's most important insight is that you must know what your objectives are, specify them in ways that can be measured, measure them and report the results. It is the only way to rationalize the process of design, production, and delivery. For schools, it is the minimum that the public can rightfully expect. (p. 2)

The assessment of educational outcomes can take many forms, but regardless of the specific decisions about who, what, and how to assess, good programs all share some common attributes. These guiding principles should help to ease some of the distrust that often surfaces when faculty are asked to provide evidence of what and how much students are learning in addition to the single letter grade that faculty assign to each student in each course. In planning a program to assess student learning, one strategy is to collect and report data in ways that minimize the probability that they can be misused, while maximizing information that can be used to improve the teaching–learning continuum.

GENERAL GUIDELINES FOR GOOD PRACTICE

In thinking about assessing the outcomes of education, it is often better to keep broad principles in mind than to decide on the specifics of any program because the general principles can be used to guide programmatic decisions and keep all of the stakeholders focused on the reasons why we engage in educational assessment as they plan for the "how" of educational assessment.

1. **The purpose of student outcomes assessment is to improve teaching and learning. It is important to keep this goal in mind because it can be used to guide the many decisions that have to be made when designing an assessment program.** Therefore, one feature of a good outcomes assessment program is that it is student-centered (Halpern et al., 1993). Information about individual students should be used to help them select courses, plan careers, and develop life views. The information gained from an outcomes assessment is best provided in a way that students can monitor their own cognitive and attitudinal gains (or losses) while they are enrolled in college.

   Faculty should receive information that they can use to improve individual classes and the way they teach, and institutions can use the data to direct curricular change and development. For example, in my former department we sampled senior research projects from six different sections of the course and assessed them on many dimensions, including how well the students understood the principles of the research method they used in their projects, how well they reported and analyzed their own data, writing, and knowledge of the content area. We used these assessments to identify what we were doing well in our instruction in the major and what areas needed improvement. We then went back to examine where in the curriculum these topics were being taught and used. We worked on ways to strengthen those areas in which student scores were lowest. In our report to the university, we explained how we were monitoring our student learning outcomes and what we were doing to improve them. Data were not reported for any individual faculty member (samples were selected from several different sections taught by several faculty), nor did we need to provide data that would make us "look good" to the administration. In this way, we avoided the potential misuse of the data, and we were comfortable in examining our own strengths and weaknesses as a department.

2. **There is no single indicator of educational effectiveness. No single number can capture the multifaceted nature of an effective college education or the cognitive growth of an adult student.** All good programs use multiple measures that

are qualitatively different. Thus, the sample of research projects by seniors was only one of several measures that we used in answering the basic question of how well we were achieving the educational goals we established for our students.

3. **Successful assessment programs are owned by faculty.** It is the faculty who are responsible for the curriculum and the process of higher education, and it is the faculty who must direct any assessment of the educational effectiveness of their courses and their teaching. Faculty know what they are teaching in their classes and the underlying rationales that were used in structuring the major (or general education program or other program that is being assessed). Decisions about the way data are generated and used rest with appropriate faculty committees.

4. **The expertise and hard work that are involved in a quality assessment of educational objectives must be recognized and rewarded in a manner that is comparable to other professional activities.** A good program of outcomes assessment requires hard work. There needs to be an appropriate reward system for the faculty who are willing to do it. They are using the skills of their discipline and advanced knowledge of student learning and their content matter. In this way, student outcomes assessment is similar to any other research project. It is a prototypical example of the scholarship of learning (Halpern et al., 1998). Directors of assessment programs should receive the same consideration in the retention, promotion, and tenure process as faculty engaged in the more traditional research and committee assignments. Similarly, departments that engage in a thoughtful analysis of their programs and follow sound educational practices should reap some of the rewards that are customary in higher education such as increases in budget or support staff.

5. **Outcomes assessment programs create natural links with the other segments of higher education (i.e., high schools, two- and four-year colleges, doctoral programs).** These activities create opportunities for real learning partnerships across educational institutions and levels of education. Institutions can form regional collectives for the purpose of tracking student progress and monitoring the variables that are associated with student success, such as course-taking patterns, contiguous enrollment, and preparation for transfer. When the focus is on student learning, it is not meaningful to separate learning outcomes into discrete "packets" that correspond to community college, baccalaureate degree programs, and

graduate school because, ideally, the learning is connected (from the learner's perspective). Student outcomes assessment encourages a holistic view of learning.

6. **No program can succeed unless care is taken to ensure that data are not misused. Student outcomes assessment should not be used as an indicator of faculty performance.** I understand that there are many experts in higher education who vehemently disagree with this principle, arguing that the best measure of a teacher's effectiveness is what and how much students learn. I maintain that student outcomes assessment data are not appropriate for use in the faculty promotion, retention, and tenure process. If faculty believe that the data will be used in this manner, the entire enterprise will be subverted. It is fairly trivial to devise "look good" measures of student learning. We can hardly expect faculty to examine student learning critically if they will be punished if they find any shortcomings or areas that need improvement.

7. **The greatest strength of American higher education is its diversity. There is no single set of desirable outcomes that would apply to all psychology majors or all psychology departments for example.** Although there must be some commonalities among majors of the same discipline, homogenization of majors or campuses is not good for education. Each program of outcomes assessment will depend on the nature of the curriculum and the faculty who teach and design the curriculum. A long list of outcomes is not better than a short one, nor is a short one evidence of greater depth of knowledge. We must appreciate and value differences in our programs. Our goals for student learning need to be consistent with our institutional missions. We are not all the same, nor should we strive to be.

Programs that adhere to these seven general principles will avoid many of the pitfalls and pratfalls that have been associated with educational assessment programs. For most of us, the question is not whether we should be examining the educational outcomes of our programs, but when and how. Student outcomes assessment should not be thought of as a one-shot report that is finished and filed once it is completed. It is an integral component of the teaching–learning process, and the results should be useful and used to redirect further teaching and learning.

When assessment is designed to improve the teaching and learning process, the focus is on what and how much is learned. Usually, we assess students and courses on a course-by-course basis. By shifting to a learning outcome model, we can examine academic majors and other programs like the general education curriculum or the entire baccalaureate program by determining what and how much students know when they graduate or at some other point in time. Leach, Neutze, and Zepke (2001) maintain that learner-centered assessments empower adult learners by providing them with information they can use as evidence of their own learning. Good tests reflect course goals and content and provide feedback to the students and the instructors. The same benefits should accrue when a major or general education program, as a whole, is assessed.

To examine outcomes from an academic major or program, faculty need to have a clear vision of the objectives of that program and then devise ways to determine whether the goals have been achieved. Often departments report that the act of coming together to discuss what faculty want students to know and be able to do when they graduate can create greater coherence in the curriculum. Thus, it is not just the result of the assessment that is valuable, but the very process of articulating learning goals can be a stimulus for educational improvement.

The central question that should guide the process is, What should we expect a graduating senior from your campus to know and be able to do? When we pose the question by focusing on the students, we shift the focus from, What have I taught? to What have the students learned? The change is from Does this student have the appropriate number of units? to What does this student know and what can he or she do? Increasingly, credit units will become extinct because students will be learning at distant sites, with multiple forms of media, and at times that are unmonitored. It is possible that the "credit unit" will go the way of the cuckoo bird or perhaps just become endangered, like the bald eagle. Learning outcomes may prove to be a useful alternative to credit units, which correspond to the number of hours students sit in classrooms, without regard to what or how much is learned. The change from credit units to an alternative measure of learning will not be easy, but radical changes in how we conceptualize familiar and fundamental constructs never are.

WHAT SHOULD WE EXPECT A GRADUATE FROM YOUR PROGRAM TO KNOW AND BE ABLE TO DO?

Although the nature of the assessment will vary among institutions, there are several general areas that most programs will include. I present here a brief set of suggested outcomes as examples to complete the overview on student outcomes assessment. More detailed explanations and more creative alternatives are presented in the following chapters and in the Task Force on Undergraduate Psychology Major Competencies (American Psychological Association, 2002); Allen, Noel, Deegan, Halpern, and Crawford (2000); and McGovern, Furumoto, Halpern, Kimble, and McKeachie (1991).

Content Knowledge of the Disciplines

Every psychology major should know who Freud is and the basic premises of his famous theories. They should know important basics about the relationship between brain activity and behavior, classical conditioning, and definitions of mental illness, among many other concepts that are central to our discipline, even as we argue about them.

Methods and Basic Research Concepts in the Discipline

For example, students should be able to read and critique a newspaper account of psychological research, such as a study that claims that self-esteem is important for success in school or that adherence to gender roles causes eating disorders.

Language and Literacy Skills

Language skills include reading and writing complex prose. Graduates from a quality program in psychology should be able to comprehend journal articles in psychology that they could not comprehend when they entered the curriculum (e.g., general articles from publications like the *American Psychologist* or *Developmental Psychology*). They should also be able to present a coherent and persuasive argument on a contemporary topic in both written and oral form at a high level of proficiency.

Critical Thinking Skills

Critical thinking skills include recognizing the need for control groups, not confusing correlation with cause, understanding the concepts of likelihood and uncertainty, and identifying valid and invalid conclusions on the basis of empirical evidence. There is a large literature showing that students can be better thinkers when they are specifically taught with this goal in mind (Halpern, 2003).

Information Gathering and Synthesis

All college graduates should be able to find information in the library (which has become a computer-assisted skill) and voluntarily read more than when they entered college. The flood of materials available on the Internet means that it is increasingly important that students develop the habit of determining the credibility and reliability of information sources. They should be able to synthesize information from a variety of sources in order to derive a conclusion or reach a decision.

Knowledge of and Appreciation for the Arts—in Any or All Forms

Although an appreciation for the arts is not usually included in goals for psychology majors, we are educating "whole persons," and the arts are one part of the whole. Ideally (and arguably), graduates should be more likely to attend a concert, see a play, write a poem, or attend an art exhibit than they would have been without their education.

Skills Gained Through Practical Experience

A quality education should help students develop problem solving and communication skills while also exposing them to different segments of the society than they are likely to encounter in college. Student and employer perceptions about the value of such an experience should also be included in an outcomes assessment.

Ethics and Values

There are ethical principles and standards that are an integral part of our everyday experiences. Undergraduates should be able to use these principles to understand conflicts, to generate alternative responses, and to act on their judgments. It is far easier for students to recite the ethical standards of their discipline than it is to live by them. In the abstract, most students will agree that cheating is wrong, but when they are faced by a friend who "needs a good grade," it is far more difficult to refuse to allow that friend to cheat than a simple recitation of ethics would imply.

Interpersonal Skills

A "noncognitive" gain that I consider to be as important as all of the other objectives is increased tolerance for differences, especially as they relate to all types of minority groups. Education is more than stuffing heads with facts. Knowledge about prejudice, aggression, communication styles, helping, and so on should be applicable to students' lives and life choices.

There are endless other possibilities. It is constructive for faculty to work toward a common definition of what should be learned by their students. The process of identifying desirable outcomes can promote greater coherence in the structure of any major and can create a tangible emphasis on teaching and learning excellence.

MEASUREMENT ISSUES

Given a diverse array of desirable outcomes, it is clear that different models of measurements will be needed. A brief list of measurement alternatives is presented here. Additional alternatives with more extensive rationales are presented in many of the following chapters in this book. (See Allen et al., 2000, and Doherty, Riordan, & Roth, 2002, for additional suggestions for assessing learning outcomes.)

"Off the Shelf" Normed Instruments

The major testing companies have swarmed to outcomes assessment like ants at a picnic. They have anticipated our every need by marketing instruments that are normed in a variety of ways so that colleges and departments can compare their graduating seniors with those at comparable institutions, the nation as a whole, or many other comparison groups. But unless they are administered to entering freshmen or some similar group, they cannot be used as an index of student gains. Many of these normed instruments (e.g., Major Field Tests) use multiple-choice questions, which are limited in the kind of information they can provide. They cannot be used to measure objectives such as the ability to explain a controversy or present an articulate argument; moreover, nationally normed examinations are usually expensive and may not match the objectives in the curriculum of any specific department very well.

Locally Written Comprehensive Exams

Learning objectives for a specific department can be measured with comprehensive examinations, written and graded by the department's own faculty. Local examinations offer the advantage of being tailored for the specific topics emphasized at each institution and thus reflect what the faculty teaching the courses believe to be important. Some disadvantages of comprehensive examinations include the problem of unknown psychometric properties and the time and expense of writing and grading broad-spectrum exams. These problems can be mitigated somewhat if groups of institutions establish an outcomes measures data bank containing questions coded by type of content or skill (e.g., basic content question or thinking skill) and type of question (e.g., multiple-choice, essay; see chap. 6, this volume). Participating institutions could contribute to and sample from the data bank of coded questions. In this way, the task of constructing good outcomes measures could be shared among faculty at several institutions while allowing each institution to individualize its own assessment.

Capstone Course Work and Other Culminating Experiences

A senior capstone course in general education or in psychology can also be incorporated into an assessment program. The general goal of the capstone is to require the students to bring together the skills that have been developed in their program of study. There are several alternatives available. Capstone courses could involve a lengthy integrative paper, debate, or other experiences in which assessment is tied to learning.

Use of Available Data

Colleges and universities already collect a considerable amount of data about their incoming students. These data typically include scores on college entrance examinations, placement tests in English and mathematics, data about course patterns and success at previous institutions, and student perceptions about advising, faculty quality, personal educational goals, and satisfaction with their educational programs. In addition to providing a benchmark for assessing gains, entry data can be used to advise students about appropriate course selections and to help them identify their strengths and weaknesses, which should be useful in academic and career planning.

There are many theoretically important relationships in higher education that we know very little about that we could begin answering with wise use of these data. For example, it is important to know which college courses are associated with cognitive growth and the development of thinking skills and what sort of high school curriculum predicts success in college. I am not aware of any university that has this type of information. The establishment of a relevant database will allow us to begin to answer questions like these.

Nonintrusive Measures

These measures refer to information that is collected without student awareness—that is, they do not "intrude" in the ongoing processes of learning. For example, it is often possible to determine how many books of various kinds are checked out of the library during an academic year and how many students have checked out books. If one goal is to foster the development of writing skills within the major, then a simple count of how many courses require a term paper or other writing assignment could be instructive in determining how well that goal is being met because students cannot be improving their writing skills if they are doing very little writing.

Student, Alumni, and Employer Surveys

Surveys of students and alumni are also important in determining educational quality and in directing programmatic change. Graduates can be asked if they wish that they had taken more mathematics or computer or literature courses when they were students. Do they believe that they were well prepared for their careers? How many are working in jobs that require a college degree or are engaged in some other employment that they consider meaningful or useful or lucrative? Employers of our students should also be included in an outcomes assessment. What skills do they want their employees or your alumni to have when they are hired? How do they perceive the education being provided for their current and future employees?

Unfortunately, much of this information is fragmented, difficult to access, and rarely used for academic decision making. When coordinated, it can be used to understand why students drop out of school or change colleges, how students feel about the academic advising they receive, and what alumni believe to be the most valuable aspects of their education.

Nontraditional Qualitative Measures

A large number of student-centered, performance-based methods can be used to provide information about student and programmatic outcomes. Here are a few that are relatively easy to administer.

Portfolio Analysis

Portfolio analysis was originally developed as a means of assessing art work, but is adaptable to the assessment of a variety of educational goals. Portfolios are simply files of students' work, selected to represent various educational objectives, which are periodically reviewed. Portfolios may be developed at the level of the individual course, the major, or the entire college experience. Portfolios can also include video and audiotapes that provide samples of student achievement. Seldin and Associates (1993) have advocated for the creation of portfolios as an alternative means of assessing the quality of teachers at all levels of education. Thus, portfolios can be applicable in a wide variety of situations, but have as a disadvantage the psychometric problems of unknown reliability and validity. They are also very expensive to grade and maintain (see chap. 10, this volume).

Interviews

Interviews with students may be conducted periodically during their academic careers or as part of their senior experience. They may broadly address a student's experiences in the major or in the college as a whole. In planning interviews, consider questions that are likely to be most useful in understanding the college experience from the students' perspective and leave some questions open-ended so students can be sure to include what they want you to know.

Performance-Based Assessment

Performance-based assessment asks students to demonstrate what they have learned through class discussion, projects, speeches, and other active learning situations. For example, in a seminar course, students may be assigned related articles to read that provide them the opportunity to assert, challenge, and defend various points of view. The exercise provides the opportunity to practice and assess the critical thinking skills of evaluation and analysis and the personal characteristics of nondefensiveness, open mindedness, and tolerance of ambiguity. Performance-based assessment provides faculty, students, and external constituencies with particularly clear indicators of students' skills. Effective performance-based assessment requires careful attention to the specification of goals and criteria for assessment and multiple opportunities for student learning.

The diversity in this list of assessment techniques highlights two basic and inescapable facts: Educational goals are complex and all measurement is imperfect. Assessment will be most useful to the extent that a variety of methods are used to examine clearly specified objectives. I know that there are many naysayers among us. Psychometricians confirm that these measures are flawed and cannot capture the essence of what is learned in college. There are no perfect assessments, but it is time to start using them anyway. A response to all of the doubting Thomases was eloquently framed by Curry and Hager (1987): "To assess outcomes, we must overcome enormous problems of procedure and analysis, but we cannot refuse to look at what the instruments enable us to see" (p. 57). In other words, it is time to take steps in the right direction, even if we are not completely sure where we are going.

A disgruntled faculty member once complained that he was already overworked and "this outcomes assessment busy-ness" was just one more thing. I told him that the assessment of student learning is not "one more thing." It is the only thing—it is the only way of knowing whether students are achieving the learning goals that you have established for them and, if they are not, it provides information for making changes. It closes the loop between teaching and learning and provides the information we need to enhance learning.

REFERENCES

Allen, M. J., Noel, R. N., Deegan, J., Halpern, D. F., & Crawford, C. (2000). *Goals and objectives for the undergraduate psychology major: Recommendations from a meeting of California State University faculty.* Retrieved November 22, 2003, from http://www.lemoyne.edu/OTRP/otrpresources/otrp _outcomes.html

American Psychological Association, Board of Educational Affairs, Task Force on Undergraduate Psychology Major Competencies. (2002, March). *National standards and learning outcomes for the undergraduate psychology major.* Retrieved January 1, 2004, from http://www.apa.org/ed/pcue/taskforcereport2.pdf

Arnone, M. (2003, January 3). The wannabes: More public universities are striving to squeeze into the top tier. *Chronicle of Higher Education,* A18–A20.

Bishop, J. H. (2000). Curriculum-based external exit exam systems: Do students learn more? How? *Psychology, Public Policy, and Law, 6,* 199–215.

Boyer Commission on Educating Undergraduates in the Research University. (1998). *Reinventing undergraduate education.* Retrieved January 3, 2003, from http://www.sunysb. edu/pres.

Council for Higher Education Accreditation. (2002, September). *The fundamentals of accreditation: What do you need to know?* Washington, DC: Author.

Curry, W., & Hager, E. (1987). Assessing general education: Trenton State College. In D. F. Halpern (Ed.), *Student outcomes assessment: What institutions stand to gain* (pp. 57–66). San Francisco: Jossey-Bass.

Doherty, A., Riordan, T., & Roth, J. (Eds.). (2002). *Student learning: A central focus for institutions of higher education.* Milwaukee, WI: Alverno College.

Doyle, D. P. (1991, April 15). Without tests, we flunk. *The Washington Post.* Retrieved January 1, 2004, from www.thedoylereport.com

Halpern, D. F. (1988). Assessing student outcomes for psychology majors. *Teaching of Psychology, 15,* 181–186.

Halpern, D. F. (2003). *Thought and knowledge: An introduction to critical thinking* (4th ed.). Mahwah, NJ: Erlbaum.

Halpern, D. F. (with Appleby, D. C., Beers, S. E., Cowan, C. L., Furedy, J. J., Halonen, J. S., Horton, C. P., et al.). (1993). Targeting outcomes: Covering your assessment needs and concerns. In T. V. McGovern (Ed.), *Handbook for enhancing undergraduate education in psychology* (pp. 23–46). Washington, DC: American Psychological Association.

Halpern, D. F., Smothergill, D. W., Allen, M., Baker, S., Baum, C., Best, D., et al. (1998). Scholarship in psychology: A paradigm for the 21st century. *American Psychologist, 53,* 1292–1297.

Leach, L., Neutze, G., & Zepke, N. (2001). Assessment and empowerment: Some critical questions. *Assessment & Evaluation in Higher Education, 26,* 293–305.

McGovern, T. V., Furumoto, L., Halpern, D. F., Kimble, G. A., & McKeachie. W. J. (1991). Liberal education, study in depth, and the arts and sciences major—psychology. *American Psychologist, 46,* 598–605.

National Center for Education Statistics. (2000). *Pursuing excellence: Comparisons of international eighth-grade mathematics and science achievement from a U.S. perspective, 1995 and 1999* (NCES 2001–028). Washington, DC: U.S. Government Printing Office.

National Commission on Excellence in Education. (1983). *A nation at risk: The imperative for educational reform.* Washington, DC: Author.

Perlman, B., & McCann, L. I. (1999). The structure of the psychology undergraduate curriculum. *Teaching of Psychology, 26,* 171–176.

Secretary's Commission on Achieving Necessary Skills. (2000). *The workforce skills website.* Retrieved January 3, 2003, from http://www.scans.jhu.edu/NS/HTML/Skills.htm

Seldin, P., and Associates. (1993). *Successful use of teaching portfolios.* Bolton, MA: Anker.

II

MODELS FOR DEPARTMENTAL ASSESSMENT AND EVALUATION

2

SEVEN GOALS FOR EFFECTIVE PROGRAM ASSESSMENT

MICHAEL L. STOLOFF, KEVIN J. APPLE, KENNETH E. BARRON,
MONICA REIS-BERGAN, AND DONNA SUNDRE

At James Madison University (JMU), the process of program assessment is vital to program success. We view assessment not as an examination or survey, but rather as an organizing process that helps our faculty develop a shared perspective on what our program should be accomplishing. It helps us connect our individual courses to create a coherent program. It provides continuous feedback as we use assessment findings to inform decisions about how to best implement our psychology major. In this chapter we describe the assessment process for the JMU psychology major and how the process has improved our program. Specifically, this chapter is organized around seven goals that guide our assessment efforts, and we share examples from various assessment projects that we have conducted to help illustrate each of these goals.

The authors wish to thank the following individuals for their contributions to the process of developing the assessment program we describe in this chapter: Jim Benedict, Jim Couch, S. Lynn Cameron, Jane Halonen, David Hanson, Alan Hoffman, and Eileen Nelson.

THE ASSESSMENT CULTURE AT JAMES MADISON UNIVERSITY

James Madison University is a comprehensive state university located in a rural area of Virginia. In 2002, 704 full-time and 274 part-time faculty taught 14,402 undergraduate and 1,210 graduate and special students. The undergraduate program in psychology is one of the most popular majors on campus with 940 declared majors in 2002.

Both the academic and the nonacademic divisions of JMU use an assessment-based model to demonstrate institutional effectiveness, making our university a very assessment-friendly environment. Substantial university resources support all phases of assessment. For example, the Office of Institutional Research collects data useful for institutional planning, policy analysis, and the demonstration of how well the university is accomplishing its goals. The Office of Academic Advising and Career Development completes an annual survey of alumni activities. The Center for Assessment and Research Studies helps faculty develop measurable educational objectives and valid instruments for measurement of outcomes and provides administrative support for the process of collecting and interpreting information. The center also offers a doctoral program in assessment and measurement. This level of assessment support provides us with tremendous opportunities to collect information about our program. These resources, in combination with an interested and energetic faculty, make an elaborate assessment program feasible.

James Madison University expects students to participate in assessment activities and makes participation a requirement stated in our undergraduate catalog. Students participate in assessment activities during their first year, when they are sophomores, and again when they are seniors. The university even sponsors an Assessment Day each spring. Classes are canceled so students can participate in university-wide and departmental assessments throughout the day. This assessment-focused culture, when embraced by academic programs, fosters cooperation by faculty and students in assessment efforts.

There is no doubt that assessment works at JMU, in part, because the administration is steadfast in its requirement that programs use feedback from assessment instruments to inform program operations and curricular change. The psychology faculty do not find this assessment-centered administrative philosophy to be a threat to their programs or to their academic freedom. Perhaps our assessment culture does not intimidate most faculty because the faculty still design and control the curriculum. Although we are required to engage in assessment, faculty set their own goals and design their own methods of assessment. The requirement to engage in assessment is satisfied when programs can demonstrate that they are using assessment data as developmental feedback for their programs.

SEVEN GOALS OF PROGRAM ASSESSMENT

In our opinion, program assessment should be done on a continuous basis as an organizing principle for program development. We use the process of program assessment at JMU to frame faculty decisions regarding long-term program goals. Assessment helps us with decisions regarding curriculum, instructional delivery, and course-schedule planning as well as measuring the extent to which students achieve our stated goals. Assessment provides us with a constant stream of information that affects all decision making.

The seven goals that guide program assessment in our psychology department are as follows:

1. Focus faculty attention on shared program curriculum objectives.
2. Collect assessment data.
3. Use findings to guide program administration.
4. Demonstrate program strengths.
5. Identify program weaknesses.
6. Use information as a tool to inform instructional delivery.
7. Use information as a tool to evaluate program change.

Below, we describe each goal and provide examples of how each goal is implemented and what we have learned through that process.

Goal One: Focus Faculty Attention on Shared Curriculum Objectives

James Madison University recruits faculty members with strong teaching interests and skills. Each faculty member can teach wonderful classes with virtually no input from other faculty. However, we want the program to be much more than a list of classes. We want psychology majors to develop a common core of knowledge and skills. Our students should learn to think about behavior in a sophisticated way, in a manner that draws from many theoretical models of psychology. They should be able to apply skills developed in college to new problems that they will encounter in their post-graduation experiences. They will only be able to do this if they encounter topics more than once, building on their ability to analyze situations and address problems with increasing sophistication. Coursework needs to address and readdress key themes in a manner that reinforces and extends understanding. We strive to create a coherent, interdependent, integrated program of study.

We have devoted substantial energy into putting overall curricular objectives to paper and deciding which courses within our curriculum need to address each objective. The program objectives document is not static, but a living document in a near-constant state of review and revision. We refine our objectives to incorporate information we receive from assessment, to benefit from the input that new faculty bring to our program, and to incorporate national trends for "best practices," such as those expressed in the American Psychological Association (APA) Task Force on Undergraduate Psychology Major Competencies report (Halonen et al., 2002) and other published sources (e.g., Brewer et al., 1993; McGovern, Furumoto, Halpern, Kimble, & McKeachie, 1991; McGovern & Reich, 1996).

We expect faculty to incorporate common objectives into their course syllabi. This expectation helps to formalize the relationship between each course and our overall major curriculum. We require all faculty to conduct student evaluations of teaching at the end of each semester. On a 5-point scale, students are asked to rate how well the instructor made it possible for them to achieve course goals and objectives. With these procedures, each individual course contributes to our overall curricular objectives in a formal and measurable way.

Goal Two: Collect Assessment Data

Our psychology instructors use many sources of information to meet our second goal of program assessment, gathering information that can be used as feedback to program development. Formal assessment of the psychology major began at JMU in 1989. Our program of assessment has grown substantially since those early days.

Many of our assessment instruments that measure the skills, experiences, and content knowledge of our seniors are administered on the annual Assessment Day. One month prior to Assessment Day, all students who will be graduating in May or December of that calendar year with a psychology degree are notified that they must participate in the department's Assessment Day activities. More than 80% of our graduating class typically attends our Assessment Day testing sessions. All students begin Assessment Day activities by completing a checklist of psychology courses taken and the Academic Skills-Experience Inventory described below. One hundred students who are expected to graduate in May complete the content instrument used that year. All other May and December graduates complete either the Information Literacy Assessment or the Writing Assessment. All students finish Assessment Day activities with the Motivation Student Opinion Scale (SOS). A student who fails to attend our sessions on Assessment Day is required to complete several online tests, including the Information Literacy Inventory. Each of these test instruments is described below.

Academic Skills-Experience Inventory

Psychology majors have experiences and develop skills that prepare them well for a variety of future careers. We evaluate graduating psychology majors using the 90-item inventory developed by Kruger and Zechmeister (2001). The survey defines 10 fundamental skills often developed through a psychology major in a liberal arts baccalaureate program. The items measure activities that reflect skill development and demonstration. The survey not only provides us with assessment data but also helps students reflect on the domains of skill development that have been part of their college experiences.

Content Assessment

We have used two different content assessment tools: the Austin Peay Psychology Area Concentration Achievement Test (ACAT) and the Educational Testing Service (ETS) Major Fields Achievement Test in Psychology (MFAT). We began measuring psychology content knowledge in 1989 by asking all students enrolled in our required senior-level History and Systems course to complete the Statistics, Experimental Psychology, and History and Systems subtests of the ACAT. Over time we added additional subtests, but switched to administration of the MFAT on Assessment Day in 1994 because an unpublished validation study conducted at JMU (Kellard & Sundre, 1993) did not demonstrate that ACAT scores were highly correlated with student course grades in the areas we were assessing and because faculty had concerns about the ACAT's content and item quality. We expected the MFAT to be highly correlated with Psychology Subject Area Graduate Requisite Examinations (GRE) scores since the MFAT was created from the same test item pool as that examination. One of our program goals is to prepare students for graduate school admission, so it seemed logical to assess their knowledge in a manner that might be consistent with this often-used graduate admission examination.

In 2002 we decided to abandon the MFAT and return to the ACAT. Again we switched because a validation study failed to show a strong correlation between MFAT subtest scores and the courses in the areas that matched the MFAT subtests (Stoloff & Feeney, 2002). Only 4 of the 28 psychology courses frequently taken by our students significantly predicted MFAT subtest scores. We plan to continue to use the ACAT in the future, repeating our validation studies.

Information Literacy Test

Since 1998, a sample of senior psychology majors is selected on Assessment Day to complete an information literacy test that was designed at JMU. This test is presented in an online, split-screen format. Questions appear in a bottom frame, while the top frame is available to students to access online databases or other reference materials. The current version of the test consists of 59 multiple-choice items that measure students' ability to find and evaluate the quality of information from a variety of sources, including the electronic library catalog, PsycINFO, and the Internet. Additional items ask students to rate their satisfaction with library resources and services and the frequency with which they use various types of computer applications such as word processing, database searches, statistical software, and so on. We have recently added questions regarding APA style citations and references to this instrument.

Writing Assessment

In 2001, in response to faculty concerns about the quality of our students' writing and student suggestions on our senior-exit survey that we should help them improve their writing abilities, we began a systematic focus on improving writing in our curriculum. Part of that effort was the development of a writing assessment to be given to a sample of seniors during Assessment Day. Improvement in writing skills resulting from curricular changes could then be monitored by improvements in student scores on this instrument in the future. We have conducted two writing assessments so far. After our first attempt, we substantially revised our procedures.

The current version of our test uses a one-and-a-half-page, locally written summary of an article on gender differences in memory (Herrmann, Crawford, & Holdsworth, 1992). We expected that students would be familiar with the issues raised by this research, but not the specific study. After reading the research summary, students wrote brief essays in a computer lab. We asked them to summarize the research, describe its strengths and weaknesses, and suggest applications of the findings. We told them they would be evaluated on their general writing competence. We developed our grading rubric from the results of a faculty survey that identified the elements of writing considered most important. Two teams of faculty gathered for an afternoon of training and rating these papers.

In 2002, while student writing was not uniformly excellent, every student worked hard on this task. Student motivation was a problem during our 2001 writing assessment, but we believe this was corrected in 2002 through several changes that we would now recommend:

1. We started Assessment Day activities with a pep talk by our program director and we had a faculty member (rather than a graduate student) proctor the writing assessment lab to demonstrate that this activity was important to us.
2. We kept the article summary short. This allowed students to begin writing soon after they entered the writing lab, reducing boredom and frustration.
3. We told students that feedback about their writing would be made available to them.

Motivation Scale

The SOS (Sundre & Moore, 2002) is a 10-item measure of examinee motivation that provides three scores: an overall total motivation score, and two subscales measuring importance and effort. All scales have reliabilities exceeding .85, and considerable validity evidence has been observed to date with a variety of JMU samples. We collect this information at the end of each Assessment Day because it gives us a way to monitor whether we can draw valid inferences from the data collected, especially since students complete Assessment Day activities with no personal consequences regarding their individual performance.

In addition to the measures that we collect during Assessment Day, we also use the following instruments or other sources of information to complete our assessment analysis.

Senior Exit Survey

This instrument has evolved substantially since it was initially developed in 1992 to evaluate the quality of academic advising. We currently use 84 close-ended response items and 16 open-ended response items to obtain student self-reports on a wide range of issues related to advising, performance of departmental administration and staff, departmental communication, and involvement with special learning opportunities. We also ask students to describe their rationale for choosing the psychology major, how well they feel they achieved the objectives of the psychology major through normal classroom experiences and special learning opportunities, and their overall satisfaction with the major. Finally, we ask them to describe their future plans. We administer the survey in a Web-based format that allows easy data importation for analysis with statistical software. We have excellent survey participation (around 95%), because we have tied completion of the senior-exit survey to each student's graduation application. The number and depth of relevant written comments on the open-ended items lead us to believe that students are taking the time to complete this survey carefully and thoughtfully.

Alumni Survey

Our department head completed the first systematic survey of our alumni in the 1970s by conducting a structured telephone interview with every graduate of the program that he could find (E. Nelson, personal communication, November 23, 2002). This method is still in use in some of our graduate programs, such as our MA in psychological sciences, which typically has about 10 graduates each year, but it is less feasible in a large undergraduate program. James Madison University now systematically conducts alumni surveys for all majors every five years. The survey begins with questions regarding students' overall university experience and continues with a series of questions developed for the students' major. Most questions ask alumni what they are doing now and how well their JMU experience prepared them. Many of the questions are similar to the senior-exit survey, but now that the students have been away from campus for several years, they are in a better position to tell us how applicable and useful their JMU learning experiences have been.

University Employment Survey

The JMU Office of Academic Advising and Career Development conducts an annual employment survey of all students who graduated approximately 10 months earlier. Follow-up mailings are sent at two-month intervals to increase the response rate. With the help of student organizations, non-respondents and graduates initially classified as "still seeking employment" are contacted by telephone. These methods typically result in a response rate of about 75% of the students for whom a forwarding address or telephone number is available or about 57% of the entire graduating class. The survey collects information regarding employment status, graduate school status, and salary. For example, we are able to estimate that typically 30% of our psychology majors attend graduate school the year after they complete their undergraduate degree, and the mean first-position salary for psychology graduates seeking employment in 2001 was $28,912, which is comparable to other liberal arts majors at the university.

Institutional Research Reports

The JMU Office of Institutional Research has as its mission the development, collection, and communication of measures of overall institutional effectiveness. The information collected by this office is primarily derived from official university records and surveys of deans, department heads, and faculty. For psychology, the data from this office has been invaluable by providing us with information regarding majors, faculty, numbers of students taught, and graduation rates. We can use these data to compare our students to the university population at large. These data provide context for interpretation of specific information collected about our students, our program, and our faculty. Many of the office's reports are made available to the public through its Web site.

Short-Term Projects

In the assessment culture that has evolved at JMU, whenever we make curricular changes or when the value of particular practices comes under scrutiny, we ask ourselves whether we have any assessment data available that will allow us to address the issues at hand. We have so many forms of assessment already in place that previously collected information from assessments is often available, although it sometimes requires further analysis to address specific concerns. Sometimes new information is needed, so we conduct a short-term project to address specific concerns. Some examples of these projects are discussed later.

Informal Student Input

Long before there was assessment at JMU, we asked students how they felt about their experiences in our program. Formal assessment is not a substitute for informal input. A formal assessment process simply allows us to confirm or disconfirm what we hear from students informally. It allows us to separate common beliefs from empirical facts, a process comparable to research done in many psychological laboratories. One regular source of informal student input comes from a group of students who volunteer to serve on a student advisory panel that meets monthly to discuss issues, concerns, and proposed changes with the undergraduate program director.

Informal Faculty Input

It may seem too obvious a source of information to even list here, but we are compelled to note that informal faculty input is a vital source of information for a comprehensive assessment program. Faculty talk to one another about what is going on in their individual classes and about how their classes fit into the curriculum as a whole. We mention this because several of us have served as consultants to departments in which this form of communication is extremely limited, and consequently an overall curriculum plan is virtually nonexistent. Our curriculum is more than a collection of independent courses; it is a collection of individually valuable experiences that impact student development through synergy. Regular communication among faculty is vital for coherent program design and delivery.

Goal Three: Use Findings to Guide Program Administration

The information that we collect through the methods noted above is used in many ways to help guide our program. We created Table 2.1 to capture the range and impact our assessment plan has had on our program.

We would like to share just a few examples starting with our use of findings to guide program administration.

Improve Academic Advising

Our original senior exit survey was conducted in response to a university-wide effort to improve the quality of advising (Nelson & Johnson, 1997). We found that students were generally satisfied with the academic advising they had received—more satisfied than university averages as measured by a university-wide survey. However, there was higher than acceptable variability on a few items about advisors such as "informed of services," "respectful of feelings," "helpfulness," "effectiveness," and "overall satisfaction."

On the basis of this input, we took a number of actions to improve the quality of advising: Each year we conducted a one-hour advising workshop for faculty. In addition, our undergraduate program coordinator presented a two-minute advising tip at the start of every faculty meeting. We expanded and further formalized the training program for our peer advising program (Nelson & Fonzi, 1995). We diversified the range of advising services by expanding newsletters (now distributed on paper four times each year) and

TABLE 2.1
Psychology Assessment Plan

Assessment Instrument	Findings	Use of Findings
Skills-Experience Inventory	Seniors score equal or higher on all domains compared to available norms.	We began to explicitly focus student attention on the marketable skill sets developed through the major.
Content Assessment (ACAT/MFAT)	Test performance and selected courses correlated.	We increased the availability of certain courses.
Information Literacy Test	New teaching approaches are as effective as old ones.	We identified new, more effective role for liaison librarian.
Writing Assessment	Confirmed problems with writing.	We encouraged more writing assignments in all courses.
Motivation Scale (SOS)	Scores increased when faculty were present during tests.	Faculty continued active participation in Assessment Day.
Senior Exit Survey	Identified problems with advising and writing.	We developed peer advising, expanded use of newsletters and e-mail news, started our writing improvement effort.
Alumni Survey	Identified most valuable features of our program.	We expanded and encouraged participation in mentoring activities.
Employment Survey	Identified what students do upon graduation.	We expanded career advising for baccalaureate-level jobs.
Institutional Research Reports	Determined retention rate for psychology majors.	These data informed enrollment-management plans.
Short-Term Projects	Studied effectiveness of multimedia classrooms and methods course sequencing.	We continued to develop multimedia classes. Ideal order of methods classes still under investigation.
Informal Student Input	Confirmed other findings.	Validated formal measures.
Informal Faculty Input	Confirmed other findings.	Enhanced confidence in assessment culture.

archiving articles from the newsletter on our Web site. We now also distribute a weekly e-mail newsletter that receives high marks from students on recent senior exit surveys.

Faculty members and the psychology director review individual advising feedback from the exit survey and discuss it informally at annual evaluation meetings. We have decided that we can improve the overall quality of advising with flexible workload assignments. We no longer expect all faculty to serve as advisors for individual undergraduate students. Some faculty are assigned to advise only graduate students. Other faculty members may not have any individual student advisees, but they address our undergraduate advising mission by conducting workshops on career development or by being a designated resource person for students (and faculty advisors) who need specific advice about pursuing particular career goals such as counseling psychology or art therapy.

Inform Course Scheduling

One of our program goals is to prepare students for graduate study in psychology, and one of the ways that graduate programs measure content-knowledge preparation is performance on the Psychology Subject Area GRE. We had been using the MFAT to measure content knowledge, in part, because we believed that it would measure students' knowledge in a manner that would be comparable to the Psychology GRE. We conducted an analysis of the impact of taking particular psychology courses on MFAT performance and found that, in addition to General Psychology and Statistics and Research Methods courses (taken by all students), only four courses appeared to predict MFAT subtest scores: Abnormal Psychology, Social Psychology, Biopsychology, and Counseling Psychology (Stoloff & Feeney, 2002). We do not want to simply "teach to this test," and we do not think this information is sufficient reason to revamp our curriculum. However, we realized that many students may have been denied the opportunity to take some of these courses due to limited section offerings. We now offer a sufficient number of these four courses so that every psychology major who wants to take these courses can complete them before they graduate. We also have lowered the priority of History of Psychology in our scheduling scheme because taking this course did not contribute to improved MFAT scores. We believe this course is important, but essential content of history is probably sufficiently well covered within our other courses.

Expand One-on-One Activities

Data from our senior exit and alumni surveys agree with informal student feedback and general faculty impressions that some of the most valuable features of our psychology major program are the experiences that students have when they help faculty with research or service projects. It is in these contexts that students develop mentor relationships with faculty. Students who help faculty with projects demonstrate problem solving skills, motivation, and their ability to bring their full range of skills to bear on problems. These activities build student resumes and, later, permit faculty who supervise them to write excellent letters of recommendation on their behalf. The positive feedback from assessment regarding the value of these activities has led to the expansion of these opportunities for psychology majors. Currently, most undergraduate psychology faculty supervise six or more students each semester in courses in which students earn academic credit for research or service-learning activities. In addition, we typically have 25 students completing a field placement each semester and approximately nine students working on their senior honors theses. This practice requires a tremendous faculty-resource investment, but our assessment findings indicate that it is well justified.

Goal Four: Demonstrate Program Strengths

The greatest rewards for university professors are often in the realm of the intangible. Salary is generally not comparable to that of professionals with similar education, skills, and experience in the nonacademic workplace. For job satisfaction, we rely on the knowledge that what we do is important and valuable. Unfortunately, most people (even our supervisors) are only marginally aware of our accomplishments. Reinforcement is sporadic and often takes place only after a long delay. Assessment data can provide evidence that a program is making a difference in students' lives. For example, at JMU we know from our university employment survey that our graduates are frequently admitted to graduate programs, and from our alumni survey we hear that they are "well prepared." Data from our alumni survey indicate that most graduates believe that we "effectively prepared them for employment."

In addition to discussing these findings among ourselves, as self-reinforcement for our achievement, we use these data when we meet with potential students and their parents. The bottom line question for parents is often, How well prepared will my daughter or son be after attending this university? We can use these data to quantify the merit and marketability of our program. In addition, we regularly use these data on administrative reports. We are confident that we are doing a good job and have several strong sources of empirical data to support this claim.

Goal Five: Identify Program Weaknesses

Our data also suggest that we could be doing a better job in particular areas. This result is sometimes difficult for faculty to hear because it invariably means that change is necessary, and change is almost always more difficult than continuation of the status quo. However, if faculty use the knowledge that they are doing excellent work as a primary source of motivation, they will likely be motivated to take steps to correct weaknesses. A number of examples of weaknesses that have been identified through assessment have already been noted, but we would like to highlight two recent cases.

Career Advising

In a generally excellent program, identified program weaknesses are sometimes easy to address. This was the case for the following example. Many students completing our 2001 senior exit survey remarked that they were tired of hearing that they need to go to graduate school to get a psychology-related job. We also knew from our student employment survey that most students were actually getting satisfying jobs with their bachelor's degrees and we knew from alumni surveys that we were preparing students well for these jobs. Why were we so focused on graduate school as the primary option? Why not discuss more popular post-graduation positions that could be obtained without additional training as enthusiastically as a graduate school application?

We responded by encouraging our peer advisors, who regularly conducted symposia on graduate school, to diversify and make presentations on such topics as "Jobs for Psychology Majors" and "Marketing Yourself With a Bachelor's-Level Psychology Degree." For our quarterly newsletter, the peer advisors wrote complementary articles on these topics. We used our e-mail news to announce positions available for psychology majors with a bachelor's degree. (Often these job announcements are reprinted from the local newspaper.) These advertisements helped a few graduating students to get the specific jobs advertised but, more important, it made our younger students aware of job opportunities that might be available when they completed their program. We strengthened our relationship with the university Office of Academic Advising and Career Development and now regularly advertise events they sponsor that help students write resumes, practice job-interview techniques, and meet with potential employers. Our career advising is now more diverse and more appropriate for our students' likely career directions. If these efforts prove successful, we should see fewer student complaints on future senior exit surveys regarding the orientation of our career advising.

Writing

It was clear from informal student and faculty input that our students are deficient in their writing skills. We considered the problem to be acute when both seniors and alumni used the open response areas of their survey forms to remark that writing skill development is an important area that needs attention. Unlike the career advising concern described above, this problem was not easy to address. Improving student writing would certainly take substantial faculty time and, in a program with a high student–faculty ratio, this would be even more challenging. Writing was already required in two of our mandatory courses: our sophomore-level Research Methods course and our senior-level capstone seminars. An analysis of the graded activities that are listed on our course syllabi revealed that written work was only sporadically required in most other courses.

We took up the challenge of improving student writing with a multifaceted assessment-based approach. First, we decided to assess students' writing regularly. This monitoring would provide us with a baseline measure of student writing skill and could be used to measure any improvement in writing ability that developed among our students as a result of curricular change. We discussed the problem at faculty meetings and had faculty share techniques they had developed for requiring written work in large classes without tremendously expanding the grading workload. The suggestions included requiring students to write very short (well-edited) papers or implementing peer review and rewrite of written assignments before they are submitted for instructor grading (Stoloff & Rogers, 2002). Another approach, known as "Just-In-Time-Teaching," requires students to prepare for class by writing brief answers to online questions the night before each class session (Benedict, 2001). During class, poor answers and excellent answers are anonymously displayed and discussed. The excellent answers serve as models that students can emulate on their next assignment. In addition, several faculty met to discuss teaching writing as part of the process of evaluating our writing assessment samples.

We reexamined the syllabi from all of our courses one year later and found an increase in the proportion of student grades derived from writing assignments in many courses. We will continue to encourage faculty to find ways to get students to practice writing in their courses and we will continue to monitor student writing outcomes.

Goal Six: Use Information as a Tool to Inform Instructional Delivery

One can see a culture of assessment developing within JMU's psychology program because our psychology faculty are applying their skills as researchers to virtually every question that emerges regarding curricular innovation. The following are a few examples.

Do Multimedia Classrooms Enhance Student Learning?

In 1993, when the technology was available to install computer- and video-based multimedia equipment in lecture classrooms, psychology led the way by pioneering what was then known at the university as the "Classroom of the 21st Century." Our university president was very excited by the project and arranged for hardware and software purchases, faculty training, and a lecture-classroom renovation. As we started to use the classroom, three separate faculty groups conducted assessments regarding the effectiveness of instruction using this modality (Brewster, 1996; Erwin & Rieppi, 1999; Stoloff, 1995). Students liked taking classes in the multimedia classroom. Students especially liked those classes that used keypad technology, that incorporated short video clips into lectures, or that took advantage of the computer to incorporate animated demonstrations or game-format content reviews. However, we could not demonstrate that these strategies significantly enhanced learning. Students did as well on examinations when they took multimedia classes taught in this room as they did in comparable classes in standard large lecture halls or small classrooms. Although our assessment data did not provide strong evidence for expanding multimedia classrooms from a content learning perspective, the university continues to develop these classrooms. Whether instruction with this technology significantly improves student learning or whether it in fact stifles spontaneity and discussion is still an issue that requires additional research. That research continues at JMU.

How Should We Teach Information-Seeking Skills?

Since 1994, our required research methods course has included a presentation by our liaison librarian about finding and evaluating information from a wide range of sources. This practice was reinforced by a series of information-seeking exercises packaged in a workbook completed as homework following the presentation. Since 1998, we have assessed the information literacy of a sample of graduating seniors and we have consistently found them to be good but not excellent in most areas. Our librarian liaison modified her presentation and workbook each year to keep up with advancing technology, including more online resources, and to try to enhance student learning as might be reflected in annual assessments. These changes did keep her presentation and workbook current, but it never improved our students' skill level as measured during the senior year. In 2000, some of the instructors teaching our research methods class decided to limit the library presentation to an explanation of how to use PsycINFO. They replaced the workbook activities with other assignments. Despite this more dramatic change in teaching methods, we found that students performed similarly on our information literacy test. From these data we have concluded that these new teaching methods produce a comparable level of skill development in our students compared to the methods used in the past. We continue to look for ways to improve student skill development. We suspect that reinforcing the skills first introduced in our research methods course as students take their more advanced courses is probably the answer.

What Is the Most Effective Order in Which to Teach Statistics and Research Methods?

There has been a near-perennial debate among our faculty who teach in this area regarding the ideal learning sequence for our methods courses. We currently require students to take a three-credit general education statistics course, followed by a four-credit psychological statistics course, followed by a four-credit research methods course. Is the general education statistics course necessary or does it sometimes turn students off, frighten or confuse them, making it harder to teach psychological statistics later? Should our research methods course precede psychological statistics, or should the content of both courses be taught concurrently in a year-long course?

We are currently addressing these questions with an assessment-based approach. During fall 2002, psychology started a learning community program for first-year students. Eighteen students from our incoming class were recruited to live together to participate in some community-building activities, and take some of their courses together. Among the common courses was a new approach to learning research methodology. These students were exempted from the general education statistics course and instead enrolled in a year-long course that used an integrated approach to statistics and research methods. The skill level of these students will be compared to students who complete our traditional course sequence (including some with the same instructor). These findings will be part of the dataset that will be used to inform future decisions regarding the importance of the general education statistics prerequisite and a possible alternate sequence for these courses.

Goal Seven: Use Information as a Tool to Evaluate Program Change

With every proposed change in our curriculum, we ask which curriculum objectives are addressed by this proposal. We ask not only how this change will improve the curriculum but also how we can measure the improvement in student outcomes that results from this change. We have been collecting so much information, for so long, that often we have data available to address these questions. Sometimes we do not have the data on hand to address the specific question but, because of our strong interest in these issues, often a faculty member steps forward to conduct the assessment. Many of these assessment projects are of general interest to faculty who teach psychology everywhere, so assessment projects can become publishable scholarship in the field of effective teaching of psychology.

Throughout this chapter, we have tried to highlight many examples of how we are using the process of assessment to evaluate a particular teaching approach or to examine whether a new approach might be better. We also recently applied for a course, curriculum, and laboratory improvement grant to develop laboratory classroom experiences for psychology majors. Our comprehensive assessment program provides us with a strong baseline against which to measure any effects that these curricular improvements might have on student content knowledge and skill development.

HOW USEFUL ARE OUR ASSESSMENT METHODS?

We clearly collect a considerable amount of assessment information, and we often use that information, but how effective is the assessment process in the JMU Psychology Program? We believe that it is very effective. The culture of assessment certainly provides structure that might not otherwise be in place to design and review our curriculum in a manner that promotes coherence among our courses. There is a sense of common purpose to our overall curriculum, and our faculty share this common understanding of what we collectively need to do. Perhaps assessment works for us at JMU because we have faculty who meet the four criteria outlined by Angelo (2002)—they experience assessment activities as stimulating, they apply their disciplinary research methods and high standards of assessment practice, and they directly link their assessment results to teaching and learning. For us as research-oriented psychologists, the assessment-oriented approach to curriculum development is easy to adopt. It requires us to use methods that are familiar to most psychologists. We collect data and make decisions based on our interpretations. To most psychology faculty at JMU today, this approach seems quite natural.

Based on our experience with program assessment, we make the following recommendations: (1) Start small. Don't be overwhelmed by the comprehensive assessment programs that are described in this book! Don't try to do everything at once. The important thing is to just start! (2) As you collect data, analyze and interpret your findings. Use the information you gather to adjust your program and your assessment methods. (3) Clarify your program objectives. If you are doing this right, you will start this process but you will never finish it. Sorry! (A special tip for the Program Director: Every few years, give your faculty a break and stop talking about your objectives; but don't stop for long!) (4) Frame all future program development projects in terms of better meeting your program goals. Whenever possible, use assessment data to show where improvements are needed, implement the desired changes, and then evaluate again to see how well things are working. We wish you good luck in your assessment efforts.

REFERENCES

Angelo, T. A. (2002). Engaging and supporting faculty in the scholarship of assessment: Guidelines from research and best practice. In T. W. Banta & Associates (Eds.), *Building a scholarship of assessment* (pp. 185–200). San Francisco: Jossey-Bass.

Benedict, J. O. (2001, July). *Using just-in-time-teaching for teaching psychological statistics.* Workshop presented at the meeting of Project Kaleidoscope, Snowbird, Utah.

Brewer, C. L., Hopkins, J. R., Kimble, G. A., Matlin, M. W., McCann, L. I., McNeil, O. V., et al. (1993). Curriculum. In T. V. McGovern (Ed.), *Handbook for enhancing undergraduate education in psychology* (pp. 161–182). Washington, DC: American Psychological Association.

Brewster, J. (1996). Teaching abnormal psychology in a multimedia classroom. *Teaching of Psychology, 23,* 249–252.

Erwin, T. D., & Rieppi, R. (1999). Comparing multimedia and traditional approaches in undergraduate psychology classes. *Teaching of Psychology, 26,* 58–61.

Halonen, J. S., Appleby, D. C., Brewer, C. L., Buskist, W., Gillem, A. R., Halpern, D., et al. (Eds.). (2002). *Undergraduate major learning goals and outcomes: A report.* Washington, DC: American Psychological Association. Retrieved November 30, 2000, from http://www.apa.org/ed/pcue/ taskforcereport2.pdf

Herrmann, D. J., Crawford, M., & Holdsworth, M. (1992). Gender-linked differences in everyday memory performance. *British Journal of Psychology, 83,* 221–231.

Kellard, L. E., & Sundre, D. L. (1993). *Validation study of the Austin Peay Psychology Area Concentration Achievement Test (ACAT).* Harrisonburg, VA: Office of Student Assessment, James Madison University.

Kruger, D. J., & Zechmeister, E. B. (2001). A skills-experience inventory for the undergraduate psychology major. *Teaching of Psychology, 28,* 249–253.

McGovern, T. V., Furumoto, L., Halpern, D. F., Kimble, G. A., & McKeachie, W. J. (1991). Liberal education, study in depth, and the arts and sciences major—Psychology. *American Psychologist, 46,* 598–605.

McGovern, T. V., & Reich, J. N. (1996). A comment on the quality principles. *American Psychologist, 15,* 251–255.

Nelson, E. S., & Fonzi, G. L. (1995). An effective peer-advising program in a large psychology department. *National Academic Advising Assocation (NACADA) Journal, 15,* 41–43.

Nelson, E. S., & Johnson, K. A. (1997). A senior exit survey and its implications for advising and related services. *Teaching of Psychology, 24,* 101–105.

Stoloff, M. L. (1995). Teaching physiological psychology in a multimedia classroom. *Teaching of Psychology, 22,* 138–141.

Stoloff, M. L., & Feeney, K. J. (2002). The MFAT as an assessment tool for an undergraduate psychology program. *Teaching of Psychology, 29,* 92–98.

Stoloff, M. L., & Rogers, S. (2002). Understanding psychology deeply through thinking, doing, and writing. APS *Observer, 15*(8), 21–22, 31–32.

Sundre, D. L., & Moore, D. L. (2002). The Student Opinion Scale: A measure of examinee motivation. *Assessment Update, 14(1),* 8–9.

3

LEARNING OUTCOMES ASSESSMENT OF THE UNDERGRADUATE PSYCHOLOGY MAJOR: A MODEL IN PROGRESS

MICHAEL FIRMENT, PATRICK J. DEVINE, AND VALERIE WHITTLESEY

In a major effort that encourages assessment, the American Psychological Association Board of Educational Affairs has published suggested learning outcomes for the undergraduate psychology major (see Appendix 3.1; Halonen, J. et al., 2002). When departments use learning outcomes to improve curricula, those outcomes become powerful tools for improving teaching and learning. In this chapter, we describe how the Kennesaw State University (KSU) Psychology Department's assessment process began and how that process changed over time.

THE FIRST PHASE OF THE KSU ASSESSMENT PLAN (1995–2001)

KSU is a regional state university that is part of the university system of Georgia. The University has an enrollment of approximately 16,000 students, most of whom commute, and is located in a suburban area north of

Atlanta, Georgia. The KSU Psychology Department has approximately 600 undergraduate majors and 12 full-time faculty. The undergraduate psychology program is based on a liberal arts model of higher education that provides a background in both the scientific and applied areas of psychology. The program requirements are general psychology; careers in psychology; a two-course research sequence; one course in each of four content areas (variability, individual/social, applied, and scientific areas of psychology); senior seminar; and three upper-level psychology electives.

Identifying Student Learning Outcomes

Although the Psychology Department at KSU has, since its inception, periodically assessed its alumni as a means of getting feedback on the quality of the psychology program, the department developed its first formal assessment plan in 1995. Our department used the "quality principles" (McGovern & Reich, 1996) from the 1991 St. Mary's Conference on Undergraduate Education in Psychology as well as other contemporary sources (Halpern, 1988; McGovern, Furumoto, Halpern, Kimble, & McKeachie, 1991; Sheehan, 1994) to develop the assessment plan.

Ten student-learning outcomes that psychology majors should develop provided the structure for the assessment plan:

1. Understanding of experimental approaches used to study behavior;
2. Understanding of non-experimental approaches used to study behavior;
3. Competence in scientific writing;
4. Competence in skills needed to make oral presentations of theoretical and empirical work;
5. Understanding of statistical concepts and reasoning used in psychological research;
6. Understanding of variability in human and/or animal behavior;
7. Understanding of individual and social perspectives on human behavior;
8. Knowledge of scientific areas of study in psychology;
9. Knowledge of applied areas of study in psychology; and
10. Understanding of the major ethical issues related to research and application in psychology.

We constructed a matrix from the outcomes and five assessment methods. During the 1996–1997 academic year, we used four of the five assessment methods to assess students on the ten learning outcomes. During the 1997–1998 academic year, we used all of the methods. Table 3.1 provides a matrix of the assessment plan.

TABLE 3.1
Original Matrix of Learning Outcomes and Assessment Methods

Knowledge Areas	Senior Seminar Assignments	Senior Exit Surveys	Alumni Surveys	Research Proposals	Sequence Exam
1. Experimental psychology				X	X
2. Non-experimental psychology				X	X
3. Scientific writing skills		X	X	X	
4. Oral presentation skills	X	X	X		
5. Statistical reasoning				X	X
6. Variability of behavior	X	X	X		
7. Individual and social perspectives	X	X	X		
8. Scientific psychology	X	X	X		
9. Applied psychology	X	X	X		
10. Ethical issues				X	X
11. Career and graduate study	X	X	X		

Selecting Assessment Methods

We employed five assessment methods to determine whether students had achieved learning outcomes. Several of these methods are still in use.

1. Student Senior Seminar Assignments

The capstone course, Senior Seminar in Psychology, which was offered for the first time in the fall of 1995, facilitates integration of prior academic experiences for graduating psychology students. Two faculty members rated assignments in the course in terms of a subset of the learning outcomes.

2. Senior Exit Survey

The senior exit survey, a 59-item written questionnaire, prompted seniors to rate on a scale (from [1] "poor" to [5] "excellent") their present level of knowledge and skills in areas of psychology. We coded responses in terms of the learning outcomes.

3. Alumni Survey

This 58-item questionnaire used a 5-point scale from "poor" to "excellent," in which alumni rated their level of knowledge and skill in areas of psychology (many of the questions are identical to those in the senior exit survey). They also rated the usefulness of their knowledge and skills in their present job or in graduate school. Again, the responses are coded in terms of our learning outcomes.

4. Student Research-Sequence Proposals

Psychology majors must take the research sequence courses as part of their major requirements. We collected a random sample of anonymous research sequence proposals from these courses. Two research-sequence faculty rated the proposals in terms of how well they incorporated learning outcomes relevant to this method.

5. Research Sequence Exam

This exam assessed knowledge of statistical procedures and research methods. Students took this test at the end of their last sequence course, Experimental Psychology.

Interpreting Assessment Results

Both graduating seniors and alumni rated their scientific writing and oral presentation skills as *strong*. Both groups also rated their content knowledge of psychology (variability, individual and social perspectives, scientific, and applied understanding) as *strong*. In contrast, they rated their understanding of academic course requirements and of career information as limited; they also were dissatisfied with their exposure to research and applied practicum opportunities.

Other assessment measures (research sequence exam, senior seminar assignments, and research sequence proposals) demonstrated "satisfactory" to "fair" oral presentation skills, written communication skills, and knowledge of the four psychology content areas. The research sequence exam and analyses of research sequence proposals produced mixed results concerning statistical reasoning and ethical understanding, with the weakest results seen in statistical understanding.

Psychology majors and alumni seem to have at least satisfactory levels of communication skills and understanding of the four content areas of psychology, although the apparent strength of the knowledge and skills varied depending on the assessment method used. There were several possible limitations in the validity and reliability of the individual measures that could have caused this variability. Self-ratings of knowledge and more direct measures of knowledge may be measuring very different things. Garhart and

Hannafin (1986) found little similarity between undergraduates' statements concerning their understanding and later test results. Hacker, Bol, Horgan, and Rakow (2000) discovered somewhat better accuracy, although accurate predictions were limited to the best performing students. Second, although we used a grading guide in the senior seminar assignments and the research sequence proposal grading, interrater reliability was low. A third difficulty existed in attempting to gather information concerning outcomes such as ethical knowledge and statistical reasoning from the research proposals or various other types of knowledge from the senior seminar assignments (see Table 3.1). Depending on the area of research and the complexity of the research design, the amount of information related to the outcome measure and the difficulty for the student in adequately meeting the outcome measure varied.

Modifying the Curriculum

The assessment results led us to modify the curriculum in three ways.

1. Student Academic and Career Advisement

We developed an 11th learning outcome, Career and Graduate Study Preparation. An academic advisement center was developed for psychology majors, and a faculty member became the Coordinator of Advisement for the department. We developed a one-hour Careers in Psychology course and made it required for all psychology majors beginning in the fall of 1998. The course later became a three-hour course.

2. Applied and Research Practicum Opportunities

The Field Practicum course, previously offered once a year in the spring, was offered twice a year beginning in the fall of 2000. We developed a Research Practicum course and offered it once a year beginning in the fall of 1998. The course places students in sites in the community that allow them to use their research skills.

3. Research Sequence Courses

We reconfigured the three-course sequence (Statistics, Research Methods, Experimental Psychology) to a two-course sequence (Research Methods and Experimental Psychology, both with labs) in the fall of 1998. We integrated statistics into the labs of the Research Methods and Experimental Psychology courses in the hope that students would more easily connect statistics with design.

Modifying the Assessment Plan

The initial years of implementing the department assessment plan provided information about the knowledge and skills of our students and about their opinions concerning the strengths and weaknesses of the department. There were, however, difficulties with the validity, reliability, and completeness of the knowledge measures and with the efficiency of the assessment plan as a whole.

The only direct test of knowledge in the old assessment plan was the research sequence test. We had made the decision during the initial development of the assessment plan to use in-house tests. A benefit of this approach was that we could gear them specifically toward our outcome measures. There were two weaknesses to this approach. One was the amount of work needed to develop and revise the tests to ensure the reliability and validity of the measures. The other was our inability to compare our students' results with those obtained at other universities.

The research sequence test, given at the end of the third course in the initial three-course sequence, contained only questions dealing with material from Statistics, Research Methods, and Experimental Psychology. The earliest version of the research sequence test, given from 1994 through 1996, consisted of multiple-choice questions taken from one instructor's research-sequence tests. Some of the faculty thought that the questions selected were too difficult; they may have feared that low scores would be held against the department. It was also impossible to persuade all of the instructors to allow class time for the test. The later versions of the test were much better accepted. They consisted of a short research article (either a correlational design for the research methods class or an experimental design for the experimental class) followed by 15 multiple-choice questions dealing with the article. We gave this test as a portion of the research methods and experimental psychology finals, where it served as an excellent means of testing comprehension of research articles.

Our other measures of knowledge included senior seminar assignments, research sequence proposals, and alumni surveys. The seminar assignments, generally group oral reports, were judged by members of the assessment committee on their correct use of psychological knowledge. Those reports generally dealt with a limited subset of psychological knowledge and provided information only on students' preparation in those specific areas. Similar to the sequence tests, the research proposals were measures primarily of research methods and statistics. The senior and alumni surveys contained questions such as, "Please rate from 1 to 5 how adequate your education at Kennesaw State was in the following areas: A. Experimental/scientific areas of psychology." Such ratings were of some use but, as mentioned in an earlier section, they probably provided different results than what would have been obtained from other measures. These surveys were, however, very useful in letting us know the areas, such as career advising, in which students noticed program deficiencies.

In 2001, the psychology faculty as a whole met to review our assessment plan. We observed that we were spending a great amount of time and faculty resources on assessment, but realizing only limited gain in program improvements from the information collected. The assessments of research papers and senior seminar presentations were labor intensive and yielded limited information on overall program effectiveness. The research sequence exams that we rewrite each semester were not producing the breadth of information needed to make program-change recommendations. Although we were collecting a lot of information, we were using very little of it. What we learned from this analysis was that, in the process of selecting and developing assessment measures, we need to ask not only what a measure assesses, but also how we will use the information gained.

SECOND PHASE OF THE KSU PLAN (2001 TO THE PRESENT)

During the 2001–2002 school year, the department simplified the method of assessment to lead to more easily compared results. We retained the senior exit survey and alumni survey components from the old techniques and we added the Educational Testing Service (ETS) Psychology Major Field Test. This changed the assessment process by placing more emphasis on the measurement of knowledge and less on measures of the presentation and use of that knowledge (see Table 3.2). This change resulted in greater reliability, validity, efficiency, and breadth of knowledge measured, although it entailed some loss of assessment depth.

Adopting the ETS Major Field Test

We chose the ETS test over alternative tests because of the broad range of its question topics and the large number of schools (more than 200) that can serve as a comparison group. The ETS measure is made up of 140 questions that examine students' ability to interpret and make inferences as well as lower-level abilities.

The ETS grade report gives individual scores for each student as well as group assessment means for the areas of memory and thinking, sensory psychology and physiology, developmental psychology, clinical and abnormal psychology, social psychology, and methodology. We administer the test each semester to our senior seminar classes. Students pay a $24.00 fee for the test during registration and take the test in the first half of the term. ETS scores the exams often enough to return the scores by the end of the term. To encourage students to do their best on this test, their test grade influences their final grade for the course. Depending on the instructor, between 10 and 15% of the points given in the class come from the major field test. However, instructors structure the grades so that poor performance on the ETS exam will not have significant adverse impact on a student's final course grade. Students who score in the top 30% of the students in that class who are

TABLE 3.2
Revised Matrix of Learning Outcomes and Assessment Methods

Knowledge areas	Senior Exit Surveys	Alumni Surveys	Major Field Test
1. Scientific writing skills	X	X	
2. Oral presentation skills	X	X	
3. Statistical reasoning			X
4. Variability of behavior	X	X	X
5. Individual and social perspectives	X	X	X
6. Scientific psychology	X	X	X
7. Applied psychology	X	X	X
8. Ethical issues	X	X	
9. Career and graduate study	X		
10. Critical thinking	X		

taking the test receive As for the ETS test; those who score in the 30th to 70th percentiles receive Bs; those who score below the 30th percentile receive Cs. Informally gathered information dealing with the acceptance of the test by students seems to be mixed. Some students do not appreciate the necessity of paying for and taking the test, but they are typically very curious to find out how they did in comparison to students in other universities.

Before making the major field test a part of our assessment program, the comparison of our students' knowledge and skills with those of students from other schools was impossible. Adding the ETS Field Test improves this situation, but it still presents some difficulties. Different colleges offer this test in different ways. For some, students must get a passing score to graduate; for others, the score on the test has no academic consequences. There are also large differences in the academic abilities of students at different colleges. For an additional fee it is possible to make up a sample of similar schools that use the major field test as a comparison group. We are currently considering this option.

ENHANCING ACADEMIC AND CAREER
ADVISEMENT THROUGH ASSESSMENT

During these two phases we have made a sizeable investment in faculty resources and time in assessing and developing our academic and career advisement program. We believe the potential gains in student satisfaction, success, and retention justify the investment. Faculty and administrators "recognize that students who formulate a sound educational/career plan on the basis of their values, interests, and abilities will have an increased chance for academic success, satisfaction, and persistence. Academic advising remains the most significant mechanism available on most college and university campuses for aiding and abetting this important process" (Habley as quoted in Kramer, 1995, p. 1). Additionally, student persistence in college is positively related to contact with faculty (Pascarella & Terenzini, 1991). Therefore, we have administered three advisement surveys over the past several years at two-year intervals to assess the quality of our faculty–student interaction with respect to academic and career advisement.

We developed the first academic advisement survey in 1997 to assist the department in identifying what students were looking for in a sound advisement program. The department's rapid growth in majors and not-so-rapid growth in faculty forced the department to realize that our one-on-one assigned faculty advisor program was becoming cumbersome, if not inadequate, in meeting the needs of 60-plus majors per faculty advisor. Therefore, we geared the initial survey toward evaluating student satisfaction with the existing advisement program as well as identifying what they wanted from the department with respect to academic and career advisement.

In the first survey (1997–1998) we included an extended series of biographical questions that helped us learn about our psychology major respondents. These data proved very useful in helping us learn more about our majors and their needs. The statistics confirmed that a large percentage of our majors (69%) were transfers from other institutions, indicating that a new advisement system would need to provide for one-on-one consultation with an advisor well versed in working with transfer credits. Additionally, a fair number of students identified themselves as both day and evening students. Written comments clarified the reason for this result: Our scheduled course offerings forced them to attend both day and evening classes to earn the credits required to graduate in a timely manner. We incorporated this feedback into our scheduling of classes in future semesters to correct for this problem. Interestingly, the biographical data did not differentiate response patterns concerning the evaluation of quality or satisfaction with advisement.

The survey also contained several questions that gave us specific information about how frequently students sought advisement with their assigned faculty advisor and the reasons why they did not go to advisement often, if that was the case. The reason cited most often for not going to advisement regularly was time schedule conflicts between advisor and advisee. Anticipating this response and knowing that the system required change, we included questions concerning their preferences for other advisement delivery systems. Although they were unhappy about their ability to schedule one-on-one appointments with their faculty advisor, 89% of the respondents indicated a continuing preference for one-on-one advisement over other forms of advisement, such as pooled or group advisement.

The core of the 15-item advisement survey (see Exhibit 3.1) assesses the student's perception of both the quality and importance of a variety of ad-

EXHIBIT 3.1
Core Advisement Survey Questions

QUALITY
A - Excellent - extremely helpful and knowledgeable
B - Good - very helpful
C - Fair - helpful
D - Poor - advisor seemed uninformed
E - Not discussed in advisement sessions

IMPORTANCE
A - Very important to me
B - Important to me
C - Somewhat Important to me
D - Not important to me
E - Not applicable, not expected of advisor

ACTIVITY	QUALITY	IMPORTANCE
1. Discussed general education requirements (core).	A B C D E	A B C D E
2. Discussed major requirements	A B C D E	A B C D E
3. Discussed minor and elective options	A B C D E	A B C D E
4. Discussed career opportunities	A B C D E	A B C D E
5. Discussed my work schedule/load and made course and hours per term recommendations accordingly	A B C D E	A B C D E
6. Suggested courses that will help me complete my degree requirements	A B C D E	A B C D E
7. Suggested or recommended campus resources, such as the counseling or placement center, writing lab ...	A B C D E	A B C D E
8. Discussed graduate education opportunities and options	A B C D E	A B C D E
9. Discussed my career goals with me	A B C D E	A B C D E
10. Helped to select courses in line with my career path	A B C D E	A B C D E
11. Advisor was professional	A B C D E	A B C D E
12. Advisor answered my questions	A B C D E	A B C D E
13. Advisor seemed genuinely concerned with helping me	A B C D E	A B C D E

Transfer students only. Please advance to question 16 if you are not a transfer student.

	QUALITY	IMPORTANCE
14. Advisor was helpful in assisting me to identify how my prior course work fits into KSU's program of study	A B C D E	A B C D E
15. Advisor was genuinely interested in helping to transfer or substitute as many courses as possible	A B C D E	A B C D E

visement activities, including general education and major field requirements, career issues, and the professionalism of the advisor. We developed core questions from extensive faculty discussion of our desired outcomes for academic and career advisement. We also solicited and incorporated feedback from a group of students participating in a tests and measurements course.

We wanted to measure both the quality and importance of each advisement activity. In this survey situation we thought that assessing importance was as significant as assessing quality to reengineer our advisement program for greater effectiveness and efficiency. Quality ratings would indicate areas in need of improvement, whereas the importance rating would help us to decide where to spend our energy and limited resources first.

We incorporated student feedback in developing the scale anchors. On the basis of their input, the anchors for the quality scale ranged from "terrible," the students' preferred term, to "excellent," with an additional alternative of "not discussed in advisement session." The importance scale ranged from "not important to me" to "very important to me" with the additional alternative of "not expected of advisor."

The advisement items indicated that 81% of the respondents believed that the faculty advisors were performing in the "good" to "excellent" range with respect to quality of advisement, receiving the highest marks in knowledgeable course planning, professionalism, openness to student questions, and genuine interest in advisees. Students indicated that they desired greater discussion of career options, objectives, and planning as well as discussion about balancing work schedules with school workloads. Campus resources were another area about which they desired to learn more.

We administered the resulting 37-item, 15-minute survey to all psychology majors in our upper-division classes during the fall semester. We chose upper-division courses over the introductory courses so that we would be soliciting input from students who had at least a year's experience with our advisement program.

On the basis of the survey findings and the need for change in our advisement delivery process, we developed an advisement center model that provides one-on-one advisement with faculty members. Faculty sign up for two to three hours of advising time per week for the four- to five-week period during which the center is in operation during a semester. Students call for an appointment and may request a 15-minute appointment time with a particular advisor, although most instead select an appointment at a time that is convenient to them. The advisement center model, therefore, met the needs of both faculty and students in providing easy access and an efficient advisement system. Students no longer had the frustration of the constraints of scheduling appointments with an assigned faculty member, and faculty no longer thought they had to be on 24-hour call throughout the semester for students needing advisement.

The 15-minute time limit provided only enough time to discuss course selection and planning in relation to workload considerations. It did not provide an opportunity to discuss the career issues that the students had rated so highly. Consequently, the department required a one-credit-hour Careers in Psychology course that would directly address career opportunities in and outside the field with a bachelor's degree as well as with graduate degrees. The course also incorporated vocational assessment, career exploration, and career-planning exercises. A portfolio assessment process was used to evaluate student performance.

With the careers issue tackled, the task of advising transfer students remained. We resolved this challenge by creating a department support role of Coordinator of Advisement, wherein a faculty member receives a one-course reassigned time for one-on-one advisement of the transfer students. The Coordinator is also responsible for managing the Academic Advisement

Center and keeping current various advisement materials as well as administering future advisement surveys.

With these changes in place the department decided to assess the new system after two years. We conducted a second advisement survey that contained the same 15 core advisement items and added several items to evaluate the students' opinions about the effectiveness of the new advising center. We also included questions concerning the new Careers in Psychology course and whether students believed the course was meeting their career advisement needs.

The results of the second survey (1999–2000) indicated an increase in overall satisfaction with advisement from 81% to 88%. When asked which system they preferred, 66% indicated preferring the new academic advisement center approach compared with 34% who preferred the assigned advisor system. Faculty also liked the advisement center approach, but most felt rushed by the 15-minute advisement time, preferring a slightly longer session length of 20 minutes. So on this survey, we questioned the students about the adequacy of the 15-minute advisement time interval and whether it should be raised to a 20, 25, or 30-minute appointment. Sixty percent of the respondents indicated favoring an increase to 20 minutes. We implemented the 20-minute advisement session the following semester on the basis of the demonstrated student support.

The questions addressing the Careers course indicated "high" satisfaction with the course in respect to the information that it provided on career opportunities and career exploration, but 60% of the respondents thought they needed additional advisement beyond the course. Students concurred with the faculty position that the course should be expanded from a one-credit hour course to a three-credit hour course. We extended the course to three credit hours the following academic year, providing more time for career exploration exercises and discussion.

With the above changes in place we conducted a third advisement survey two years later, during the 2001–2002 academic year. Again we presented the 15 core questions along with follow-up questions on the advisement center process and the Careers course. We added a new set of questions to find out whether students were accessing advisement materials that had been placed on the department's Internet site since the prior survey. Students affirmed the high satisfaction with the quality of academic advisement, with a slight increase to 90% indicating "good" to "excellent" ratings. Most notable here was an increase in the number of students awarding an excellent rating. Seventy percent of the respondents indicated that the 20-minute advisement center appointment was adequate for the primary advising activities of course planning and scheduling as well as discussion of course selection on the basis of career interest. The added time for discussion in the Careers course must have influenced this response. The overall satisfaction with the Careers course increased with the added credit hours; 65% of the students thought that they received an acceptable level of career advisement through the course.

On the basis of the most recent survey, there is strong support for the current academic advisement center model and the Careers in Psychology course as effective means of providing needed career information and guidance to students. The success of the Careers in Psychology course goes along with findings indicating that these courses are becoming popular and inform majors of the realities and opportunities in psychology (Dillinger & Landrum, 2002; Landrum, Shoemaker, & Davis, 2003). A significant number (35%) thought that additional career advisement is needed beyond the careers course, even with its expanded format. This outcome may be due to the timing of the Careers course in their academic program as many take it in their second year of coursework and plans are likely to change between then and their senior year. This issue will be assessed in a fourth advisement survey that we are planning for the upcoming 2003–2004 course year.

The department, faculty, and students have benefited greatly from the advisement survey information collected over the years. A new advisement system has been implemented and adjusted over the years on the basis of student feedback to make it more effective and student friendly. The career advisement process has been strengthened through the introduction and expansion of the Careers in Psychology course. We hope that our plans for an alumni mentor program and other initiatives will meet student needs in this area and will be assessed in future years to determine whether they have, in fact, enhanced the career advisement process.

With respect to the assessment process itself, a two-year interval seems more than adequate with respect to frequency of assessing our advisement program. A three-year interval will probably suffice once we have settled into a system and stopped adding major components.

During this period of working to improve our advisement program we have seen not only a rise in satisfaction scores from students, but also an increase in the number of psychology majors, despite increasing competition from recently added allied discipline programs, such as sociology, human services, and criminal justice. We see the increasing popularity of psychology as an additional measure of our success. Also, because of the reputation the department has developed for effective delivery of student advisement across the campus, several other major programs have implemented similar outcomes assessment programs and adopted the department's advisement center model.

IDEAS FOR THE FUTURE

Assessment is of little use unless it results in improvements in students' knowledge and skills. Assessment tasks will not be done (at least not for long) if sufficient resources are not available. As part of our future planning, we will consider both the costs of assessment techniques and the ways in which our program could be modified if the results of those techniques show that our outcomes are not met. This review should lead to a more stable and efficient assessment process. A tentative conclusion from our experiences is that broad and relatively easily done assessment measures, such as surveys, can capture significant problems that, when resolved, lead to important program gains. More focused and resource-intensive assessments may be required to ensure that changes actually result in specific improved performance.

We will continue to investigate new methods for assessing each of the learning outcomes with an eye on broader (as opposed to very focused) assessment methods. Stivers, Campbell, and Hermanson (2000) provide an excellent description of the process of implementing a departmental assessment process in an accounting department. The article provides practical advice for anyone beginning such a program. One of their recommendations is to begin an assessment program with a "buckshot" approach—to capture as many types of information as possible at a basic level but also to be sure that the data you take in are important data, not just data that are easy to measure.

Greater faculty involvement in and support for the assessment process is a desired future outcome. The more information communicated to the faculty about the process, goals, and outcomes of assessment, the more likely they are to envision it as a valued part of the program. In our early years of assessment, the program was championed only by a few, and information obtained was shared on only a limited basis with the larger faculty group. As assessment methods broadened and the information obtained became more useful and discussed more frequently with the faulty as a whole, faculty interest and involvement have steadily increased. Greater faculty "buy-in" has led to their participation in the assessment process and making their classes available for collecting needed data.

Learning outcomes are most directly affected by the actions of the instructor in the classroom. We plan to encourage assessment techniques that occur within the classroom and that could result in immediate improvements. These techniques include such things as structured midterm evaluations, peer evaluation, the comparison of test and paper grades to desired course outcomes, and pre- and post-tests. Of course, the effectiveness of such measures depends on the willingness of the instructor to be flexible in his or her teaching and on whether the information gained is used for faculty performance appraisal or purely developmental purposes.

RECOMMENDATIONS

A comprehensive student learning outcomes assessment plan should be an ongoing process, continuously used for program planning and improvement (Astin et al., 2003). As we navigated our way through the process, we learned several lessons:

1. Implement assessment processes gradually. It is easy to attempt to do too much, too fast. It is helpful to concentrate on one aspect of the plan at a time.

2. Do not assess each outcome every semester or every year. We have developed an assessment regimen that places all but the ETS exam on a two-or-more-year interval assessment schedule.

3. Keep faculty involved in the process. Take time to communicate and discuss learning outcomes, assessment methods, and assessment data results at department meetings and retreats.

4. Communicate the outcomes to psychology majors and show how those outcomes are tied to the curriculum. Appleby (2002) notes the importance of communicating the department's curriculum goals to students. At Indiana University-Purdue University at Indianapolis, he has developed a document to explain the department's goals to their majors.

5. Take opportunities to benchmark and to learn from what other departments (psychology and non-psychology, on-campus and off-campus) are doing. This practice keeps us from reinventing the wheel.

6. Stay at the practical level. The most important reason for assessment is to improve the quality of student learning. Data should address needed changes in any program so as to realize stated learning objectives and outcomes.

We additionally recommend that the assessment plan remain developmental in focus, and that outcome information not be incorporated into individual faculty performance evaluations. This strategy is particularly important when faculty "buy-in" is important in getting new assessment programs started. Faculty should view program assessment as a development tool or process that is at their disposal to help improve their teaching and degree program. We have experienced significant growth in our program, both in quality and in student numbers, as the result of this philosophy.

REFERENCES

Appleby, D. (2002). *The first step in student-centered assessment: Helping students understand our curriculum goals.* American Psychological Association. Retrieved September 1, 2003, from http://www.apa.org/ed/ helping_students.html

Astin, A., Banta, T., Cross, K., El-Khawas, E., Ewell, P., Hutchings, P., et al. (2003). *Nine principles of good practice for assessing student learning.* American Association for Higher Education. Retrieved September 1, 2003, from http://www.aahe.org/assessment/principl.htm

Dillinger, R., & Landrum, R. (2002). An information course for the beginning psychology major. *Teaching of Psychology, 29,* 230–232.

Garhart, C., & Hannafin, M. (1986). The accuracy of cognitive monitoring during computer-based instruction. *Journal of Computer-Based Instruction, 13,* 88–93.

Hacker, D. J., Bol, L., Horgan, D. D., & Rakow, E. A. (2000). Test prediction and performance in a classroom context. *Journal of Educational Psychology, 92,* 160–170.

Halonen, J., Appleby, D., Brewer, C., Buskist, W., Gillem, A., Halpern, D., et al. (2002). *Undergraduate psychology major learning goals and outcomes: A report.* American Psychological Association. Retrieved September 1, 2003, from http://www.apa.org/ed/pcue/reports.html

Halpern, D. (1988). Assessing student outcomes for psychology majors. *Teaching of Psychology, 15,* 181–186.

Kramer, G. L. (1995). Reaffirming the role of faculty in academic advising. *National Academic Advising Association Monograph, 1.* Manhattan, KS: National Academic Advising Association.

Landrum, R., Shoemaker, C., & Davis, S. (2003). Important topics in an introduction to psychology major course. *Teaching of Psychology, 31,* 48–50.

McGovern, T., Furumoto, L., Halpern, D., Kimble, G., & McKeachie, W. (1991, June). Liberal education, study in depth, and the arts and sciences major—psychology. *American Psychologist, 46,* 598– 605.

McGovern, T., & Reich, J. (1996, March). A comment on the quality principles. *American Psychologist, 51,* 252–255.

Pascarella, E. T., & Terenzini, P. T. (1991). *How college affects students: Findings and insights from twenty years of research.* San Francisco: Jossey-Bass.

Sheehan, E. (1994). A multimethod assessment of the psychology major. *Teaching of Psychology, 21,* 74–78.

Stivers, B. P, Campbell, J. E., & Hermanson, H. M. (2000). An assessment program for accounting: Design, implementation, and reflection. *Issues in Accounting Education, 15,* 553–581.

APPENDIX 3.1

UNDERGRADUATE PSYCHOLOGY LEARNING GOALS

Knowledge, Skills, and Values Consistent With the Science and Application of Psychology

Goal 1. Knowledge Base of Psychology

Students will demonstrate familiarity with the major concepts, theoretical perspectives, empirical findings, and historical trends in psychology.

Goal 2. Research Methods in Psychology

Students will understand and apply basic research methods in psychology, including research design, data analysis, and interpretation.

Goal 3. Critical Thinking Skills in Psychology

Students will respect and use critical and creative thinking, skeptical inquiry, and, when possible, the scientific approach to solve problems related to behavior and mental processes.

Goal 4. Application of Psychology

Students will understand and apply psychological principles to personal, social, and organizational issues.

Goal 5. Values in Psychology

Students will be able to weigh evidence, tolerate ambiguity, act ethically, and reflect other values that are the underpinnings of psychology as a discipline.

Knowledge, Skills, and Values Consistent With Liberal Arts Education That Are Further Developed in Psychology

Goal 6. Information and Technological Literacy

Students will demonstrate information competence and the ability to use computers and other technology for many purposes.

Goal 7. Communication Skills

Students will be able to communicate effectively in a variety of formats.

Goal 8. Sociocultural and International Awareness

Students will recognize, understand, and respect the complexity of sociocultural and international diversity.

Goal 9. Personal Development

Students will develop insight into their own and others' behavior and mental processes and apply effective strategies for self-management and self-improvement.

Goal 10. Career Planning and Development

Students will emerge from the major with realistic ideas about how to implement their psychological knowledge, skills, and values in occupational pursuits in a variety of settings.

From the Undergraduate Learning Goals and Outcomes document authored by the Task Force on Undergraduate Psychology Major Competencies appointed by the American Psychological Association's Board of Educational Affairs. Retrieved September 1, 2003, from www.apa.org/ed/pcue/reports.html.

4

DESIGNING AND IMPLEMENTING PSYCHOLOGY PROGRAM REVIEWS

THOMAS P. PUSATERI, RETTA E. POE, WILLIAM E. ADDISON,
AND GEORGE D. GOEDEL

As a result of greater accountability pressures in higher education (e.g., Halpern, 2003; chap. 1, this volume, 2002), preparation of self-study reports, as part of both internal and external academic program review requirements, has become a regular feature of academic life. This chapter is an effort to provide psychology department chairs and faculty with advice on using the review process to advance departmental goals, preparing for the program review process, writing the self-study report, selecting an external reviewer or review team, planning a site visit, and implementing the recommendations that emerge from the program review.

USING THE REVIEW PROCESS TO ADVANCE DEPARTMENTAL GOALS

The departmental chair usually plays a critical role in accomplishing a successful program review. In many respects, the daily activities of a skilled chair continually involve program assessment, in one form or another, to garner resources to maintain program integrity, to realize short and long-term departmental goals and objectives, and just to "keep all of the trains running on time." For example, the chair engages in program assessment activities when constructing course schedules, preparing budget requests, conducting performance reviews and making salary recommendations, working with the department's faculty members to develop curriculum changes or new course initiatives, and so forth. In completing these tasks, the chair must draw upon a variety of data to support and justify his or her conclusions. In addition, chairs who submit data-driven requests for resources generally have higher rates of success. Deans and provosts are typically more persuaded by and responsive to empirically supported arguments.

Perhaps the most critical of all assessment documents, especially for any long-term planning and program improvement, is the program review self-study. Although program review is a challenge and involves a good deal of work, it is in the best interests of the department for both department chairs and faculty members to embrace program review as a welcome opportunity to compile a wealth of data that can be used to improve their programs. The process of assembling a self-study report also provides an opportunity for the members of the department to reflect on the purpose and quality of the programs they offer. Ideally, the self-study report combines useful information about the department in one comprehensive document and provides an overall picture for the chair, the faculty, and those who administer the institution.

Another potential benefit associated with the program review process is that it may help psychology departments in their efforts to acquire institutional resources when they are competing with programs in other disciplines that have national certification or accreditation standards (Wesp, 2002). In some cases, these other disciplines will bolster their requests for resources by maintaining that they risk losing accreditation unless certain changes are made. With the exception of some specialized graduate programs (e.g., school psychology), psychology departments currently do not have this kind of leverage. However, psychology departments may gain some leverage by referring to a recent American Psychological Association (APA) task force report (2002) on undergraduate learning goals and outcomes for psychology majors. Additionally, other documents such as guidelines for animal research (e.g., American Psychological Association Committee on Animal Research and Ethics, n.d.) may be used to support the case for resources. However, a department's best hope for improved funding and scarce institutional resources may be a well done, comprehensive program review, with convincing assessment data clearly presented and effectively interpreted.

PREPARING FOR THE PROGRAM REVIEW PROCESS

Clarifying the Purpose of Academic Program Review

A necessary first step is to determine the purpose of the program review at your institution and the context in which the review occurs (Nichols &

Nichols, 2000). Depending on the economic and political climate on your campus at the time of the self-study, your review may have several related but different purposes: program expansion or enhancement, program continuance at current levels of support, or program reduction with a decrease in resources. Because these different purposes should probably be addressed in different ways, you may wish to request that your chief academic officer clearly define the purpose of the review.

Having a more explicit goal may provide better direction or focus for your review, suggesting specific areas for emphasis. For example, if your review has possible expansion or enhancement as a purpose, then it would be reasonable to explore needs that are not currently being met and fertile opportunities for growth. A well-documented needs analysis could provide support and emphasis for growth in new areas. However, if the program review is being done primarily for purposes of determining program continuance or reduction, then it may be important for your department to reflect seriously on the relative costs and benefits of maintaining the program at a current or reduced level. Such an analysis could determine whether some reduction in services or an internal reallocation of resources is warranted. Although painful, such actions may actually be in the best interests of your program and institution. Regardless of purpose, a comprehensive program review should provide a candid appraisal of the strengths and weaknesses of your current program. Strengths should be highlighted and tied to institutional mission and goals. All identified weaknesses critical to the integrity of your program should be reported with reasonable recommendations for amelioration.

If regional accrediting boards or state boards of higher education are primarily driving the review, as may be the case in the review of some graduate programs, those groups typically indicate the primary criteria for institutional reaccreditation or meeting established state standards and the contingencies for failing to meet those criteria. In general, such criteria tend to be fairly broad, are generally not discipline-specific, and are usually easily met by an established, functioning department. Under such circumstances, an institution's limited resources will be primarily directed toward meeting glaring institutional deficiencies rather than enhancing programs that make a "passing grade." Therefore, unless the self-study reveals some serious deficiencies that threaten institutional reaccreditation, it is not likely that your program review will lead to any increase in resources for your department.

On the other hand, reviews may be primarily internally driven by institutional strategic planning activities. Under these circumstances, your review may be taken very seriously in helping either to establish or to meet long-term institutional priorities. Strategic planning documents can often provide important information about issues that your review should address. Administrators are likely to allocate institutional resources to those departments that contribute to strategic planning initiatives. Another important factor to consider is any recent administrative restructuring that may have occurred on your campus. For example, suppose that your institution has recently established an office for community outreach or distance learning. If your review contains recommendations for program initiatives or enhancements in these areas, your chances of receiving additional funding may improve.

Finally, before you begin the self-study, you should develop realistic expectations about how seriously the institution will regard the self-study review and its likely outcomes. The department chair and faculty should ascertain how the institution has handled departmental program reviews conducted in prior years. Unless significant changes have occurred in your administration, prior administrative follow-up to past reviews may well predict the response a new review will receive. Another predictor of how seriously higher administrators will regard the self-study may be their willingness to commit institutional resources to support the review process. For example, the dean or provost may be willing to provide reassigned or release time for the faculty member who is appointed to serve as the overall writer and editor of the self-study report. A third predictor may be how willing administrators are to commit in advance to providing a timely written response to the final report recommendations.

Collecting Resources and Reference Materials

Once you understand both the task and the approach you must take, the next step is to determine what you need to know to prepare the self-study report. In addition to examining the specific requirements of your institution's self-study process, you should review how other institutions approach the academic program review process. Also, you may need some "benchmarking" information, and you may want to see some examples of other psychology programs' self-study reports. See Appendix 4.1 for a list of online resources and Appendix 4.2 and the References for lists of print resources related for preparing self-study reports.

Because the report must include detailed information about faculty activities, the department chair will be dependent on faculty cooperation to obtain information about publications, presentations, grants, institutional service activities, public service, and so on. One way to simplify the collection of faculty information is to develop a template. If all faculty members report their information in the same format and submit the information electronically, the task of developing a master list of faculty activities becomes one of simply cutting and pasting from the documents submitted.

Developing a Departmental Mission Statement and Goals

You will need a thoughtfully developed, clearly articulated departmental mission statement as well as a mission statement and a set of goals for each program; if you lack these, creating them should be a high priority. In addition, your departmental and program mission statements should be tied to your institution's mission statement, and the linkage between institutional and departmental and program mission statements should be obvious (Nichols & Nichols, 2000).

You should choose your mission statements and goals carefully. Because some accrediting bodies may expect you to demonstrate that you are accomplishing your mission and goals, be sure that they are measurable and attainable. For example, if you say that you intend to produce graduates who are globally competitive, think about whether and how you can demonstrate that you have succeeded in this. Similarly, if research and service activities are part of your institution's mission (and therefore part of the department's mission), be prepared to provide an accounting of your success in accomplishing these aspects of your mission.

An important part of program review is the ongoing assessment of program/departmental effectiveness in terms of student learning outcomes (Halpern, chap. 1, this volume). You should identify the expected outcomes for each program, the means of assessing those outcomes, and the criteria for determining success in meeting the outcomes. You should include a plan for collecting relevant data, making any necessary program improvements suggested by the data, and documenting that you have made the changes. For assistance in developing student learning outcomes, you may wish to review the APA task force report on undergraduate learning goals and outcomes for psychology majors (2002) and APA's Assessment CyberGuide (http://www.apa.org/ed/guidehomepage.html). Additional examples of statements of student learning outcomes may be found on the institutional Web sites that are listed in Appendix 4.1.

Soliciting Faculty Cooperation and Participation

Preparing a self-study report is ideally *not* a task for the department chair alone. Sharing the responsibility is important for several reasons, not the least of which is the amount of work that may be involved. Faculty members who assist in the preparation of the self-study report may also develop a greater understanding and appreciation of the department as a whole and may gain insight regarding its strengths and weaknesses. Also, a collaborative process will make it more likely that the recommendations for change that emerge from the self-study will be "owned" by the faculty who will have to implement the changes. Begin by scheduling an early departmental meeting to review the goals and process of program review and to formulate a plan.

Although the division of responsibilities will depend on situational variables, some roles for which volunteers may be solicited include the following: (a) overall writer and editor of the self-study report; (b) writers and editors of various sections (faculty, facilities, curriculum, assessment plan and results, etc.); (c) chair of the external review process (finding a suitable external reviewer, arranging the site visit, etc.); and (d) chair of the assessment committee (collecting and organizing effectiveness data, preparing tables and charts, etc.).

PREPARING THE SELF-STUDY REPORT

Time Frame

Depending on the size of the department, the ideal time to begin preparing for the self-study report is one or two semesters. For example, if a department schedules the external review for the spring semester, initiate the self-study process during the spring semester or summer term of the preceding calendar year. This schedule would allow sufficient time to gather and organize the necessary information for the report.

The optimal time frame for the preparation of the report also depends on the number of faculty members involved in the process. It is a good idea to begin the report writing process in the summer prior to a review scheduled for spring. Although it may be more difficult to obtain some information during the summer (e.g., faculty vitae), the chair and other faculty working on the review are less likely to be distracted by other demands. If the preparation of the report must be done during a single semester (e.g., during the fall semester for a review the following spring), assistance from a faculty committee on some aspects of the report is probably essential.

Components of a Strong Report

A strong self-study report should provide a detailed account of fundamental information relevant to the review process (e.g., faculty positions, number of majors, courses offered). Additionally, the report should include a realistic appraisal of the challenges and opportunities facing the department. A strong report should be relatively candid, comprehensive, and detailed. In particular, an effective report should provide a thorough accounting of the department, the faculty, the students, academic support, and the curriculum as well as information about facilities and equipment, assessment activities, and activities related to external relations and fund-raising. See Appendix 4.3 for a list of suggested items to be included in the report. The following sections discuss some of these items in more detail.

Departmental Information

This section of the report should begin with the department's mission statement and goals. In addition, this section might include a history of the department and information concerning the department's external and internal patterns of administration. External patterns of administration include such information as the division or college in which the department is housed and the channels of communication from the department to the upper administration (e.g., direct report by the department chair). Internal patterns of administration include formal policies governing the responsibilities of the chair and any program coordinators (e.g., coordinators of an undergraduate honors program or graduate program), the department's committee structure, and the schedule for department meetings and retreats. Departmental information should also include budgetary information such as the size of the department's base budget, the extent to which the budget is decentralized, and typical allocations for travel, equipment, discretionary funds, and so on.

The Faculty

The report should include, or refer to, current copies of faculty vitae and information regarding the allocation of faculty lines within the department. For example, the report should indicate the number of current positions including the number of tenure-track and annually contracted faculty, the number of full-time and part-time faculty, and the areas of psychology represented by faculty training. Additionally, if the department makes use of any graduate or undergraduate teaching assistants, the report should denote the number of assistants and their responsibilities. Faculty information should also address, in a fairly detailed manner, the evaluation process for promotion and tenure, including any formal guidelines or requirements.

Students

Key information about students includes the student/faculty ratio for the psychology department and recent trends in the number of majors per program. Additional information that might be helpful to both the department and the external reviewers can be addressed in a "student profile" that would include average SAT or ACT scores and other relevant demographics such as the proportions of traditional and nontraditional students, the proportions of residential and commuting students, and the diversity of the student population in gender, age, and ethnicity.

Academic Support

The report should include specific information about the institutional support available for the department's academic programs. Much of this support consists of personnel who work directly with the department (e.g., secretary or administrative assistant, graduate assistants, work-study students) and those who indirectly support the academic work of the faculty by providing expertise in a variety of technological areas (e.g., computer assistance, training in Web-enhanced or Web-delivered courses). Additional indirect support includes library personnel and resources as well as materials and expertise available through an office of faculty development, a center for teaching and learning, or an office of grants and research.

The Curriculum

Much information regarding the curriculum is likely to be found in the institution's undergraduate and/or graduate catalog; thus, references to pertinent sections of the catalog may be appropriate. The report may include passages from the catalog that contain details about the degree program(s) offered by the department, including requirements for the major, the minor, any concentrations or options within the major, and course listings with descriptions. Other relevant information regarding the curriculum, which may not be readily accessible from the catalog, includes course enrollment patterns, service learning opportunities, and the department's contribution to other programs such as the institution's general education program or supporting courses for majors in other disciplines.

Other sections of the report should address the department's available facilities and equipment, including classroom and laboratory space; information about the department's assessment activities; and activities related to external relations and fund raising, such as alumni outreach efforts. For example, if the department publishes an alumni newsletter on a regular basis, the report may include a representative copy.

Some sections of the report may include references to print documents related to "best practices" in psychology education to familiarize readers who may not have backgrounds in the discipline. For example, your department's mission statement could make reference to the APA's "Principles for Quality Undergraduate Psychology Programs" (McGovern & Reich, 1996) or to the report of the APA Task Force on Undergraduate Psychology Major Competencies (APA, 2002). Some sections of the report may also be strengthened by comparisons of your program with similar programs at other institutions. A report of a survey by APA's Research Office of undergraduate psychology programs (Kyle & Williams, 2000) provides useful information on programs that may be similar to yours. To compare your department's undergraduate degree requirements with those of other institutions, consult surveys of the typical structure of the psychology major and most frequently listed courses (e.g., Perlman & McCann, 1999a, 1999b). Examine how departments at other institutions are assessing the achievement of learning outcomes for their majors (e.g., Graham, 1998; Jackson & Griggs, 1995; Kruger & Zechmeister, 2001; Lawson, 1999; Levy, Burton, Mickler, & Vigorito, 1999;

Nelson & Johnson, 1997; Sheehan, 1994; Stoloff & Feeney, 2002; refer also to the institutional Web sites listed in Appendix 4.1).

SELECTING AN EXTERNAL REVIEWER OR REVIEW TEAM

Many institutions expect departments to arrange for one or more external reviewers who will write an evaluative report following a site visit. We recommend gaining commitments from the identified reviewer or review team at least one semester prior to the site visit. Two excellent sources of potential reviewers may be found online: the Departmental Consulting Service listed on the Office of Teaching Resources in Psychology (OTRP) Web site, and the Council on Undergraduate Research (see Appendix 4.1). An essential criterion for selecting your reviewer should be the match between your institution and that of the reviewer. Not only are the reviewer's recommendations likely to be better informed if the reviewer comes from an institution similar to yours, but the similarity may give the reviewer more credibility with senior administrators at your institution. Some of the relevant criteria for seeking a good match are: (a) the size and selectiveness of the reviewer's institution; (b) the nature of the reviewer's institution (public, private, religious); (c) the similarity of programs offered (doctoral, master's, baccalaureate only, psychology specialty areas); (d) the reviewer's knowledge of the expectations of the regional accrediting association; (e) geographical and cultural similarities between the reviewer's institution and yours; and (f) the kinds of students served (many potential graduate students, mostly terminal baccalaureate students, many commuter or nontraditional students, etc.).

If your department is seeking feedback about specific aspects of your program, you may want to identify a reviewer with specialized expertise (Korn, Sweetman, & Nodine, 1996). Examples include: (a) curriculum issues (e.g., writing across the curriculum, service learning, internships, technology in the classroom); (b) cross-cultural or international awareness; (c) academic and career advising; (d) development of new programs or concentrations; (e) methods of assessing outcomes; and (f) personnel issues (e.g., faculty evaluation).

Providing Information to and Questions for the External Reviewer

At least 3 weeks prior to the site visit, provide the reviewer or review team with the department's self-study report and supplemental materials describing the department, the institution, and the purpose for the program review. Appendix 4.4 identifies materials that might be included in the packet sent to your reviewer(s). The packet should include a cover letter with an inventory of enclosed materials and a list of key questions or issues, approved by the department and administration, to guide the reviewer(s) in examining the materials and preparing questions for the site visit.

THE SITE VISIT

Appendix 4.5 presents a recommended schedule of activities for the site visit for departments of eight or fewer faculty members. This schedule presupposes one reviewer will be selected and will visit for 1 1/2 days, arriving mid-afternoon the first day and completing the visit no later than 5 p.m. the second day. Larger departments, or departments that have several programs to review, may need to select two or more reviewers and may need more days for the site visit. If you recruit two or more reviewers, they may separate to interview different individuals or groups. However, the ideal arrangement is for all reviewers to be present during key meetings (e.g., those that deal with the dean or provost), and time should be scheduled to allow reviewers the opportunity to share notes on site. The following paragraphs provide our recommendations for the purpose and focus of each meeting.

Initial Meeting With Representative(s) of the Administration

The department chair should ask appropriate members of the institution's administrative team who have oversight of the program review process to meet with the reviewer at the beginning of the site visit. This meeting could provide the reviewer with information concerning the administration's perception of your department within the context of the institution, its mission, and its strategic plan. This meeting may also help the reviewer clarify the purpose of the program review and expectations for the contents and structure of the reviewer's report.

Tour of Facilities

The department should schedule a tour of relevant facilities early in the site visit. This tour helps the reviewer develop familiarity with issues that may arise during meetings with the department's faculty members, students, and other campus representatives. Appendix 4.5 lists some sites to consider including on the tour. You might want to ask the reviewer to view these sites from the perspective of a prospective student entering the facilities for the first time, particularly the common areas, such as hallways leading to faculty offices and departmental bulletin boards. Ask your reviewer to comment on how welcoming the facilities appear to be, how accessible the facilities are for individuals with disabilities, and how easy it is to find information and resources that a prospective student might want from the department, such as advising materials, career information, and schedules of departmental activities. Such information from the reviewer may help your department consider ways to renovate or restructure your facilities to make them more useful for current and prospective students.

Dinner With the Department

Scheduling a dinner for the reviewer to meet the department's chair and faculty members can help to clarify the purpose of the review process and the reviewer's role. Ideally, all members of small departments should attend this dinner, and large departments should select key members to attend (e.g., the department chair, members of the committee that wrote the self-study report, or program coordinators). An ideal outcome of this dinner meeting is a spirit of collaborative inquiry during the rest of the site visit.

Meetings With the Department's Faculty Members

Ideally, each member of the department should have time for a private meeting with the reviewer. However, the size of the department, time constraints, and scheduling conflicts may require some faculty to meet in groups with the reviewer. The reviewer(s) and members of the department should agree on a list of questions to help focus conversation during these meetings and allow all faculty members to provide responses to key questions for the review. What follows are some suggestions for general questions that could be adapted depending on the needs of the department. Three or four general questions like these can be discussed during a 30-minute meeting and still leave sufficient time for faculty members to address other relevant issues.

1. What are the current strengths of the department? What are some essential aspects of the department's functioning that should not change in the future?
2. What are areas in which the department needs to improve? What areas are currently not working at a desirable level?
3. Where would you like to see the department develop within the next 5 years? How might the department devote resources to that development?
4. How well and in what ways does the department address the mission of the larger institution? How might the department change in ways that would further support the institutional mission?

Group Interview With Students

This meeting might be scheduled at breakfast or lunch and student meals may be paid for from the review budget in order to give them incentive to attend the meeting. The students in attendance should be a representative sample of students served by the department in demographics (e.g., gender, age, ethnicity), class rank (e.g., senior, junior, graduate student), career interests (e.g., graduate school, terminal baccalaureate degrees), and other variables relevant to the department and the larger institution (e.g., commuter and residential students). Departments that offer graduate programs may wish to schedule separate meetings for undergraduate and graduate students. The department may request that reviewers start the interview by asking students to complete a questionnaire similar to the following.

1. What is your current year or status in college (e.g., first year, senior, graduate student)?
2. What major(s), minor(s), or program(s) are you pursuing?
3. (For undergraduates) Do you plan to apply to graduate school? If yes, in what area?
4. What career(s) are you considering?
5. In your opinion, what are the strengths of the program in psychology?
6. In your opinion, how might the program be improved in the future?

Students can then discuss their responses as a group and write additional comments on their surveys during the discussion.

Typically, faculty members tend to recruit their most successful undergraduate students for the group interview, which biases the group composition towards seniors applying to graduate school. If this is likely, faculty may wish to ensure input from a more representative sample of undergraduate students by distributing the same brief questionnaire in selected classes either during or prior to the reviewer's visit and providing the reviewer with the results.

Meetings With Other Relevant Campus Representatives

Depending on the department's needs, individual or group meetings may be arranged between the reviewer and individuals from other institutional offices or departments. For example, you should consider having reviewers meet with faculty members from departments that have or are developing interdisciplinary programs with psychology, offer support courses for psychology majors, or require their majors to enroll in psychology courses. Also consider scheduling meetings with clerical or academic support staff. For example, if a department's self-study raises questions related to current library resources that support the major or program, you may want to arrange for the reviewer to meet with library staff to discuss relevant library acquisitions and services. Similarly, if the department's faculty members are interested in incorporating more technology into their courses, a meeting with technology support staff might help the reviewer gauge the feasibility of the department's plans.

Meeting With the Department Chair

If practical, a meeting between the reviewer and the department chair should be the last scheduled meeting prior to the reviewer's report. This arrangement allows the department chair an opportunity to discuss with the reviewer any sensitive issues that may have been raised during earlier meetings and that may not be appropriate for inclusion in the reviewer's report.

Preliminary Reports to the Department and/or Administration (Optional)

At some institutions, the department and/or administration may wish to hear a preliminary oral report from the reviewer at the conclusion of the site visit. An experienced external reviewer may be able to provide general impressions from the visit, but neither the department nor administration should expect the reviewer to offer specific recommendations until he or she has had sufficient time to consider the wealth of information collected during the visit. Prior to delivering the oral report, the reviewer should be permitted some private preparation time. If two or more reviewers are involved in the site visit, the preparation time might require 60 minutes or more so that reviewers may share their observations, particularly if they conducted separate interviews during the site visit. If the reviewer provides a report to the department, the meeting should allow time for faculty members to discuss the reviewer's general impressions.

The Reviewer's Report and the Department's Response

The department should request that the reviewer provide a written report within 1 month of the site visit, with copies sent directly to the dean or chief academic officer and to the department chair, who then shares the report with the rest of the department. Within 1 month of receiving this report, the department should draft a response to the report and forward it to the chief academic officer.

IMPLEMENTING THE RECOMMENDATIONS FROM PROGRAM REVIEW

An external reviewer's report will include a number of recommendations such as changes in curriculum and the resources available to departments (Korn, Sweetman, & Nodine, 1996). Regardless of whether the department chair and faculty accept the reviewer's recommendations, the department should provide a written response to all recommendations, either proposing plans (including a reasonable timetable) to implement the recommendations it supports or offering a rationale for rejecting the recommendations with which it disagrees. The department should also identify which changes are feasible and which are not.

The department's response to the review recommendations should be submitted to the dean with a request for a written response, especially to those items that may involve additional resources. In a sense, the department's response and timetable for implementation, along with the dean's reactions, may serve as an implied contract regarding shared expectations and any needed resource allocations. There should be agreement on what the department is doing well and how it contributes to the institution's mission, goals, and objectives. Such agreement ensures that the department will continue to be valued and it makes the case for additional resources where current funding levels are inadequate. In addition, implementation of any recommendations that may require a shift in resources can be viewed in terms of how such a shift may affect current operations.

Some of the recommendations may be implemented without the need for any additional resources. If so, the department should implement these low-cost recommendations as soon as possible. Such immediate action suggests to administrators that the department takes its review seriously. In addition, the department should show initiative in its attempts to obtain external sources of funding to make recommended changes. External or "soft" money that a department obtains for a short period may eventually turn into institutional "hard" money to continue a project. Moreover, even if your grant applications for external support fail to bear fruit, your attempts to obtain such support will likely strengthen any future request for internal funding. Finally, the department should explore "matching fund" grants. Many agencies (e.g., National Science Foundation) typically require a commitment of matching funds from your institution. Thus, even if you do not receive the grant, you can argue for those partial funds that the institution was willing to commit as its match.

Perhaps the most difficult task following the completion of a program review is keeping the document alive and having its recommendations serve as a continuing priority for both the department's faculty and higher administrators. We offer a number of suggestions for preventing your review from accumulating dust. First, review recommendations should be thoroughly integrated into annual and long-term departmental goals and objectives. The department can do this either in a very subtle manner or explicitly, such as by adding to any stated goal or objective the phrase, "as recommended in the department's program review." It is a good idea to keep the dean well informed every time a recommendation has been implemented and how that implementation has contributed to institutional goals and objectives. This practice will serve as a continuous reminder to the dean that the review remains a priority for the department and it will give the dean a reason to talk to others about how well your department is performing. Fly your department's flag whenever you can, publicizing successes, acknowledging assistance, and giving credit where credit is due (i.e., primarily to those who have provided resources).

Many institutions require an annual departmental report to summarize faculty achievements, new initiatives, and so forth. Such a report should emphasize all review recommendations that have been realized, those that could have been realized had adequate funding been available, and those yet to be realized. This practice helps to keep reviews alive for several years after completion. Wherever feasible, you should integrate both appropriate data generated by a review and review recommendations into *all* resource requests, including those related to the annual operating budget, additional faculty and staff lines, instructional equipment and technology, additional space and capital construction, library and software acquisitions, faculty and staff training and development, support for student organizations, community outreach initiatives, and curricular enhancements. Given that a well-done, comprehensive program review provides a wealth of data, the department should continue to refer to the report when competing with other programs for limited resources.

REFERENCES

American Psychological Association Committee on Animal Research and Ethics. (n.d.). *Guidelines for ethical conduct in the care and use of animals.* Retrieved March 27, 2003, from the APA Science Directorate Web site: http://www.apa.org/science/anguide.html

American Psychological Association Task Force on Undergraduate Psychology Major Competencies. (2002). *Undergraduate psychology major learning goals and outcomes: A report.* Retrieved January 14, 2003, from http://www.apa.org/ed/pcue/taskforcereport2.pdf

Graham, S. E. (1998). Developing student outcomes for the psychology major: An assessment-as-learning framework. *Current Directions in Psychological Science, 7*(6), 165–170.

Jackson, S. L., & Griggs, R. A. (1995). Assessing the psychology major: A national survey of undergraduate programs. *Teaching of Psychology, 22*(4), 241.

Korn, J. H., Sweetman, M. B., & Nodine, B. F. (1996). An analysis of commentary on consultants' reports on undergraduate psychology programs. *Teaching of Psychology, 23*(1), 14–19.

Kruger, D. J., & Zechmeister, E. B. (2001). A skills-experience inventory for the undergraduate psychology major. *Teaching of Psychology, 28*(4), 249–253.

Kyle, T. M., & Williams, S. (2000). *1998-1999 APA survey of undergraduate departments of psychology*. Retrieved January 14, 2003, from http://research.apa.org/9899undergrad.html

Lawson, T. J. (1999). Assessing psychological critical thinking as a learning outcome for psychology majors. *Teaching of Psychology, 26*(3), 207–209.

Levy, J., Burton, G., Mickler, S., & Vigorito, M. (1999). A curriculum matrix for psychology program review. *Teaching of Psychology, 26*(4), 291–294.

McGovern, T. V., & Reich, J. N. (1996). A comment on the quality principles. *American Psychologist, 51*(3), 252–255.

Nelson, E. S., & Johnson, K. A. (1997). A senior exit survey and its implications for advising and related services. *Teaching of Psychology, 24*(2), 101–105.

Nichols, J. O., & Nichols, K. W. (2000). *The departmental guide and record book for student outcomes assessment and institutional effectiveness* (3rd ed.). New York: Agathon Press.

Perlman, B., & McCann, L. I. (1999a). The most frequently listed courses in the undergraduate psychology curriculum. *Teaching of Psychology, 26*(3), 177–182.

Perlman, B., & McCann, L. I. (1999b). The structure of the psychology undergraduate curriculum. *Teaching of Psychology, 26*(3), 171–176.

Pusateri, T. P. (2002). A decade of changes since the St. Mary's conference: An interview with Thomas V. McGovern. *Teaching of Psychology, 29*(1), 76–82.

Sheehan, E. P. (1994). A multimethod assessment of the psychology major. *Teaching of Psychology, 21*(2), 74–78.

Stoloff, M. L., & Feeney, K. J. (2002). The major field test as an assessment tool for an undergraduate psychology program. *Teaching of Psychology, 29*(2), 92–98.

Wesp, R. (2002, Summer). From the chair. *CUPP Newsletter, 12*, 1.

APPENDIX 4.1

ONLINE RESOURCES FOR
PREPARING SELF-STUDY REPORTS

Sample Guidelines for Assessment, Student Learning Outcomes, and Academic Program Review

- Arizona State University: http://www.asu.edu/graduate/news_publications/apr/APRtoc.html
- Ball State University: http://web.bsu.edu/IRAA/AA/WB/contents.htm
- California State University, Chico: http://www.csuchico.edu/community/assessment.html
- Concordia College: http://www.cord.edu/dept/assessment/ahbcontents.html
- East Tennessee State University: http://www.etsu.edu/outcomes/academic_program_ review.htm
- George Mason University: http://assessment.gmu.edu/AcadProgEval/index.shtml
- James Madison University: http://www.jmu.edu/assessment/
- North Carolina State University: http://www2.acs.ncsu.edu/UPA/assmt/index.html
- San Francisco State University: http://www.sfsu.edu/~apd/5thcycle4.html
- Southeast Missouri State University: http://www2.semo.edu/provost/aspnhtm/busy.htm
- Southern Illinois University - Edwardsville: http://www.siue.edu/~deder/assess/
- Southwest Missouri State University: http://www.smsu.edu/Assessment/
- Texas A & M University: http://www.tamu.edu/marshome/assess/Manual.html
- University of Central Florida: http://www.oeas.ucf.edu/
- University of Colorado at Denver: http://www.cudenver.edu/academicaffairs/APR.htm
- University of Saskatchewan: http://www.usask.ca/vpacademic/spr/selfstudyguidelines.html
- University of Washington: http://depts.washington.edu/grading/slo/SLO-Home.htm
- University of Wisconsin-Madison: http://www.ls.wisc.edu/handbook/ChapterFive/chV-4.htm
- Western Carolina University: http://www.wcu.edu/facctr/assessment.html

Lists of Web Resources Related to Assessment

- APA's Assessment CyberGuide for Learning Goals and Outcomes in the Undergraduate Psychology Major: http://www.apa.org/ed/guidehomepage.html
- American Association for Higher Education: http://www.aahe.org/assessment/web.htm
- Texas A & M University: http://www.tamu.edu/marshome/assess/oabooks.html

Departmental Consulting Services (External Reviewers)

- Council on Undergraduate Research: http://www.cur.org/consulting.html
- Office of Teaching Resources in Psychology: http://www.lemoyne.edu/OTRP/memberservices.html#dcs

Documents on Student Learning Outcomes for Introductory Psychology and Undergraduate Psychology Majors

- APA's High School Standards for Introductory Psychology: http://www.apa.org/ed/natlstandards.html
- APA Task Force Report: http://www.apa.org/ed/pcue/reports.html
- California State University Report: http://www.lemoyne.edu/OTRP/teachingresources.html#outcomes

Statistics Related to Psychology Majors

- APA Research Office (Enrollment and employment of psychology graduates): http://research.apa.org/
- APA Survey of Undergraduate Departments of Psychology: http://research.apa.org/9899undergrad.html
- National Center for Education Statistics: http://nces.ed.gov/pubs2001/2001177.pdf

Psychology Knowledge-Based Tests

- Area Concentration Achievement Test—Psychology: http://www.collegeoutcomes.com/ACATS/psych.htm
- Major Field Test–Psychology: http://www.ets.org/hea/mft/discipline.html

Examples of Psychology Program Review Self-Studies

- Old Dominion University: http://web.odu.edu/webroot/orgs/ AO/assessment.nsf/pages/PsychologyBS_page
- State University of West Georgia: http://www.westga.edu/ ~psydept/programreview.htm
- Western Carolina University: http://www.wcu.edu/stratplan/ PrgrmRvw/Psychology.htm

Sites Related to Graduate Study in Psychology

- APA's site on graduate study in psychology: http://www.apa.org/ ed/graduate/
- Council of Graduate Departments of Psychology (COGDOP): http://psych.psy.wfu.edu/COGDOP/
- APA's report, "Analyses of Data from Graduate Study in Psychology, 1999–2000": http://research.apa.org/grad00contents .html
- APA's site on accreditation guidelines and procedures: http:// www.apa.org/ed/accreditation/
- National Association of School Psychologists (NASP) Standards for School Psychology: http://www.nasponline.org/certi-fication/index.html

APPENDIX 4.2

PRINT RESOURCES FOR PREPARING SELF-STUDY REPORTS

Borden, V. M. H., & Rajecki, D. W. (2000). First-year employment outcomes of psychology baccalaureates: Relatedness, preparedness, and prospects. *Teaching of Psychology, 27*(3), 164–168.

Friedrich, J. (1996). Assessing students' perceptions of psychology as a science: Validation of a self-report measure. *Teaching of Psychology, 23*(1), 6–13.

Halpern, D. F., & Reich, J. N. (1999). Scholarship in psychology: Conversations about change and constancy. *American Psychologist, 54*(5), 347–349.

Korn, J. H. (1999). Recognizing teaching as teaching. *American Psychologist, 54*(5), 362–363.

McDonald, D. G. (1997). Psychology's surge in undergraduate majors. *Teaching of Psychology, 24*(1), 22–26.

McGovern, T. V. (1993a). The past and future of the undergraduate psychology curriculum. *The Psychology Teacher Network, 3*(1), 2–6.

McGovern, T. V. (1993b). The past and future of the undergraduate psychology curriculum. *The Psychology Teacher Network, 3*(2), 2–4.

McGovern, T. V., Furumoto, L., Halpern, D. F., Kimble, G. A., & McKeachie, W. J. (1991). Liberal education, study in depth, and the arts and sciences major-psychology. *American Psychologist, 46*(6), 598–605.

Messer, W. S. (1997). Undergraduate psychology curricula in North Carolina. *Teaching of Psychology, 24*(2), 127–130.

Messer, W. S., Griggs, R. A., & Jackson, S. L. (1999). A national survey of undergraduate psychology degree options and major requirements. *Teaching of Psychology, 26*(3), 164–171.

Myers, D. G., & Waller, J. E. (1999). Reflections on scholarship from the liberal arts academy. *American Psychologist, 54*(5), 358–361.

Perlman, B., & McCann, L. (1993). The place of mathematics and science in undergraduate psychology education. *Teaching of Psychology, 20*(4), 205–208.

Sheehan, E. P. (1993). Assessment in the major: A model psychology program. *College Student Journal, 27*, 256–258.

Stache, C., Perlman, B., McCann, L., & McFadden, S. (1994). A national survey of the academic minor and psychology. *Teaching of Psychology, 21*(2), 69–74.

APPENDIX 4.3

RECOMMENDED MATERIALS TO INCLUDE IN THE DEPARTMENT'S SELF-STUDY REPORT

General Information About Department

- Mission or vision statement (including program goals, objectives)
- History of the department
- External and internal patterns of administration
- Budget information

The Faculty

- Current faculty vitae (including rank, years of service, research productivity, etc.)
- Allocation of faculty lines
- Teaching loads (including any release time for research, service activities)
- General information regarding salary (e.g., averages by rank; recent trends in salary)
- Evaluation process for promotion and tenure

Students

- Student/faculty ratio for the psychology department
- Number of majors per program (including any recent trends)
- Student profile and demographics

Academic Support

- Staff support (e.g., secretary, graduate assistants, work study students)
- Technology support
- Library resources, including budget for psychology periodicals and books
- External support (e.g., faculty development office, center for teaching and learning)

The Curriculum

- Degree programs (including requirements for major, minor, options)

- Course listings and descriptions
- Department's contribution to general education
- Course offerings required or recommended in other programs
- Service learning opportunities
- Enrollment patterns

Facilities and Equipment

- Allocation, utilization of physical space for teaching, research
- Computer support for faculty
- Technology support for teaching and research
- Availability of computer labs for students

Academic Assessment

- Current assessment plan, including goals, objective, outcomes
- Recent assessment reports, including measures of student learning, satisfaction

External Relations and Fund-Raising

- Alumni outreach efforts (e.g., alumni newsletters)
- Faculty, student involvement in local community and professional organizations
- Local (i.e., department fund-raising efforts)

APPENDIX 4.4

RECOMMENDED MATERIALS TO PROVIDE TO THE EXTERNAL REVIEWER(S) PRIOR TO THE SITE VISIT

Information About the Larger Insitution (To Place the Program Review in an Appropriate Context):

- College or university undergraduate and graduate bulletins (as appropriate)
- College or university mission, vision, or goals statement
- Documents related to the institution's expectations for program review and long-range planning

Information About the Department

- Departmental self-study report (which may itself include some of the following materials)
- Departmental mission, vision, or goals statement
- Curriculum vitae of the department's faculty members (including part-time and adjunct faculty)
- Sample course syllabi from classes recently taught by each faculty member
- Course offerings and enrollment figures for the department for the past several years
- A list of relevant journal subscriptions and electronic search engines in the campus library
- Annual reports or minutes of department meetings for the past 1–2 years
- Report of alumni placements for the past several years
- Departmental brochures
- Graduation checklists or advising sheets or both
- Previous self-study reports or reports from external reviewers
- Reports from the department (e.g., assessment studies, proposals for new majors/programs)

Institutional and Departmental Web Sites

The external reviewer may find relevant materials about the institution and department by visiting the institution's Web site. Some of the materials described above are often available at these Web sites (e.g., bulletins, mission statements, course descriptions and syllabi, course offerings, and enrollment figures).

APPENDIX 4.5

RECOMMENDED SCHEDULE OF EVENTS FOR THE SITE VISIT BY THE EXTERNAL REVIEWER

Day 1: Mid-Afternoon

- Initial meeting with representative(s) of the administration. (45 minutes–1 hour)
- Tour of facilities (1–2 hours, depending on the extent and location of facilities)
  - Offices of the department's faculty members
  - Offices of the department's support staff (e.g., secretarial, clerical, laboratory, technology, student help)
  - Classrooms frequently used by the department—include technology classrooms if appropriate
  - Laboratory facilities used by the department
  - Campus library: particularly library areas and resources relevant to departmental needs
  - Offices of other departments or support services with which the department interacts: (e.g., instructional technology center, faculty development center, counseling center)
  - Common areas used by the department (e.g., hallways, bulletin boards, meeting rooms)

Day 1: Evening

- Dinner with the department or key members of the department

Day 2, Option 1: Review With a Preliminary Oral Report

Day 2: Morning to Early Afternoon

- Interviews
- Individual/group interviews with the department's faculty members (30–45 minutes each)
- Group interview with students (approximately 1 hour)
- Interviews with other relevant campus representatives (20 minutes–1 hour)
  - Faculty members from other departments with which the department interacts, and/or
  - Secretarial/clerical/technology/library support staff relevant to the department's needs

- Meeting with the department chair

Day 2: Late Afternoon

- Time for reviewer to develop the preliminary oral report (30 minutes–1 hobur)
- Final meeting with the department (1 hour)
- Final meeting with appropriate representative(s) of the administration (30 minutes–1 hour)

Day 2, Option 2: Review Without a Preliminary Oral Report

Day 2: Morning and Afternoon

- Interviews
- Individual or group interviews with the department's faculty members. (30–45 minutes each)
- Group interview with students (approximately 1 hour)
- Interviews with other relevant campus representatives (20 minutes–1 hour)
  - Faculty members from other departments with whom the department interacts, and/or
  - Secretarial, clerical, technology, library, or other support staff relevant to the department's needs
- Final meeting with the department chair

5

THE PSYCHOLOGY CHAIR PORTFOLIO

KENNETH A. WEAVER

The psychology chair's role is rich with expectations and opportunities. Tucker (1993) lists the following "bedrock" (p. 530) responsibilities for serving the department well: See that work is accomplished; handle the flow of management tasks required by superiors; communicate effectively with both faculty and administration; exercise supervisory authority over the faculty while respecting their professionalism; obtain and manage the fiscal resources to realize the department's mission; and plan, plan, plan.

In this chapter, the term "psychology chair" refers to any administrative head of a unit responsible for psychology education. In college, university, and community college contexts, these can be departments, divisions, or schools of psychology. Psychology units also exist as part of larger behavioral or social science collectives. In high schools, psychology typically exists within social studies.

To set the stage for evaluating how well a psychology chair meets expectations, a series of questions can be asked: What are the psychology chair's administrative strengths and weaknesses? Is the chair seeking to understand more clearly the department, division, or school of psychology? What is the chair's administrative philosophy? Is the chair encountering a problem with a faculty member? Does the chair want to improve communication with the faculty? Is the chair preparing to enter the job market for an administrative position? Is the chair searching for a good evaluation procedure now that the institution requires review of administrators?

To answer these questions, the psychology chair can create a chair portfolio. This chapter describes how to create this portfolio, providing chairs with new insights about their leadership ability and the relationships among themselves and their faculty, staff, and students. Although administrative responsibilities may differ across high schools, community colleges, colleges, and universities, the design of the chair portfolio accommodates these differences because it is based on job descriptions, accomplishments, and contexts rather than a single set of characteristics against which administrators from all backgrounds are judged.

Academic administration is more complex, more pressured, and more businesslike than it was 10 years ago (Seldin & Higgerson, 2002b). Higher expectations mean greater accountability. A midwestern adage suggests that "if you're riding ahead of the herd, take a look back every now and then to make sure it's still there." Although this adage is relevant to department leadership, evaluating department chairs is substantively more complicated because the chair manages the faculty yet is also a faculty member. Faculty, principals, deans, and vice presidents evaluate the chair in managerial, political, and academic areas (Tucker, 1993). How well is the chair assigning teaching and other duties? How well is the chair communicating expectations? How successfully is the chair managing the department? How much is the chair aware of the latest intellectual developments in the fields included in the department? How accomplished is the chair in teaching and, for higher education, research? How equitably is the chair distributing departmental resources? Is the chair modeling effective service contributions?

Given the psychology chair's considerable responsibility in a number of different areas and the institution's reliance on chairs for maintaining smoothly running departments, institutions may have formal procedures for evaluating the chair's performance. Complementing such traditional approaches to chair evaluation is a new methodology that applies the same assessment used for creating a teaching portfolio to producing a chair portfolio (Seldin & Higgerson, 2002b).

PROFESSIONAL ASSESSMENT THROUGH PORTFOLIOS

A Portfolio for Teachers

The teaching portfolio nurtures effective teaching through valuable self-reflection. It is an evidence-based assessment of teaching that principals and department chairs can use for accountability purposes. The portfolio describes one's teaching strengths and accomplishments and includes support materials and facts that together reflect the scope and quality of the teaching performance (Seldin, 1997). Effective teachers demonstrate passion for learning and for their subject (Brewer, 1996), listening, flexibility, humor, caring, nurturing (LeBlanc, 1999), distinctive character (Tralina, 1999), intellectual vibrancy (Feinburg & Mindess, 1994), a memorable personality, and success at meeting learning outcomes (Zigmond, 1996). These characteristics can be documented and are fact-based, and the teaching portfolio provides a coherent outlet for faculty to organize the evidence and reflect upon it to improve their teaching and their students' learning (Seldin, 1997). Performance-based learning (American Psychological Association, 1997; Barr & Tagg, 1995) has supplanted teacher-centered efforts as the focus of assessment (Lucas, 2000), and the teaching portfolio is a logical product of this change.

A Portfolio for Psychology Chairs

The psychology chair portfolio presents "selected information on administrative activities along with solid evidence of their effectiveness" (Seldin & Higgerson, 2002b, p. 5). Its components depend upon the intended purpose, the chair's institutional context (e.g., small liberal arts institution, major research university), the chair's weighing of what to include, and what the institution may require (Seldin & Higgerson, 2002b). Rather than the "flashlight" approach of traditional evaluations that illuminate only those administrative skills and abilities that fall within its beam, the portfolio is a "searchlight" whose broader beam encompasses administrative philosophy, attitudes, abilities, skills, and accomplishments (Seldin & Higgerson, 2002a, p. 3) supported by empirical evidence.

Examples of empirical evidence include comparative lists of present and past departmental activities; copies of changed policies, procedures, forms, and documents; photographs of department changes (e.g., renovated classroom, department picnic); articles authored by the chair; and letters from faculty and administrators attesting to administrative acumen. Self-analysis of administrative effectiveness occurs from compiling, organizing, and reflecting on the evidence.

CONSTRUCTING THE PSYCHOLOGY CHAIR PORTFOLIO

The typical portfolio is contained in an easily accessible format, such as a three-ring binder. The narrative is approximately 8 to 12 double-spaced pages followed by appendices that support the claims made in the narrative. The portfolio takes between 12 and 15 hours if the administrator is already doing annual reviews (Seldin & Higgerson, 2002a, 2002b). Appendix 5.1 lists the contents of the typical portfolio (Seldin & Higgerson, 2002b).

Seldin and Higgerson (2002b) offer 13 examples of portfolios created by administrators in a variety of different higher education contexts (e.g., university or college, public or private). These portfolios are also excellent models for department chairs in high schools.

Choosing the Audience

Who will read the portfolio is determined by why the portfolio was created. As an exercise in self-assessment or preparation for administrative job application, the portfolio is a private, personal document. Chairs have flexibility and autonomy in what goes into their portfolio and determining who will read it. For example, the chair may want no one to read the portfolio, only the faculty, just the principal/dean, or everyone.

On the other hand, as a required evaluation tool for administrative review, the chair creates the portfolio for formative or summative assessment by an audience, which may include a faculty review committee, the principal, the dean, or the vice president. Regardless of the portfolio's purpose, chairs should be willing to share their administrative philosophy with the faculty.

Writing the Administrative Philosophy

Articulating one's administrative philosophy means explaining the convergence (or lack thereof) between the chair's beliefs about effective administration and subsequent administrative behaviors. Reflecting about administration, psychology chairs ask themselves questions such as: What do I as department chair believe an effective chair should be and do? How do my behaviors as chair reflect my beliefs about administration? What have I done and what am I doing to be an effective chair? What areas of improvement have I identified and what plans have I developed to convert these areas of improvement into strengths? How can I use what I know about psychology to improve my administrative effectiveness?

This exercise in self-reflection "addresses the issue of *how* the administrator carries out responsibilities from the standpoint of *why* they do what they do" (Seldin & Higgerson, 2002b, p. 12). A chair's administrative philosophy results from a challenging, metacognitive analysis that brings coherence to the chair's actions and ideas while illuminating areas of strength and improvement. At least two approaches for organizing the chair's actions and ideas prior to writing the philosophy exist.

Higgerson's (1996) Administrative Lenses

Successful department chairs carry out responsibilities collaboratively with the faculty, thus effective communication skills are extremely important (Higgerson, 1996). Higgerson views this communication through three administrative lenses: promoting the department culture, working with faculty, and presenting the department to external groups (e.g., the principal or dean, alumni, civic and business organizations). To promote the department's culture, successful chairs work collegially to articulate a well-defined department mission, building consensus around shared values. Chairs recognize the qualities of a healthy department climate and regard their behaviors and decisions as building or destroying a productive, collegial work environment. Chairs model ethical behavior and encourage faculty to do the same.

Working with faculty entails monitoring their performance, managing conflict, and implementing proactive change. The effective chair meets regularly with individual faculty, discussing professional development and evaluation; setting and meeting professional goals; providing support for those goals; updating tenure, promotion, or post-tenure status; and reflecting on their professional contributions in light of professional goals. Supporting the development of new faculty as teachers and scholars is especially important (Bensimon, Ward, & Sanders, 2000).

Conflict is a normal byproduct of human interaction. Conflict can be healthy, but the chair should act to minimize destructive conflict. Higgerson (1998) proposes three steps for managing conflict. First, the chair minimizes conflict potential by working to hire qualified faculty and staff with well-defined performance expectations and regular performance evaluations. Second, the chair sets the tone for airing disagreements by maintaining open and effective communication and working constantly at building and maintaining a positive department climate. The chair's credibility positively influences conflict management if the chair is perceived as knowledgeable, well-intentioned, and trustworthy. Third, the chair focuses on managing rather than resolving the conflict by intervening early, establishing rules for airing differences of opinion constructively, and encouraging discussion of disagreements in constructive ways.

Besides resolving tensions that normally arise in a department, managing conflict may involve legal issues. "The threat of lawsuits in the academic environment is an offensive obstacle to the exercise of seasoned academic judgment. . . . the complexities of the law have become a constant of academic life" (Bennett & Figuli, 1990, p. 139). The chair's traditional role of preparing faculty for tenure and promotion has changed with the prospect of litigation if the faculty member is unsuccessful. A chair may be liable if the department milieu tolerates prejudice, discrimination, or harassment; thus, training about personnel law (e.g., Human Resources Council, 1996) is critical to effective department functioning.

Lucas and Associates (2000) see leading academic change as the essence of a department chair's responsibilities. They advocate training the chair as the leader of a team made up of the faculty. Developing the department mission, working through budget crises, changing the curriculum (Halonen et al., 2002), developing new programs, reviewing old policies and establishing new ones, and maintaining quality are daunting tasks for a department chair and cannot be accomplished in isolation. Instead, successful leadership requires developing shared goals, motivating all team members, maintaining excellence, creating a climate of trust, managing conflict effectively, making problem solving rather than winning the basis for deliberation, and involving faculty in decision making (Lucas, 2000).

Higgerson's (1996) third lens for viewing effective chair communication is interfacing with constituencies outside of the department. Through this lens, the chair actively communicates department needs and problems to the principal or dean and requests assistance as frequently as necessary. The chair also promotes the department to other constituencies, such as alumni and community business and civic organizations to inform them of department programs and provide opportunities for external support of department programs. Building alliances and coalitions across different groups advances department programs.

Leaming's (1998) Framework of Effective Chair Characteristics

According to Leaming, effective chairs set goals; know their departmental colleagues thoroughly; facilitate change; understand and appreciate the relationships among teaching, research, and service; are honest, forthright, and decent; are fair and evenhanded and work towards consensus using good communication skills (pp. 11–12). Each characteristic becomes a heading under which the chair lists evidence in support of these items. From this listing, the chair then composes the administrative philosophy.

Identifying Relevant Data

Appendix 5.2 contains questions keyed to Higgerson's (1996) three lenses to assist chairs in collecting the data for composing their administrative philosophy. Individual departments may have idiosyncratic characteristics for chairs to address beyond the ones covered in Appendix 5.2. The administrative philosophy does not answer the questions; instead it provides the coherent explanation for the chair's pattern of effectiveness that emerges from the aggregated answers to those questions.

Developing My Portfolio

Since 1994, I have chaired a department of 17 faculty in psychology, special education, and art therapy at a midwestern state university of 6,000 students in Kansas. The department has 200 undergraduate majors and 180 graduate students. I am formally reviewed by the department faculty every three years based on a comprehensive instrument I assisted in developing.

Although the 1997 and 2000 evaluations were positive, I realized two years ago that the department was losing momentum. After having a strong "head of steam" for six years while saying goodbye to a number of beloved and devoted faculty, attracting new faculty, introducing the department to performance-based assessment, meeting accreditation demands, and maintaining my own teaching, scholarly activity, and service, I thought I had lost touch with the essence of the department. The overall health of the department seemed to be declining, and being department chair was losing its luster. Constructing a chair portfolio was my search to recapture the department's essence, and in so doing, my search for ideas for engaging the faculty in the life, health, and vigor of the department.

To start my portfolio, I first compiled a listing of accomplishments with accompanying evidence, using many of the questions in Appendix 5.2 as guides. My accomplishments clustered into four categories: physical modifications, faculty affairs, student affairs, and curriculum and accreditation review. I then articulated my administrative philosophy; what did I believe about administering a department? The essence of my administrative philosophy was the commitment to the professional development of the faculty as my top priority. My administrative goals and my accomplishments reflected this emphasis. The total document was 16 double-spaced, typed pages.

Toward the end of the portfolio process, I realized that my administrative philosophy was based on the department as it had been when I began as chair in 1994, with a faculty of mostly full professors. Since then, the department had changed dramatically; now two-thirds of the faculty were untenured. It became clearly but painfully evident that my focus on meeting new faculty's needs, which were more substantial than the needs of tenured faculty, had "drowned out" the professional development needs of our majors. The "essence" I thought I had lost was really losing the centrality of our students to the life of the department. By reprioritizing student and faculty interests in my administrative philosophy, I then knew to ask the faculty what we can do together to make our majors' academic experiences as rich and memorable as possible. The faculty, and especially the new faculty, responded strongly.

For example, although our department mission has always been to advance students' professional development, we have expanded that development broadly in the last two years to encompass any student–faculty interaction. The department now begins the academic year with a department-wide picnic and concludes each semester with a department-wide Student Research Day and Luncheon. The department has replaced 11:00 a.m. classes on Tuesdays and Thursdays with twice weekly Professional Development Sessions including student organization meetings, all invited speakers, and faculty-led workshops on a variety of topics, such as vita construction and transcript development. Student attendance is consistently high. Although student attendance at state, regional, and national conventions has always been a departmental emphasis, student attendance at these events has increased compared with five years ago.

Faculty and students are spending more time together in departmental activities outside of class, and both are finding this increased interaction rewarding. Such interaction has helped our student recruitment and retention as well as our efforts to instill a culture of assessment in the department. In spite of difficult budget times in Kansas, department morale and the quality of academic life in the department are high. My most recent formal evaluation by the faculty occurred two months ago, producing my highest evaluations since becoming chair.

Constructing the psychology chair portfolio provided me with direction for the department at a time when I was struggling as department chair. I was so caught up working with new faculty that I had become unaware of the narrowing of my administrative focus (cf. Easterbrook, 1959). That self-knowledge has redefined me as a department chair. Now my administrative goals are infused with working with the faculty and the students to increase the number, quality, and innovativeness of opportunities to advance our majors' professional development.

Evaluating the Portfolio

The portfolio may be the sole assessment procedure or may combine with other evaluation data. The portfolio may be for formative or summative purposes. Thus, the process for evaluating the portfolio is determined by the purpose. If the purpose requires review by the principal, dean, or vice president, it is appropriate to ask for the guidelines or rubric from these superiors to ensure that the portfolio is constructed to address the specific areas being evaluated. The guidelines or rubric may be constructed collaboratively with the chair's input.

The portfolio could be part of a summative process leading to a recommendation involving a salary adjustment or renewal of the position. It is appropriate to understand *a priori* how the evaluation of the portfolio will be used to make such determinations.

THE BENEFITS OF A CHAIR PORTFOLIO

Even with well-honed time management skills, most chairs still take work home or come to the office on weekends. With so many responsibilities, why take the time to do a psychology chair portfolio? Will chairs accomplish more from this exercise than they would have if they had spent their time differently? A range of benefits from completing a chair portfolio justifies the investment of time and energy (Seldin & Higgerson, 2002b).

Stimulating Self-Knowledge

Integrating beliefs and behaviors with one's philosophy and basing this integration on evidence stimulates contemplation about one's role as an administrator. Given all of the reasons in the research literature for creating a chair portfolio, the greatest benefit is attaining clearer self-awareness about one's role as an administrator, one's successes as chair, and where improvements can be made. This valuable knowledge contributes to professional growth of the administrator that in turn contributes to a more effective department. Even chairs in departments where the chair responsibility rotates among the faculty can benefit from the knowledge obtained through the portfolio development process.

In addition, creating a future portfolio provides chairs with a second data point from which to identify how their performance has changed, what factors have contributed to their development as administrators, and additional lessons they have learned. Such longitudinal comparisons enable the chair to broaden the effectiveness of the chair portfolio in assessing professional growth.

Seldin and Higgerson's (2002b) process for developing the portfolio requires that chairs critically evaluate their work in light of the documentable evidence to identify strengths and areas of improvement. Some chairs may not want this knowledge or may undermine the process through a lack of openness, looking only for that subset of the evidence that will validate their personal preferences. Constructing the portfolio is only useful if the chair approaches the process honestly and is willing to face problems that may be uncomfortable.

Troubleshooting

The psychology chair portfolio contains answers to difficulties the chair is experiencing. For example, a new department chair hired from outside the department discerns a disconnection with the faculty at the end of her first year. To clarify the problem and generate some solutions, she creates a chair portfolio. After articulating her administrative philosophy in light of the evidence, she recognizes that her values are not congruent with the department's culture. Based on this insight, she knows that either her values or her role will need to change. My portfolio was designed to troubleshoot to find answers for energizing the department. From this perspective, the chair may find creating the portfolio therapeutic.

Formal Evaluation

Traditional evaluation of chairs involves either a survey administered to the faculty periodically or an annual review by the principal, dean, or vice president. In contrast, the portfolio contains organized evidence documenting and supporting the chair's administrative effectiveness for subsequent review and critique by others, such as the department faculty, principal, superintendent, dean, or vice president. Given the novelty of the chair portfolio, chairs may need to convince their superiors about the benefits of the exercise. Part of that convincing can include encouraging them to create their own administrative portfolios. Although the focus on this chapter is the psychology chair portfolio, Seldin and Higgerson's (2002a, 2002b) approach to portfolio construction is valid for all administrators.

Improved Communication With Faculty

Chairs can share their portfolios with their faculty. Making an administrative philosophy explicit facilitates understanding of the decisions the chair makes and the processes the chair engages in to reach a decision. Both are especially important if they conflict with a particular faculty perspective. Outlining the duties and responsibilities attached to the department chair position clarifies the difficult, but sometimes invisible, work the chair must do.

Equity

At institutions requiring faculty to create portfolios, faculty may chaffe at the thought that department chairs are not part of the same evaluation process. Creating the chair portfolio is a good faith effort by chairs to match the faculty effort and the faculty product for evaluation purposes.

Promoting Effective Leadership

An outgoing chair's portfolio can provide an incoming chair with useful information about what is expected and how the previous chair met those expectations. Likewise, sharing the knowledge and experience contained in a portfolio with other chairs may facilitate their administrative development. If the portfolio, or more specifically the administrative philosophy, is done again, then the chair can discern changes longitudinally, reflect on why these have occurred, and strive to understand what the changes mean for sustaining and improving administrative effectiveness.

Job Hunting

The portfolio may provide an advantage in the job market. The process of assembling the portfolio requires a thorough thinking through of what it means to be a department chair, how the department functions, and those personal characteristics that promote effective departments. Creating a portfolio is thus an excellent way to practice answering the types of questions one might expect on a job interview. Given that department chairs may not relocate very often, their job hunting skills are quite likely to be rusty. Assembling the portfolio forces the prospective applicant to consider issues of match between the chair's values and the prospective department's culture.

THE COSTS OF THE PORTFOLIO

Vulnerability

My ability to lead might have been compromised if I had openly shared my frustration with the department's loss of momentum and my doubts about my leadership ability. Constructing my portfolio was a private, honest attempt to reorient myself as department chair because I felt I was losing direction. During this period of vulnerability, I was not prepared or willing to share my concerns, my discomfort, or my fear with those to whom I was accountable, including the faculty and the dean.

On the other hand, the department faculty certainly deserve to know what my administrative philosophy is. I have tried to do a better job of communicating it to faculty, students, and staff. While the chair portfolio might be personal, parts of it could and probably should be publicly accessible.

Imbalance and Lack of Trust

A portfolio that does not appear to be a balanced one, favoring only a glowing view of the chair without any contrary evidence is an empty exercise. On the other hand, a dean or vice president might seize on the evidence of areas that need improvement and use it as the basis for termination.

If you do a chair portfolio, clarify why you are doing it. Who is the intended audience? What are the reasons? If it is for evaluation, is it legitimate to ask what role the portfolio will have in salary determination or renewal decisions?

TECHNOLOGY AND THE ELECTRONIC PORTFOLIO

My portfolio included photographs and was contained in a three-ring binder. Because my rationale for creating my portfolio was self-knowledge, I did not intend to share any part of it. However, several options for creating an electronic portfolio are possible with the assistance of technology. The chair can make all or a subset of the parts of the portfolio publicly accessible and control who has access depending on the format that is used—a notebook, a website, a PDF file, or a CD-ROM.

Storing the portfolio on a CD-ROM, especially a rewritable one, allows the chair to update the portfolio periodically. Navigating the CD might be more difficult than a website, but the chair can better control who has access. Digital pictures and digital video can be easily added to the electronic portfolio. Photographs and other documents can be scanned in and added as well.

CONCLUSION

Who are you as a chair? What are your beliefs about leadership? How attuned are you to the issues in your department? To borrow a term from the Palm Pilot Web site (http://www.palm.com/support/hotsync.html), how well are you and the faculty "hotsynced"? How open is the communication between you and the principal, dean, or vice president? What are you doing to provide opportunities for the department majors?

The life of the psychology chair is one rich with opportunities! Such richness can be motivating and rewarding, but it can also be consuming and tiring, limiting reflection about the department's direction, the quality of life for faculty and students, administrative effectiveness, and a variety of other issues under the chair's responsibility. Without the reflection, how does the chair establish a baseline of understanding about the department, orient administrative philosophy in the midst of so much "noise," and identify new initiatives?

Creating the psychology chair portfolio provides an interlude for reflection. Analogous to triangulating instructional objectives, teaching, and assessment (Slavin, 2003), the administrative philosophy and the evidence of the chair's accomplishments enable reflection and in turn are modified by the reflections. In turn, the validity of the reflections is ensured through its links with both the administrative philosophy and evidence. Once the cycle of triangulating philosophy, evidence, and reflection is complete, the chair is prepared for (and possibly eagerly anticipating) crafting administrative goals with the assessments to evaluate how well those goals are met.

To create a psychology chair portfolio is to open oneself to unexpected insights, to refresh one's administrative responsibilities and philosophy, and to aspire to greater effectiveness and accountability. The discovery and self-awareness imbue the portfolio process with relevance and meaningfulness regardless of the chair's motivation for creating one or the institutional setting in which the chair works.

Although the chair portfolio serves a number of useful purposes, the minimal investment of time and energy is additional enticement to chairs to create their own. Unlike chairs in departments in other disciplines, psychology chairs have an advantage because their training in psychological research methods is excellent preparation for creating a chair portfolio. For example, the department chair gathers evidence of accomplishment and concerns. After analyzing this evidence, the chair composes a narrative called the administrative philosophy, which makes sense of the evidence. Future administrative goals, based on the narrative, conclude the portfolio.

What Should You Do Now

A primer of Seldin and Higgerson's (2002a) approach to constructing the psychology chair portfolio is available at www.aahebulletin.com/public/archive/adminportfolios.asp as a downloadable PDF file. This document provides an informative overview of the steps for preparing a chair portfolio. It is an excellent complement to this chapter, and the best next step you can take after reading this chapter if you are interested in creating your own chair portfolio. It is just a mouse click away.

Next, using the questions in Appendix 5.2, pull together evidence of your administrative accomplishments. Then jot down a list of administrative strengths and weaknesses. Now write your administrative philosophy, citing the evidence and addressing your strengths and areas for improvement.

As you write, you will undertake an intellectual journey pondering leadership, yourself, and your department. Remember that the length of your administrative philosophy is not the issue; the purpose for the writing is to catalyze your reflections about what it means to be a psychology chair in your institutional context. Given openness and candor, the fruits of these reflections will be substantive, and you will emerge from the process with a renewed sense of yourself as a leader.

REFERENCES

American Psychological Association. (1997). *Learner-centered psychological principles: A framework for school redesign and reform.* Retrieved January 3, 2003, from http://www.apa.org/ed/lcp.html

Barr, R. B., & Tagg, J. (1995, November/December). From teaching to learning: A new paradigm for undergraduate education. *Change Magazine, 27*(6), 13–25.

Bennett, J. B., & Figuli, D. J. (1990). *Enhancing departmental leadership: The roles of the chairperson.* New York: American Council on Education/Macmillan.

Bensimon, E. M., Ward, K., & Sanders, K. (2000). *The department chair's role in developing new faculty into teachers and scholars.* Bolton, MA: Anker.

Brewer, C. L. (1996). A talk to teachers: Bending twigs and affecting eternity. *Platte River Review, 24*(2), 12–23.

Easterbrook, J. A. (1959). The effect of emotion on cue utilization and the organization of behavior. *Psychological Review, 66,* 183–201.

Feinburg, S., & Mindess, M. (1994). *Eliciting children's full potential: Designing and evaluating developmentally based programs for young children.* Pacific Grove, CA: Brooks/Cole.

Halonen, J. S., Appleby, D. C., Brewer, C. L., Buskist, W., Gillem, A. R., Halpern, D., et al. (2002). *Undergraduate psychology major learning goals and outcomes: A report.* Retrieved March 2, 2003, from http://www.apa.org/ed/guidehomepage.html

Higgerson, M. L. (1996). *Communication skills for department chairs.* Bolton, MA: Anker.

Higgerson, M. L. (1998). Chairs as department managers: Working with support staff. In S. A. Holton (Ed.), *Mending the cracks in the ivory tower: Strategies for conflict management in higher education* (pp. 46–59). Boston: Ankes.

Human Resources Council. (1996). *Fundamentals of personnel law for managers and supervisors.* Mission, KS: Graceland College Center for Professional Development and Lifelong Learning.

Leaming, D. R. (1998). *Academic leadership: A practical guide to chairing the department.* Bolton, MA: Anker.

LeBlanc, R. (1999, Spring). Good teaching: The top ten requirements. *The Core: Association for Experiential Education Schools & Colleges Professional Group Newsletter, 2.* Retrieved January 3, 2003, from http://www.aee.org/prof&sig/core9921.html

Lucas, A. F. (2000). A teamwork approach to change in the academic department. In A. F. Lucas & Associates (Eds.), *Leading academic change: Essential roles for department chairs* (pp. 7–32). San Francisco: Jossey-Bass.

Lucas, A. F., & Associates. (Eds.). (2000). *Leading academic change: Essential roles for department chairs.* San Francisco: Jossey-Bass.

Seldin, P. (1997). *The teaching portfolio: A practical guide to improved performance and promotion/tenure decisions* (2nd ed.). Bolton, MA: Anker.

Seldin, P., & Higgerson, M. L. (2002a, January). Adopting the administrative portfolio: A new use for a popular assessment tool. *AAHE Bulletin.* Retrieved March 3, 2003, from www.aahebulletin.com/public/archive/adminportfolios.asp

Seldin, P., & Higgerson, M. L. (2002b). *The administrative portfolio: A practical guide to improved administrative performance and personnel decisions.* Bolton, MA: Anker.

Slavin, R. E. (2003). *Educational psychology: Theory and practice* (7th ed.). Boston: Allyn & Bacon.

Tralina, R. P. (1999, January 20). What makes a good teacher? *Education Week,* p. 34.

Tucker, A. (1993). *Chairing the academic department: Leadership among peers.* Phoenix, AZ: Oryx Press.

Zigmond, N. (1996, October). What makes an effective teacher? *CEC Today, 3,* 12.

APPENDIX 5.1

CONTENTS FOR
THE PSYCHOLOGY CHAIR PORTFOLIO

1. Table of contents
2. Purpose of the portfolio (i.e., reason for completing the portfolio, such as evaluation, promotion, job hunting)
3. Description of institutional and departmental contexts
4. Administrative responsibilities
5. Administrative philosophy
6. Administrative goals (e.g., reviewing departmental priorities in light of diminishing resources, obtaining external funding, mentoring faculty for successful tenure review, completing curriculum review, preparing needs analysis for new degree, developing distance learning or evening courses for nontraditional students, modifying department's merit document, attending a department chair conference, creating partnerships with neighboring institutions)
7. Appendixes contain the supportive evidence cited by the chair to document the stated administrative philosophy and show how administrative goals have been met. Technology is useful for keeping records that provide evidence of marketing and class popularity (enrollments, recruitment, retention, course offerings), innovative budgeting practices (resources available for meeting department objectives), and faculty loads. Other evidence could include (a) hiring/retaining/terminating faculty, (b) developing or modifying policies and procedures, (c) curricular changes, (d) changes to the department's physical plant, (e) other departmental changes such as Internet courses or technology and teaching, (f) other evidence illuminating and supporting the administrative philosophy, (g) evidence supporting professional development, including articles, chapters, and books read on department chair effectiveness and the national conferences attended (e.g., Academic Chairpersons Conference, Council of Graduate Departments of Psychology annual meeting).
8. The concluding section includes letters, testimonials, and evaluations addressing the chair's effectiveness. Such letters and testimonials would come from faculty, students, and staff in the department, fellow chairs in other departments and in psychology departments at other institutions, and other administrators, such as the principal, dean, assistant superintendent, vice president, superintendent, or president. Evaluations would include formal assessments of the chair's administrative effectiveness.

QUESTIONS FOR GUIDING THE DEVELOPMENT
OF AN ADMINISTRATIVE PHILOSOPHY

Promoting the Department's Culture

1. What am I doing to promote a culture of assessment in the department?
2. What am I doing to ensure that psychology majors are active participants in the life of the department?
3. What variables contribute to the departmental environment and how does this environment facilitate student, faculty, and staff exploration and professional growth?
4. How do I nurture collaboration and collegiality among the faculty in my department?
5. Is there a relationship between faculty morale and student learning in my department, and if so, then what is it and what influence do I as department chair have on it?
6. How do I stimulate teaching excellence by the department faculty and promote high academic expectations for the students?
7. What have I done to integrate technology into the department's teaching and learning?
8. What is my influence as chair on student and faculty professional development and what am I doing to create opportunities for such development?
9. Do searches for new faculty actively involve faculty and students? How so and how do I evaluate this involvement in terms of its appropriateness?
10. What do I do to support faculty scholarship?
11. What do I do to support faculty service?
12. How do I as department chair convey that department students, faculty, and staff are valued?

Working With Faculty

1. How am I accessible to the junior faculty? What am I doing to support junior faculty?
2. How am I accessible to the senior faculty? What am I doing to support senior faculty?
3. What do I do to clearly articulate the faculty reward system; how frequently do I do this; and how well am I supporting faculty advancing in the reward system?

4. Given the institution's reward system, what is my responsibility in guiding junior faculty to successful promotion and tenure, what do I do to meet that responsibility, and what can I do better?

5. How frequently do I meet with each untenured and tenured faculty member to discuss his or her evaluation, professional goals, and continued development? Is this adequate? How do I run these meetings and what could be changed to optimize these meetings for faculty benefit?

6. How are faculty involved in changing curriculum, creating policy, setting department goals, solving problems, and assisting in decision making? Is this involvement adequate and elaborate?

7. What steps do I take to prevent, manage, and resolve conflict in the department?

8. What specifically is occurring in the department to minimize conflict and what more (or less) can be done?

9. What behaviors indicate that I model appropriate ethical conduct as department chair?

10. What do I consider to be the most significant values undergirding a quality department and what am I doing to instill and sustain those values?

11. What am I doing to foster among faculty the integration of (rather than tension among) teaching, research, and service?

Working With Students

1. What am I doing to advance students' professional development?

2. How well is the department nurturing its student organizations?

3. What is the quality of life in the department from the students' perspective?

Working With External Groups

1. What do I do to effectively communicate department needs, problems, goals, and accomplishments to the principal or dean?

2. What am I doing to promote the department in the high school, community college, college, university, and community of which it is a part? How do I know that I am effective in this promotion?

3. What am I doing to build collaborations with external groups such as civic and business organizations?

Miscellaneous

1. What are my three greatest strengths as department chair?
2. What are the three areas in which I would most like to improve as department chair?

III

BEST PRACTICES
IN ASSESSMENT

6

THE CAPS MODEL: ASSESSING PSYCHOLOGY PERFORMANCE USING THE THEORY OF SUCCESSFUL INTELLIGENCE

ROBERT J. STERNBERG

I have long been motivated to improve instruction and assessment in psychology and, particularly, in introductory psychology. When I took my introductory psychology course in 1968, I was very motivated to become a psychologist. I received a grade of C in the course. The grade was extremely discouraging to me, as was my instructor's comment that "There is a famous Sternberg in psychology, and judging from this grade, there won't be another one." I decided that I did not have the ability to major in psychology, so I switched to mathematics. This was a fortunate decision for me, because on the midterm in advanced mathematics, I got a grade of F. Now, the C was looking pretty good, so I switched back to psychology. I received higher grades

Preparation of this chapter was supported by Grant REC-9979843 from the National Science Foundation and by a government grant under the Javits Act Program (Grant No. R206R000001) as administered by the Institute of Educational Sciences (formerly the Office of Educational Research and Improvement), U.S. Department of Education. Grantees undertaking such projects are encouraged to express freely their professional judgment. This chapter, therefore, does not necessarily represent the positions or the policies of the U.S. government, and no official endorsement should be inferred.

in subsequent courses and today I am a psychologist and the 2003 President of the American Psychological Association. Incidentally, Phil Zimbardo, the previous president of the Association, also received a grade of C in his introductory psychology course.

Here is the problem: The kinds of learning and thinking that we, as psychology instructors, require of students in our courses, particularly lower level courses, do not match well with the kinds of learning and thinking that students will need to do if they choose to pursue psychology as a career. We may end up assessing the wrong things or, at best, only a subset of things that matter. For example, as a psychology professor, the principal things I need to do well are teach and mentor students; design, write up, and find a way to publish my research (often in the face of resistance from reviewers and editors); write grant proposals and somehow get some of them funded; supervise assistants; acquire office and lab space for myself and my associates; give talks to audiences of all kinds; and so forth. Not once have I had to memorize a book or a set of lectures. And, of course, practicing psychologists do not memorize books and lectures either. They treat patients, deal with managed-care companies, and often run a small business. So my view, looking back, is that skill in the introductory course was not terribly relevant to later success (or lack thereof!). Why discourage students who may have the skills they need to succeed in the field, whether or not they have the skills they need to succeed as students in entry-level courses? Why assess students only for knowledge that rather quickly will become outdated, rather than for how well they can think with this or other knowledge?

This is a problem when students who wish to pursue a career in psychology fail to do so because they think they will not succeed. If they get low grades in lower-level psychology courses, they may believe that they lack the skills to become psychologists when, in fact, what may be lacking is the fidelity of the assessments to the demands of a career in psychology. It can also be a problem if students decide to pursue a career in psychology falsely believing that success in low-level courses guarantees that they have the skills to succeed in the career. Students who do well on conventional assessments may not, in some cases, successfully transfer the skills that matter for such assessments to the skills that matter on the job. What we, as teachers, wish for all our students is the maximal success possible, and a realistic assessment of future potential.

A good goal for the teaching of psychology is to raise the achievement of all students by teaching them in a way that matches the way they learn. The question, of course, is how to do it. We think we have a way, which involves teaching to students whose preferred modes of learning embrace any or all of analytical, creative, or practical thinking or learning primarily from memory. Of course, ours is not the only way. But, so far, it seems to work for a wide variety of students of varied ages and in diverse subject-matter areas. If one teaches in this way, then one must also assess in this way.

Although the focus of this chapter is on assessment, this focus is in the context of the fact that instruction and assessment are best thought of as a unified package, rather than as separate entities.

THE PROBLEM: INSTRUCTION AND ASSESSMENT THAT WORK FOR SOME STUDENTS BUT NOT OTHERS

The problem is that some students seem to benefit just fine from the teaching and assessment they get, but others do not. Teachers try very hard to reach all students but, rather frequently, find that there are some students who just seem to be hard to reach. In introductory psychology, for example, students who start off near the top of the class often remain there, in the same way that those who start at the bottom of the class often remain there. There can be many reasons that certain students are hard to reach—disabilities, disorders, motivational problems, health problems, and so forth. One reason, though, can be the mismatch between a pattern of strengths and weaknesses on the part of the student and the particular range of methods that a teacher is using in trying to reach that student. "Teaching for successful intelligence" provides a series of techniques for reaching as many students as possible (Sternberg & Grigorenko, 2000; Sternberg & Spear-Swerling, 1996; Sternberg & Williams, 2002).

This method of teaching is based on a psychological theory, the theory of successful intelligence (Sternberg, 1997, 1999b). This theory is quite different from traditional theories of intelligence, which posit that intelligence is a single construct, sometimes called g, or general intelligence, and sometimes known in terms of the IQ measure. The methods based on this new theory are not the only series of teaching methods on the basis of a new psychological theory of intelligence. Gardner (1983, 1993, 1999) has proposed a different theory, with somewhat different, although sometimes overlapping, methods of instruction. But I believe that our methods are particularly effective; moreover, there is hard empirical data to support their usefulness.

The theory of successful intelligence holds that some students who do not do well in conventional courses may, in fact, have the ability to succeed if they are taught in a way that is a better fit to their patterns of abilities. The problem is that many students who might wish to succeed in psychology may give up because they think they cannot master the material. And if the course is taught as a straight memorize-the-book and memorize-the-lectures course, they may be right. Traditional ways of teaching and assessing psychology, especially at the lower levels, tend to shine the spotlight on some students almost all the time (those with high memory and analytical skills) and on other students almost never (those with high creative and/or practical skills, but not necessarily high memory and analytical skills). The students who are not memory-oriented may either stop taking courses in psychology after the introductory one, or even give up in the introductory course before they finish it. Teaching for successful intelligence can give these students the chance to succeed that they might not otherwise have.

WHAT IS SUCCESSFUL INTELLIGENCE?[1]

Successful intelligence is the ability to succeed in life, given one's own goals, within one's environmental contexts. Thus, successful intelligence is a basis for school achievement, but also life achievement. A key aspect of the theory is that success is defined in terms of a person's individual goals in the context in which that person lives, rather than in terms of more generalized goals that somehow are supposed to apply to everyone.

One is successfully intelligent to the extent one effectively adapts to, shapes, and selects environments, as appropriate. Sometimes one modifies oneself to fit the environment (adaptation), as when a teacher or student enters a new school and tries to fit into the new environment. Other times, one modifies the environment to fit oneself, as when a teacher or student tries to improve the school environment to make it a better place in which to work. And yet other times, one selects a new environment, as when one decides that it would be better to be in another school because attempts to adapt to and/or shape the environment of the current school have not been successful.

People adapt to, shape, and select by recognizing and capitalizing on strengths, and by recognizing and compensating for or correcting weaknesses. People do not achieve success in the same way. Each person has to find his or her own "recipe" for success. One of the most useful things a teacher can do is to help a student figure out how to make the most of what he or she does well, and to find ways around what he or she does not do so well. Certain patterns of abilities help students to do so.

Finally, people capitalize on and compensate through a balance of analytical, creative, and practical abilities (see Sternberg, 1986, 1997, 2000; Sternberg, Forsythe, et al., 2000; Sternberg & Lubart, 1995). The term "CAPS" derives from Creative–Analytical–Practical–Synthesized. The last concept (synthesized) is important, because one must not only learn how to use one's skills, but also how to synthesize them. Memory is not included as a separate element because it underlies all thinking. One cannot analyze what one knows if one does not know anything. One cannot creatively go beyond what is known if one does not know what is known. And one cannot apply

---

[1] In my earlier work (e.g., Sternberg, 1985), I proposed a "triarchic theory" of human intelligence. The present theory builds on the earlier one by defining intelligence in terms of people's ability to choose the personal and professional goals they set for their own lives.

what one knows if one does not know anything. Put another way, one needs creative skills to come up with ideas; analytical skills to decide whether they are good ideas; and practical skills to make the ideas work and to convince others of their value. How to assess performance and teach in a way that enables students to do so is the topic of the remainder of this chapter.

ASSESSING ACHIEVEMENT IN TERMS OF THE THEORY OF SUCCESSFUL INTELLIGENCE

Assessments on the basis of the theory of successful intelligence include items focusing on achievement in terms of memory as well as analytical, creative, and practical thinking, as well as the synthesis of them.

Memory-Based Assessments

We start with memory-based knowledge because such knowledge is the *sine qua non* of thinking. Memory-based assessments typically require students to recall and recognize information, such as who did something, what they did, where they did it, when they did it, why they did it, and how they did it. Here are some examples of assessments:

- **Who?**
  Who proposed that, given "a dozen healthy infants, well-formed, and [his] own specified world to bring them up in," he could "guarantee to take any one at random and train him to become any type of specialist"? [*John Watson*]
- **What?**
  What is the fundamental attribution error? [*A bias of attribution in which an individual tends to overemphasize internal causes and personal responsibility and to deemphasize external causes and situational influences when observing the behavior of other people*]
- **Where?**
  The cerebellum is in the
  a. hindbrain
  b. midbrain
  c. forebrain
  d. left brain
  e. right brain
  [*a*]
- **When?**
  Order the following individuals in terms of the time in which they made seminal contributions to psychological thinking:
  a. Wilhelm Wundt
  b. B. F. Skinner

c. John Locke
d. John Watson
[c, a, d, b]
- **Why?**
Why do many psychologists use fMRI scans in their research?
a. to compute reaction times
b. to localize functioning in the brain
c. to locate the nuclei of neurons
d. to change people's attitudes
e. to change people's cognitions
[b]
- **How?**
How does frequency theory explain people's ability to hear different pitches?
[The basilar membrane reproduces the vibrations that enter the ear, triggering neural impulses at the same frequency as the original sound wave.]

Analytical Assessments

Here one wishes students to analyze, compare and contrast, evaluate, explain, and critique. Here are examples of assessments:

- **Analyze**
Analyze the strengths and weaknesses of Skinner's account of language development.
- **Compare and Contrast**
Compare and contrast self-perception theory with the theory of cognitive dissonance as explanations for the results of the classic 1959 Festinger and Carlsmith experiment on forced compliance.
- **Evaluate**
Evaluate the levels-of-processing theory of memory.
- **Explain**
Explain, in terms of the structure of the eye, why we have difficulties in accurately perceiving colors in the dark.
- **Critique**
Critique the ethics behind Stanley Milgram's studies of obedience, discussing why you believe that the benefits did or did not outweigh the costs of such research.

Creative Assessments

Here one wants students to create, design, imagine, invent, and suppose. Consider some sample assessments:

- **Create**

  Create a very short story in which Mr. Smith, a salesman, uses several techniques to gain compliance in the process of trying to sell Mrs. Jones, a potential customer, an expensive diamond bracelet.

- **Design**

  Design and describe an experiment to test whether, on average, 12-year-old children from the remote province of Shtungis have entered Piaget's cognitive-developmental stage of formal operations.

- **Imagine**

  Imagine that, during childhood, all people were given intensive religious instruction for 4 hours each day. What effect do you think this would have on the data obtained from bystander-intervention studies of the kinds performed by Darley and Latané? Why?

- **Invent**

  Invent a test of implicit memory different from tests currently in use. Describe the test and how you would score it.

- **Suppose**

  Suppose you gave the Wechsler Intelligence Scale for Children (WISC–III) to children growing up in a remote Inuit village in the Canadian Arctic whose school language (but not home language) is English. What kinds of results might you expect in comparison to results from a large American city such as New York, and why?

Practical Assessments

Here one wants students to use, apply, implement, and employ what they have learned. Here are some examples:

- **Use**

  Use your knowledge of the Premack principle to show how reinforcements might be used to convince unmotivated students to study harder.

- **Apply**

  Apply Janis's theory of groupthink to explain why leaders of political parties sometimes put forward candidates to run for office who, because of their extreme views, have little chance of winning.

- **Implement**

  Show how you might use the technique of systematic desensitization to implement a program to help someone combat test anxiety.

- **Employ**

  How do gambling casinos employ reinforcement techniques to keep people gambling at slot machines?

EVALUATING PRODUCTS BASED ON THE THEORY OF SUCCESSFUL INTELLIGENCE

We have created a set of criteria for evaluating responses in the analytical, creative, and practical modes. Here are our criteria:

- **Analytical**—Informed, Logical, Organized, Balanced
- **Creative**—Informed, Novel, Compelling, Task-Appropriate
- **Practical**—Informed; Feasible with respect to time and place; Feasible with respect to human resources; Feasible with respect to material resources

A few notes are in order with regard to these criteria: First, in all of the criteria, we begin with the response being informed. The reason, implied earlier, is that knowledge forms the basis for all thinking. One cannot think unless one has knowledge to think with.

Second, the use of the criteria obviously requires subjective judgment. We have found that judges can be trained to show quite high reliability (Sternberg & Lubart, 1995) but, obviously, evaluations are only as good as the people doing them. Some teachers shudder at the thought that any evaluation should be subjective. This anxiety is misplaced. First, in upper-level courses, I believe it borders on the irresponsible to use only so-called objective assessments. I can scarcely imagine a senior seminar for psychology majors that culminates in nothing more than a multiple-choice final exam. Second, the coin of the realm in psychology is subjective judgments. After school is over, there are no more multiple-choice tests. The way people are evaluated is through subjective judgments. Students might as well get used to it, because that is the way the world is.

Third, we should never substitute objectivity for validity. It is more important that we measure what needs to be measured than that we measure what is easy to measure, but not particularly important in terms of the learning and thinking goals we set for our students.

SAMPLE COURSE REQUIREMENTS

How does one use the theory of successful intelligence in selecting evaluations? Here is the set of evaluations I typically use in my own undergraduate courses:

- Midterm examination(s)
  - Multiple-choice or short-answer items
  - Choice of 2 out of 3 essays (which are primarily analytical, creative, practical)
- Final examination
  - Multiple-choice or short-answer items
  - Choice of 4 out of 6 essays (which are primarily analytical, creative, practical)
- Term paper or project (assigned or unassigned topic)
- Oral presentation (assigned or unassigned topic)

I use this set of requirements in all small courses, and in large courses (such as Introductory Psychology), I omit only the oral presentation because I do not have sections and it is not feasible for each of roughly 150 students to give an oral presentation.

On the exams, I typically have multiple-choice or short-answer questions that require a broad knowledge base in order to be answered correctly. I try to avoid picky facts, but students need to know the basic material. The factual questions presented above are typical of the ones I use.

I also include essay questions, one or two of which emphasize analytical thinking, one or two, creative thinking, and one or two, practical thinking. None of them is "pure." That is, most questions require at least some combination of the three kinds of thinking skills. Thus, they differ only in emphasis. I ask students to answer two of three (or four of six) questions. The advantage of this choice is that it allows students, to some extent, to capitalize on strengths and to compensate for weaknesses. But it does not enable them only to utilize one strength. They have to utilize at least two kinds of thinking skills.

I believe a term project is important because it assesses a kind of strength that is quite different from that of a test. It requires more integrative, long-term thinking and requires students to do their own research. I usually give students a choice of any topic they wish, so long as they can relate it to the course. I also allow formats other than papers. Some students do experiments; other students write essays. I encourage students to link other interests they may have to their interest in psychology.

DOES TEACHING FOR SUCCESSFUL INTELLIGENCE WORK?

Teachers want—indeed, some demand—some level of assurance that, if they take the trouble to use a method of teaching, it really will work. We have done a series of studies showing that teaching for successful intelligence really can work, at least in the instances in which we have examined it. The common element of all these studies is the possibility that, when students are taught for successful intelligence, they are better able to capitalize on their strengths and to correct or compensate for their weaknesses, so that they learn at higher levels. Although the data from the studies are not conclusive, they are at least suggestive of the value of teaching for successful intelligence.

In a first study (Sternberg, Grigorenko, Ferrari, & Clinkenbeard, 1999), for example, we identified high school children that were gifted (a) analytically, (b) creatively, (c) practically, (d) in all three ways, or (e) in none of these ways. We then taught these children a rigorous advanced-placement summer psychology course that either fit their pattern of abilities particularly well or did not do so. The instructional conditions were memory-based, analytically-based, creatively-based, and practically-based. All students received the same textbook (an advance edition of Sternberg, 1997) and the same lectures in the morning. In the afternoon, they were divided into sections in which the emphases were different depending on the instructional condition to which they were assigned. Thus, a highly creative student might receive an instructional program that emphasized creative learning and thinking (good fit), or one that emphasized memory learning (not-so-good fit). We found that children who were taught in a way that, at least some of the time, enabled them to capitalize on their strengths outperformed students who were not so taught.

In a second study (Sternberg, Torff, & Grigorenko, 1998a, 1998b), we taught third-grade students social studies and eighth-grade students psychology in one of three ways: (a) memory learning, (b) primarily analytical (critical) thinking, or (c) teaching for successful intelligence (memory, analytical, creative, and practical learning). All students received the same quantity of instruction for the same time period, and all students received the same assessments for memory learning as well as for analytical, creative, and practical learning. We found that students who were taught for successful intelligence outperformed students who were taught either for memory or critical thinking, almost without regard to grade level, subject matter, or type of assessment. Even on memory assessments, the children taught for successful intelligence outperformed the children in the other two groups.

In a third study (Grigorenko, Jarvin, & Sternberg, 2002), we helped primarily inner-city urban students at the middle- and high-school levels develop their reading skills. At the middle-school level, reading was taught as a separate subject, whereas at the high-school level, reading was taught as part of other subjects, such as English, science, foreign languages, and history instruction. Students were taught either for successful intelligence or in a standard way that emphasized memory-based instruction. The students who were taught for successful intelligence outperformed the students taught in the more conventional way on all assessments, whether for vocabulary or reading comprehension, and whether emphasizing memory-based, analytical, creative, or practical thinking.

WHY TEACHING FOR SUCCESSFUL
INTELLIGENCE IS SUCCESSFUL

Why does teaching for successful intelligence work? There are at least four reasons:

- *Capitalizing on student strengths*. Teaching for successful intelligence helps students learn in ways that work for them, rather than forcing them to learn in ways that do not work.
- *Correcting or compensating for students' weaknesses*. Teaching for successful intelligence helps students to correct deficient skills, or at least to develop methods of compensation for these skills.
- *Multiple encodings*. This form of teaching encourages students to encode material not just in one way, but in three or four different ways (memory, analytical, creative, practical), so they are more likely to be able to retrieve the material when they need it.
- *Deeper encodings*. Teaching in this way also helps students encode material more deeply because the presentation of the material is more meaningful and more closely related to what students already know.
- *Motivation*. Teaching for successful intelligence is more interesting to most students and hence motivates them more.
- *Career relevance*. Much of what students learn, and the way they learn it, bears little resemblance to what these students later will need to succeed on the job. For example, a typical introductory psychology course may require the memorization of a great amount of material. Teaching for successful intelligence better helps students prepare for what they later will need to do on the job.

ANTICIPATED OBJECTIONS

When any new system for teaching and assessment is introduced, teachers and administrators sometimes have objections. What kinds of objections have we encountered with the system of teaching for successful intelligence, and what are our replies? Here are five typical objections:

- *It is only for gifted students*. Some teachers believe that their students have enough of a problem learning the conventional way. Why introduce other ways that will just confuse them more, especially teaching for creative thinking, which these teachers may see as unnecessary? But these teachers have things backwards. The problem is that many students simply do not learn well in conventional ways. Teaching in other ways, rather than confusing them, enlightens them. Unless they are taught in other ways, they just will not learn much. And teaching for creative thinking is not peripheral. In these times of rapid change, all students need to learn to think in a way that maximizes their flexibility.

- *It is only for weak students.* Then there are teachers who say that teaching for successful intelligence is only for weak students. Their regular students learn just fine with the current system. But do they really learn so well? And is it ever the case that their learning cannot be improved? We believe that teaching always can be improved, and that teaching for successful intelligence is one way of doing it. Moreover, many good students are "good" in the sense of having developed adequate memory and analytical skills. But later in life, they will need creative and practical skills too. Schools should help students develop these skills.

- *It takes too much time to teach everything three ways.* This objection is based on a misunderstanding of what teaching for successful intelligence requires. It does not require everything be taught three times in three ways. Rather, the idea is for teachers to alternate, so that some material is being taught one way, other material, another way.

- *It is too hard to do.* Good teachers naturally teach for successful intelligence. They need only the bare minimum of instruction. Other teachers need more time to catch on. But once one catches on—which usually does not take an inordinate amount of time— it becomes second nature. It is no harder, and perhaps even easier, than teaching in the regular way, because one begins to see alternative natural ways of teaching the same material.

- *My supervisor (department chair, dean, etc.) will not allow it.* This might be true in some instances. But our experience has been that administrators are open to almost any form of teaching that is ethical so long as it improves student achievement and motivation.

- *It won't improve test scores.* On the contrary, our data, cited above, show that teaching and assessing via the CAPS model *does* improve scores on conventional tests.

CONCLUSION

Successful intelligence involves teaching students for memory, as well as analytically, creatively, and practically. It does not mean teaching everything in three ways. Rather, it means alternating teaching strategies so that teaching reaches (almost) every student at least some of the time. Teaching for successful intelligence also means helping students to capitalize on their strengths and to correct or compensate for their weaknesses. We believe we have good evidence to support teaching for successful intelligence. Teaching for successful intelligence improves learning outcomes, even if the only outcome measure is straightforward memory learning. We therefore encourage teachers seriously to consider use of this teaching method in their classrooms— at all grade levels and for all subject-matter areas.

New techniques and programs are being developed all the time. For example, at this time, we have active research sites testing the efficacy of our programs in many parts of the United States and abroad. We also have developed a software system, "CORE," which enables teachers to communicate with us and with each other if they encounter any problems while using our materials. In this way, they can get immediate feedback to help them solve problems, rather than waiting until someone can help them, perhaps much later. CORE consists of e-mail, listservs, and chat rooms that put teachers in touch with one another so that they mutually can facilitate each other's teaching.

Teaching for successful intelligence potentially provides benefits at multiple levels. It helps students to achieve at a level that is commensurate with their skills, rather than letting valuable skills, which could be used in facilitating learning, go to waste. It helps schools reach higher levels of achievement as a whole. And, in these days of school accountability, reaching higher average scores is a goal virtually every school wants to reach. Finally, it helps society make better use of its human resources. There is no reason for a society to waste its most precious resource—its human talent. Teaching for successful intelligence helps ensure that talent will not go to waste.

Back in 1968, I got that C in the introductory-psychology course. I had the good fortune, after this disaster, to try to major in math and to do even worse in it than I did in psychology. But if I had instead turned to some other subject, such as sociology, literature, political science, or history, I probably would have done well enough to get by, and I would have ended up studying a field in which I was only cursorily interested. I might have had some success, but to the extent that we do our best work in the fields that really are important to us (see essays in Sternberg, 1999a), I probably would not have done my best work. How many students has psychology lost because the instruction and assessments in low-level courses did not fit the way the students learn and think? Let's not lose any more.

REFERENCES

Gardner, H. (1983). *Frames of mind: The theory of multiple intelligences*. New York: Basic Books.

Gardner, H. (1993). *Multiple intelligences: The theory in practice*. New York: Basic Books.

Gardner, H. (1999). *Reframing intelligence*. New York: Basic Books.

Grigorenko, E. L., Jarvin, L., & Sternberg, R. J. (2002). School-based tests of the triarchic theory of intelligence: Three settings, three samples, three syllabi. *Contemporary Educational Psychology, 27*, 167–208.

Jensen, A. R. (1998). *The g factor*. Westport, CT: Praeger-Greenwood.

Sternberg, R. J. (1985). *Beyond IQ: A triarchic theory of human intelligence*. New York: Cambridge University Press.

Sternberg, R. J. (1986). *Intelligence applied*. San Diego, CA: Harcourt.

Sternberg, R. J. (1997). *Successful intelligence*. New York: Plume.

Sternberg, R. J. (Ed.) (1999a). *Handbook of creativity*. New York: Cambridge University Press.

Sternberg, R. J. (1999b). The theory of successful intelligence. *Review of General Psychology, 3*, 292–316.

Sternberg, R. J. (2000). Creativity is a decision. In A. L. Costa (Ed.), *Teaching for intelligence II* (pp. 5–106). Arlington Heights, IL: Skylight.

Sternberg, R. J., Forsythe, G. B., Hedlund, J., Horvath, J., Snook, S., Williams, W. M., et al. (2000). *Practical intelligence in everyday life*. New York: Cambridge University Press.

Sternberg, R. J., & Grigorenko, E. L. (2000). *Teaching for successful intelligence*. Arlington Heights, IL: Skylight.

Sternberg, R. J., Grigorenko, E. L., Ferrari, M., & Clinkenbeard, P. (1999). A triarchic analysis of an aptitude-treatment interaction. *European Journal of Psychological Assessment, 15(1)*, 1–11.

Sternberg, R. J., & Lubart, T. I. (1995). *Defying the crowd: Cultivating creativity in a culture of conformity*. New York: Free Press.

Sternberg, R. J., & Spear-Swerling, L. (1996). *Teaching for thinking*. Washington, DC: American Psychological Association.

Sternberg, R. J., Torff, B., & Grigorenko, E. L. (1998a). Teaching for successful intelligence raises school achievement. *Phi Delta Kappan, 79*, 667–669.

Sternberg, R. J., Torff, B., & Grigorenko, E. L. (1998b). Teaching triarchically improves school achievement. *Journal of Educational Psychology, 90*, 374–384.

Sternberg, R. J., & Williams, W. M. (2002). *Educational psychology*. Boston: Allyn & Bacon.

7

COURSE ASSESSMENT: DEVELOPING AND ASSESSING ASSESSABLE OBJECTIVES BY USING AN INTEGRATIVE ASSESSMENT MODEL

RANDALL E. OSBORNE AND WALTER F. WAGOR

Efforts aimed at improving teaching and learning often reflect the principles outlined in the brief article by Chickering and Gamson (1987) that appeared in the Bulletin of the American Association for Higher Education (AAHE) titled, "Seven Principles for Good Practice in Undergraduate Education." Based on more than 50 years of educational research, these principles provide guidelines for improving teaching and learning in our colleges and universities. Three of these principles are particularly appropriate for our current discussion: They state that good practice in undergraduate education uses active learning techniques; communicates high expectations; and gives prompt feedback. Active learning involves more than memorizing a set of facts. It occurs as students think about, speak about, write about, and apply what they are learning. Furthermore, good practice sets appropriate goals for successful learning, challenging students with clear statements of what is expected of them. Finally, students need appropriate and timely feedback on their performance. This principle includes both frequent opportunities to practice and perform what they are learning, as well as suggestions for improvement along the way.

Similar conclusions are also drawn from the assessment literature. For example, the AAHE (1996) suggested nine principles of good practice for assessing student learning. Among the principles were:

1. Assessment is most effective when it reflects an understanding of learning as multidimensional, integrated, and revealed in performance over time.
2. Assessment works best when the programs it seeks to improve have clear, explicitly stated purposes.
3. Assessment requires attention to outcomes but also and equally to the experiences that lead to those outcomes.
4. Assessment works best when it is ongoing, not episodic.

Rogers (1991) argued that successful assessment depends on faculty defining reasonable expectations for students. Through curricula and individual courses, faculty need to provide guidance to students about the expected outcomes of their learning. Assessment can then serve as a form of feedback to improve both teaching and learning. (See also Banta & Associates, 1993, and Banta, Lund, Black, & Oblander, 1996, for examples of the AAHE principles in practice.)

CONFUSION IN TERMINOLOGY

Grading Versus Evaluation

We begin with the potentially controversial notion that grading is not necessarily formative assessment. Grading is evaluation. However, grading that is based on quality formative assessments can lead to evaluation. The two terms are not simply two ways of saying the same thing. To illustrate this point, let us take an example. Imagine that you have two students, one who received an A on an assignment and one who received a C. What do we know about these students and their learning? Do we know what they learned? Do we know what they did not learn? If they both received Cs, could we assume they both learned the same amount or that they learned the same things?

Walvood and Anderson (1998) argued that grading, properly used, can provide the type of information useful for improving teaching and learning. They suggested that a first step in achieving that end is to consider thoughtfully what you want students to learn, that is, to develop clear objectives for student learning.

With clear objectives, you can establish fair and clear standards and criteria for student performance. Learning is improved as you subsequently construct tests and assignments that both teach and test those objectives, offering feedback at numerous points along the way. At the heart of their suggestions, Walvood and Anderson argued that student learning should be the teacher's primary goal, admonishing us to be gatekeepers at the end of the process of learning, not at the beginning.

Formative Versus Summative Assessment

Summative assessment can be considered assessment *of* learning while formative assessment might best be considered assessment *for* learning. Whereas formative assessment facilitates judgments about a student's performance, summative assessment provides judgments about the student's progress. According to the Assessment Reform Group (1999), formative assessment should be concerned with shaping students' progress toward mastering a set of learning or achievement objectives.

Black and Wiliam (1998a, 1998b) suggested that formative assessment is an integral aspect of classroom work and that there is ample evidence that developing formative assessment methods can raise achievement standards. Engaging in ongoing (formative) assessment methods provides consistent feedback about performance for both student and faculty member. In addition, the feedback is specific enough (knowing exactly what concepts students miss and at what level) that areas in which improvement is needed and which methods would best be used to help students improve are more obvious.

Formative assessment is important for many reasons, including: (a) empowering students to take appropriate action, (b) allowing instructors to adjust what they are doing in a timely fashion, (c) helping students to discover what they do and do not know, and (d) keeping differences in faculty and student perceptions of learning from interfering with that learning. In contrast, summative assessment, important for overall course assessment (gate keeping) and for program assessment, does not usually provide information in a way that is timely enough to allow students to adjust what they are learning and doing while the course is still in session.

THE MECHANICS OF ASSESSMENT

According to Black and Wiliam (1998b) the practice of everyday assessment in courses is "beset with problems and shortcomings" (p. 7). They categorize these difficulties into three issues: (a) how to promote and assess appropriate levels of learning; (b) how to minimize negative impact from assessment experiences, and (c) how to manage meaningful assessment processes.

Promoting Higher Levels of Learning

One of our students once brought in a paper from another class in which the instructor had written in red ink the following marginal comment: "Don't tell me what you think, tell me what I told you to know." The student had concluded, "not only have I not been encouraged to think critically, I have been punished for it." The student's experience illustrates fairly low-level objectives for student learning.

Bloom, Englehart, Furst, Hill, and Krathwohl (1956) were among the first to articulate a framework intended to assist students to move beyond recitation of fact and to promote student work and assessment methods that move further along the cognitive continuum. Bloom's taxonomy, which distinguishes lower- and higher-order cognitive processes, provides a useful framework around which to build an assessment conversation. Traditional methods for assessing student learning typically involve the simplest levels of cognitive understanding (remembering and comprehending) while ignoring more sophisticated measures of cognitive progress (evaluating and creating). We acknowledge that Bloom's taxonomy—and Krathwohl's (2002) retooling of the model (see Exhibit 7.1)—is simply one method among many that could be used as a framework for constructing an assessment model. We use it here mainly because it is so widely known.

Optimal assessment strategies for higher-order cognitive skills should require students to demonstrate an understanding of the material or concept at the level expected. Because these assessments are formative, practice is essential (Black & Wiliam, 1998a). Therefore, feedback should identify the degree to which the work did or did not accomplish the objective along with enough detail that students can "fill in the gaps" next time.

Minimizing Negative Impact

One particularly relevant shortcoming in everyday assessment outlined by Black and Wiliam is that assessors usually mark work conscientiously but may offer little or no guidance on how work can be improved, which they referred to as "negative impact." Grading can emphasize the comparison of students' performances such that students internalize the competition for grades but not the goals of learning (e.g., Osborne, 1996). If students internalize grades—rather than valuing what they have learned and the level at which they have learned it—there is little incentive to apply that material to the resolution of issues or problems outside the classroom. In an intriguing book, Covington (1992) discusses the crisis in the current educational system in America. In contrast to some who suggest that the crisis in the American educational system is one of content, he suggests that the crisis is one of effort. The emphasis on grades and marking rather than learning and assessment prompts students to work for the grade. Competition fosters the notion

EXHIBIT 7.1
Krathwohl's Revision of Bloom's Taxonomy of Cognitive Objectives

1. **Remembering**—recognition or recitation of specific facts.
2. **Comprehending**—articulated understanding of the information.
3. **Applying**—application of information toward the solution of problems outside the classroom.
4. **Analyzing**—breaking a problem down into subparts and recognition of the connections (or lack of connections) between those subparts. During this process, useless pieces of information are identified and discounted.
5. **Creating**—an ability to take the remaining subparts (those identified as meaningful and interconnected during the analyzing phase) into a more meaningful whole.
6. **Evaluating**—assessing the degree to which an attempted solution has resolved the problem. (If the attempt has failed, the process is repeated, beginning at the analysis level or before.)

that only those with the highest scores have learned anything. Those who are less likely to succeed at the highest levels, consequently, are not motivated to try. If anything less than perfect is a failure and you do not believe you can do something perfectly, what is the motivation to try? If students try really hard and fail, it would appear to be due to lack of ability. If, however, those same students did not try and still failed, they could blame lack of effort and, thereby, would not have to internalize that failure.

Managing Meaningful Assessment Processes

The final issue mentioned by Black and Wiliam (1998a, 1998b) involves the "managerial" role of most assessments. Rather than using assessment as an opportunity to recognize progress and delineate a path for improvement, teachers may become preoccupied with and distracted by grading as a task in and of itself. Some teachers, for example, may believe that they are truly assessing student understanding by assigning a grade and making notations in a grade book without having given much consideration to the growth opportunities that formative assessments provide.

TWO FORMATIVE ASSESSMENT SYSTEMS

The more an assessment system focuses on grades rather than cognitive levels and progress in learning, the more likely it is to fall prey to the three issues outlined by Black and Wiliam (1998a, 1998b). We contend that there are some relatively simple strategies that educators can adopt to produce satisfying assessment outcomes. We will examine two approaches: the Interactive Formative Assessment Model (Cowie & Bell, 1999) and the Integrative Model of our design.

An Interactive Formative Assessment Model

Cowie and Bell (1999) articulated a model of formative assessment that differentiates between "planned" and "interactive" formative assessment. Planned formative assessment involves methods that educators develop along with the course to elicit information, actions, skills, and so forth from students. But, according to Cowie and Bell, high quality assessment also needs to have a spontaneous quality. That is the essence of Interactive Formative Assessment. With this form of assessment, faculty members monitor student performance with the intention of noticing or recognizing desired skills, actions, and knowledge. In addition, Planned Formative Assessment is more long-term and focused on the curriculum; Interactive Formative Assessment occurs in a shorter time frame and is more student-focused. Truly formative assessment, then, may need to incorporate both of these aspects of assessment. We believe the Interactive Formative Assessment model serves as a good link between more primitive forms of assessment (e.g., grading) and the integrative model that we propose.

An Integrative Model for Course Assessment

As anyone who has attempted to implement an assessment program can attest, moving faculty from the discussion phase of assessment to the implementation phase is quite challenging. Part of the challenge results from the difficulty in focusing the discussion at a level that facilitates both precise definitions of what is expected (e.g., What should a student be able to demonstrate and at what level?) and how things will be measured (e.g., How do we assess students to determine whether they can demonstrate the expected outcomes at the levels we want?). We recommend thinking about assessment as an integrative process. By delineating what is expected of students, determining what data one needs to gather, and making decisions about the degree to which students have or have not met specific assessment goals, the assessment process becomes both active and integrated.

The integrative model we propose considers formative assessment to be a five-step process:

1. **Defining** what skills and capacities students most need to acquire from the course or program.
2. **Deciding** what level of expectation there is for those skills and capacities.
3. **Detailing** what faculty will do to provide instruction in and practice with those skills and abilities and identifying what students will do to demonstrate those skills and abilities.
4. **Discovering** whether students are sufficiently demonstrating those skills and abilities.

5. **Determining** what changes to make if students do not demonstrate skills or abilities at desired levels. It is, of course, possible that the assessment data suggest that all is fine. In this case, the determination is to continue doing what one is doing.

A simple example can be used to illustrate the model. Many faculty have lower-order knowledge expectations for students (we want them to remember certain things). Perhaps the learning objective states that students will be able to "generate an accurate definition of psychology." The objective has already been defined. The next step is to decide what assessment method to use. In the case of this type of objective, a straightforward question would suffice. Students could be asked on an exam, for example, to generate an accurate definition of psychology.

The wording of the objective also helps one accomplish the third step of detailing assessment expectations to students. Students know that they are expected to be able to generate an accurate definition of psychology. The fourth step is a bit more complicated because discovering how students are doing requires that we have a clear idea of what a successful answer to the question would entail. Suppose we have decided that an accurate definition of psychology is "the scientific study of behavior and mental processes." An acceptable definition, then, would entail students stating that psychology is scientific and studies behavior and mental processes. If our goal is that 75% of our students will generate this accurate definition and they can, then little else needs to be done. If, however, we determine that students are not achieving at the desired level, we must determine what changes to make in the course to attempt to rectify that deficiency.

The integrative model can also be used to assess more difficult objectives that are not readily quantifiable. Consider the following objective, which is fairly common on Introduction to Psychology course syllabi: "Students will gain an appreciation for psychology as a science." What does it mean to appreciate something? How will we know whether students have gained such an appreciation? The *American Heritage College Dictionary* (Pickett & Pritchard, 1993) defines *appreciation* as, "to admire greatly, to show gratitude for, to be fully aware of, or to recognize the quality or significance of" something. Further analysis, however, may lead us to extract exactly what this word might mean that could influence our assessment. If students truly appreciate psychology as a science, then it means they both understand psychology and understand the implications of considering it a science. We can then create a more measurable objective that states, "students will gain an appreciation of psychology as a scientific discipline by critically assessing the scientific method and comparing that method to other methods."

Assessable objectives must be written in such a way that they are both active and measurable. This is another example of the difference between formative and summative assessment. Many times faculty know where they want students to be when they reach the end of the course (summative assessment), but have difficulty articulating what progress toward those goals (formative assessment) might look like. The five steps in our integrative model provide language that can be used to articulate performance expectations clearly.

Let us take another example from the Introductory Psychology course to illustrate how this model might be used to assess more complex objectives. One of the objectives for this course might be, "Students will be able to describe basic psychological perspectives and apply those perspectives to real world issues." Using the five-step model, we can design a method for assessing that objective, illustrating student progress (or lack of progress) on that objective, and make course changes as necessary.

1. **Defining.** What skills and capacities will students need to acquire from the course? The way the objective is written answers this question. Essentially, it involves two elements: (a) the ability to describe basic psychological perspectives, and (b) the ability to apply those perspectives to real-world issues.

2. **Deciding.** What level of expectation is there for the skills and capacities outlined within the objective? The objective states that we want students to be able to describe the perspectives and apply them in real-world situations.

3. **Detailing.** What will students do to demonstrate the skills and capacities outlined in the objective? We want students to describe and apply various psychological perspectives. A multiple-choice recognition question on an exam, then, will probably not be sufficient. Instead, we could include an essay question on an exam—in fact one of the authors includes the following question on the first and each subsequent introductory psychology exam—using a different real-world issue each time:

   > Briefly describe the 6 major psychological perspectives discussed in class. Describe each perspective (its assumptions, its major points, etc.) in enough detail that someone not taking this course would clearly understand each perspective. Imagine that you are designing a day care facility. Choose any two of the perspectives and discuss what suggestions each would make for what to include or not to include in your facility.

Writing objectives is important and may be more difficult than is first thought. The wording of the objective influences the

EXHIBIT 7.2
Articulating Objectives With Bloom's Taxonomy

Remembering = name, define, relate, report, repeat, label, record, describe
Comprehending = outline, interpret, paraphrase, accept, criticize, recommend
Applying = practice, solve, illustrate, use, demonstrate, manipulate
Analyzing = examine, discriminate, compare, dissect, subdivide, question, investigate
Evaluating = rate, judge, prioritize, decide, assess, appraise, review, judge, evaluate
Creating = produce, propose, compose, devise, forecast, formulate, prepare, organize

---

development of assessment methods, articulates expectations for students, and provides guidance as you develop your evaluative methods as well. The objective must be written at the level of your expectations or students may not know what level to strive toward. Although there are literally dozens of descriptors that could be used at each level of Bloom's taxonomy, Exhibit 7.2 may serve as a good starting point for the articulation of your learning objectives.

4. **Discovering.** Are the students meeting the objective? We have to decide what criteria will determine whether student success or performance on the objective is sufficient. The decision is twofold. First, how do we assess the individual student's progress on the objective? Second, how do we assess overall student performance to determine whether course changes need to be made before the assessment data is gathered again? Perhaps a scoring rubric could be created that assigns scores to each student. We can then have an overall assessment goal that informs the next step of the model. As example, consider the sample rubric in Exhibit 7.3 for assessing student responses to this question.

Now that we have scores, we can do several things. First, we can provide individual students with precise feedback about the nature of the score and what would need to be done differently to perform better. Second, we can decide to make changes in the course based on the assessment goals articulated for that objective. Perhaps, we decide that 75% or more of the students will receive a score of 6 or higher out of 8 on this simple scoring rubric and have raters use the form to assess the essays. Once we obtain sufficient interrater reliability, we can then use the scores in our assessment.

5. **Determining.** What changes, if any, need to be made if students do not demonstrate the skills and capacities for that objective at the articulated values? If we believe that the goal was not met because students did not understand the perspec-

EXHIBIT 7.3
A Sample Scoring Rubric

Description of Perspectives
____ fewer than 6 perspectives described (1 point)
____ 6 perspectives described but not well (2 points)
____ 6 perspectives described well (3 points)
____ 6 perspectives described extremely well (4 points)

Applications to Day Care
____ fewer than 2 applications made (1 point)
____ 2 applications made but weak (2 points)
____ 2 reasonable applications made (3 points)
____ 2 high quality applications made (4 points)

Total Score: Description _____ + Applications _____ = _____

tives well enough, then the emphasis might be on teaching the perspectives more completely or providing more in-class practice with delineating the differences among them. Remember the importance of repetition with formative assessment. It may be the case that students are not demonstrating the level of understanding that is desired because they have not had enough practice with the task. Ongoing formative assessment allows us to gather information that may point this out in time for changes in the course to be made.

SOME DATA-BASED CONCLUSIONS ABOUT PROGRAM QUALITY

For several years the Psychology Department at Indiana University East offered a critical thinking lab paired with certain sections of the Introductory Psychology course. The rationale behind the course was simple: Giving students practice with critical thinking and problem solving within a discipline would enhance skills necessary for success in college in terms of course grades and retention (Browne & Osborne, 1998). To facilitate critical thinking and problem solving, the department developed the following course themes: (a) challenging what is known, (b) exploring one's hypotheses, and (c) trying to prove oneself wrong.

The Task

As part of the assessment of the course (to inform the department about the success of the course and potential changes to make), students evaluated course activities and assignments. One particular activity was listed by 88% of the students as the most influential in illustrating the critical thinking

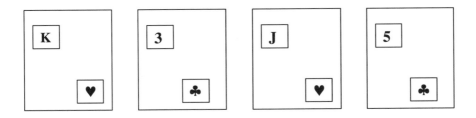

Figure 7.1. Critical thinking activity.

process. In this activity (see Figure 7.1), four cards were placed on a sheet of paper and then copied onto an overhead transparency. Once assigned to groups, students looked over the sequence of cards and generated a hypothesis that would predict what the next several cards would be (the correct answer is "face card followed by a numbered club"). Once students decided on what they believed the sequence to be, we asked them to test the hypothesis by telling either the instructor or one of the teaching assistants what they believed the next card would be. In return, they would receive a *yes* or *no* response. A *yes* response, of course, would simply indicate that the card they chose fit the sequence.

On the surface this may seem easy, but it proved extraordinarily difficult for students to do. Most groups immediately predicted that the fifth card would be the nine of Hearts (based on the hypothesis that the sequence was descending and skipping Heart cards). Shocked expressions greeted the faculty member and teaching assistants when students were told *no*.

Believing that it was the suit of the card that mattered could result in many false positive responses. Students might believe they had accurately determined part of the sequence because they had guessed the fifth, sixth, and seventh cards only to be told *no* when they guessed the eighth card. By trying to prove themselves right, or changing too many variables at once (like changing both the suit and from a face card to a numbered card in the same guess), the students had no choice but to start from scratch when they received a *no* response.

Once students tried to prove themselves wrong by inserting other suits, they made quick progress. The activity clearly illustrated for students that they were less flexible with their thinking than they needed to be. When students understood that good scientists would approach this task by trying to pick cards that might prove their hypothesis wrong rather than trying to prove themselves right, performance started to improve. Ultimately, all groups completed the task having discovered the hypothesis statement that the instructor and teaching assistants had decided upon prior to the activity.

These themes—challenging what is known, exploring one's hypotheses, and trying to prove oneself wrong—were repeated throughout the other activities in the course. Students learned to invest in their critical thinking and to understand how to reap the benefits of making that investment. Critical thinking requires more time and effort, and may force us to reveal biases and assumptions inherent in our own thinking. But, in return for such an investment, students learned they would gain more pure knowledge and could be more certain of what they knew and how they knew it. These skills, we believed, would aid students as they took other courses within their degree programs.

Linking the Example to Program Assessment

A recent analysis of our data supports our notion that this course, emulating Bloom's cognitive objectives, enhanced student success. We matched two sets of students, those who had completed the introductory psychology course with and without the lab, on a variety of entrance variables (high school rank, high school GPA, declared major, previous hours completed, etc.). Students completing the critical thinking course along with the General Psychology course outperformed the matched sample on all performance variables regardless of academic major.

Prior to this project the average "D," "F," and withdrawal ratio in our introductory course was 46%. In contrast, the average "D," "F," and withdrawal percentage was 24% across the five semesters in which introductory psychology was combined with the critical thinking lab. In addition, the graduation rate of students who completed this version of the introductory psychology course was 14% higher than for the matched cohort of students who took the traditional introductory course during the same semesters. (It is important to note that these students were also designated by the university as the most at risk for academic failure.) Finally, upon graduation, students who had completed the combined introductory psychology/critical thinking course had an overall GPA that was more than one letter grade higher than the matched cohort sample.

ASSESSMENT ASSUMPTIONS

Successful discovery of student progress on learning objectives is built upon several assumptions. First, discovery is predicated on the assumption that the faculty member has successfully completed the first three steps of active assessment. In other words, you cannot truly discover how well students are progressing on course objectives unless those objectives are well defined, outcome expectations levels have been decided, and the faculty member has clearly detailed those expectations for students. Completing the first three steps, however, does not ensure that the discovery process will be successful. A significant disconnect can exist between the expectations the faculty member has defined, decided upon, and detailed and the level at which students are assessed. We cannot measure the degree to which students can apply a concept, for example, by asking a series of multiple-choice questions that are all written at the remembering level.

If we value student progress along the cognitive continuum articulated in this chapter, then we must grapple with the question of whether the assessment methods we have developed assess at all of those levels. Multiple-choice questions *can* be written in such a way as to assess higher-order thinking and reasoning. The question is whether they *are* written in such a way as to truly assess at the desired level. Multiple assessment methods are necessary not only to get a formative picture of student progress, they can also be necessary to discover whether students have truly demonstrated the full range of higher order reasoning that we expect.

Writing learning objectives is a difficult task. Being able to write objectives effectively requires an ability to articulate many of the assumptions we make about student learning. We must also be able to articulate aspects of our discipline that may be more intuitive than concrete. Faculty may "know" what they expect students to know, or be able to do. However, defining those expectations, deciding upon levels of expectation, detailing those for students, designing methods that allow for true discovery of student progress at all desired levels, and then determining what changes, if any, might need to be made based on the outcome of those assessment efforts is a complex process. Happily, change is not always necessary. If the assessment process demonstrates that students are achieving the desired learning outcomes at desired levels, the data will reinforce our course design decisions. The key point is, we will truly know.

EFFECTIVE USE OF THE INTEGRATIVE MODEL

The Integrative Assessment Model provides a series of developmental questions (e.g., What should students be able to do? At what level should they be able to do it? How will we know whether they can do it? What do we do if they cannot?) that can be used to guide the assessment process. By clearly articulating assessable outcomes, we can maximize the likelihood that (a) students will understand and be in a position to demonstrate their progress toward those expectations, and (b) the faculty are more attuned to (paying attention to and more likely to recognize) students' progress toward achieving those expectations.

For individuals responsible for assisting others in developing assessment methods, the Integrative Assessment Model provides a framework that allows a common language regardless of discipline area, level of course, or type of program (e.g., minor, associate degree, baccalaureate degree, etc.). By addressing the assessment process as a series of questions, we can reduce tension about assessment and evaluation because faculty are used to asking and answering questions. Rather than telling faculty they must assess, the model provides a nonthreatening set of procedures that focus on the course. Once faculty have engaged in the development of assessment methods for courses and have used outcome data to make improvements to those courses, they are, perhaps, more likely to be ready to apply those same skills to programmatic assessment.

Fair Practices for Students and Faculty

Dialogue on assessment can lead to changes in faculty evaluative practices. For example, during annual performance review in the Psychology Department at Southwest Texas State University (STU) a colleague submitted documentation of effectiveness in teaching. This colleague offered a table showing the percentage of students in each of his classes who had been assigned grades of A, B, C, and so on. If grades were used to demonstrate teaching effectiveness, all faculty would have to do to earn a higher effectiveness score would be to assign higher grades to students. Teaching effectiveness is difficult, at best, to measure with grades. Consider the unknowns such as: (a) student effort, (b) evaluative difficulty, (c) student understanding of material prior to enrollment in the course, or (d) relationship between grading criteria and anticipated learning outcomes.

The STU Department also recently started to involve the departmental Personnel Committee in performance review of all faculty. Prior to this development, the chair made all the performance evaluation decisions. One of the first questions that was raised was, "Should we review faculty grade distributions?" Although, on the surface, this may appear to be a very reasonable request, there are several assumptions inherent in the question that may confuse assessment and evaluation. For example, one assumption might be that faculty who are strict about grading criteria will receive lower scores on student evaluations and vice versa. But if faculty use formative assessments successfully, students are significantly more likely to understand the relationship between the skills and abilities they are able to demonstrate (and the levels at which they can demonstrate those things) and the summative scores they earn in the course. If this understanding is clear, there is no reason to assume that grades influence course evaluations.

The Bottom Line

Why the focus on developing clear learning objectives and outcomes? Critics argue that many of us have taught for years without articulating our expected outcomes either to our students or to ourselves. Have students (at least most of them) not learned what they needed to learn? We would like to share a few thoughts on this as we conclude this chapter.

Barr and Tagg (1995) proposed the thesis that higher education is in the midst of an historic shift from a teaching-centered to a learning-centered paradigm. In this new paradigm, the primary purpose of college and universities is to produce learning rather than to provide instruction. If this is true, we suggest that the need for developing, articulating, and communicating clear expectations of what it is that students are to learn will only grow in importance. As the focus shifts to the expected outcomes, the demand to be clear about those outcomes will only increase. Only by knowing where it is that we expect students to be at the end of a course or of a program will we be able to help them get there and to know when they have arrived.

Assessment is no longer an option; it is here to stay. It is incumbent upon us to make our assessments as fair as possible. Suskie (2000) suggests a number of steps to follow in developing fair assessments. Among her suggestions are that we have clearly stated learning outcomes that we share with students so that they know what we expect; that we match our assessment to what we teach and vice versa; and that we help students learn how to assess themselves—something they can do only if they understand the desired outcome. At the heart of her suggestions, we see once again, is the importance of developing and sharing clear expectations for student learning.

Finally, in an interesting article in the *AAHE Bulletin*, Murray, Gillese, Lennon, Mercer, and Robinson (1996) proposed a set of ethical principles for college and university teaching. Embodied within their suggested principles are the ideas that what is actually taught in a course should be consistent with course objectives and should adequately prepare students for subsequent courses for which the course is a prerequisite; that both instructional methods and assessment methods should be congruent with course objectives and provide adequate opportunity for students to practice and learn skills included in the course objectives; and that students should be provided with prompt and accurate feedback on their performance at regular intervals in the course. Feedback includes an explanation of how the work was graded as well as suggestions for improvement. We propose that developing clear statements of the expected outcomes for student learning is a necessary step to engaging in ethical teaching. Good teaching is ethical teaching and both emphasize the intended outcome of student learning. And that is the goal of our endeavors after all, isn't it?

REFERENCES

American Association for Higher Education. (1996). *Nine principles of good practice for assessing student learning.* Retrieved December 11, 2003, from AAHE Web site: http://www.aahe.org/assessment/principl.htm

Assessment Reform Group. (1999). *Assessment for learning: Beyond the black box.* Cambridge, England: University of Cambridge School of Education.

Banta, T. W., & Associates. (1993). *Making a difference: Outcomes of a decade of assessment in higher education.* San Francisco: Jossey-Bass.

Banta, T. W., Lund, J. P., Black, K. E., & Oblander, F. W. (1996). *Assessment in practice: Putting principles to work on college campuses.* San Francisco: Jossey-Bass.

Barr, R., & Tagg, J. (1995, Nov/Dec). From teaching to learning. *Change,* 13–25.

Black, P., & Wiliam, D. (1998a). *Inside the black box: Raising standards through classroom assessment.* Retrieved December 11, 2003, from http://www.pdkmembers

Black, P., & Wiliam, D. (1998b, March). Assessment and classroom learning. *Assessment in Education,* 7–74.

Bloom, B. S., Englehart, M. B., Furst, E. J., Hill, W. H., & Krathwohl, O. R. (1956). *Taxonomy of educational objectives: The classification of educational goals. Handbook 1: The cognitive domain.* New York: Longman.

Browne, W. F., & Osborne, R. E. (1998, June). *Critical thinking: Developing a model for lifelong learning.* Poster session presented at the International Conference on the Application of Psychology to Quality Teaching and Learning, Hong Kong, China.

Chickering, A. W., & Gamson, Z. F. (1987, March). Seven principles for good practice in undergraduate education. *AAHE Bulletin.* Retrieved December 12, 2003, from http://aahebulletin.com/ public/ archive/sevenprinciples1987.asp

Covington, M. V. (1992). *Making the grade: A self-worth perspective on motivation and school reform.* New York: Cambridge University Press.

Cowie, B., & Bell, B. (1999). A model of formative assessment in science education. *Assessment in Education: Principles, Policy & Practice,* 6, 101–116.

Krathwohl, D. R. (2002). A revision of Bloom's taxonomy: An overview. *Theory into Practice,* 41(4), 212–218.

Murray, H., Gillese, E., Lennon, M., Mercer, P., & Robinson, M. (1996, December). Ethical principles for college and university teaching. *AAHE Bulletin.* Retrieved December 12, 2003, from http://aahebulletin.com/public/archive/ Ethical%20Principles.asp

Osborne, R. E. (1996). *Self: An eclectic approach.* Needham Heights, MA: Allyn & Bacon.

Pickett, J. P., & Pritchard, D. R. (Eds.). (1993). *The American Heritage College Dictionary* (3rd ed.). New York: Houghton Mifflin.

Rogers, B. (1991). Setting and evaluating intended educational (instructional) outcomes. In James O. Nichols (Ed.), *A practitioner's handbook for institutional effectiveness and student outcomes assessment implementation* (pp. 168–187). New York: Agathon.

Suskie, L. (2000, May). Fair assessment practices. *AAHE Bulletin.* Retrieved December 12, 2003, from http://aahebulletin.com/public/archive/may2.asp

Walvood, B. E., & Anderson, V. J. (1998). *Effective grading: A tool for learning and assessment.* San Francisco: Jossey-Bass.

8

DEVELOPING SCIENTIFIC INQUIRY SKILLS IN PSYCHOLOGY: USING AUTHENTIC ASSESSMENT STRATEGIES

THEODORE N. BOSACK, MAUREEN A. McCARTHY,
JANE S. HALONEN, AND SHIRLEY P. CLAY

Authentic assessment provides a direct measurement of what students know and can do as the result of educational experiences (Resnick & Resnick, 1996). The use of the term "authentic" emphasizes that the assessment task should be as true to life as possible. Other names applied to this form of evaluation are performance assessment, direct assessment, alternative assessment, and performance-based assessment (Baker, O'Neil, & Linn, 1993).

We are grateful for a Carnegie Foundation CASTL Grant that supported the development of the rubric reported here. Other members of the Assessment All-Stars of the Psychology Partnership Project (P3) contributed to the original project, and we acknowledge the valuable participation of Dana Dunn, Bill Hill, Rob McEntarffer, Chandra Mehrotra, Robbye Nesmith, and Kristen Whitlock. We are deeply grateful to the P3 Steering Committee that brought this group together and especially to Virginia Andreoli Mathie, whose inspirational leadership and support helped us at every turn. We also appreciate critiques and suggestions for the rubric from sessions at the Southeastern Teaching of Psychology Conference, the University of Green Bay Psychology Teachers Conference, the Steering Committee of the Rhode Island Teachers of Psychology, and the Northern Kentucky University High School Psychology Teachers' Institute. Finally, we thank Paul C. Smith, Rebecca McKenzie, and Monica Reis-Bergan, who provided feedback on various drafts of the rubric and the original manuscript published in *Teaching of Psychology*.

Implementing authentic assessment methods (and authentic teaching, proposed by Halonen, Bosack, Clay, & McCarthy, 2003) has many advantages for both teachers and learners. For example, such assessments permit evaluation at each stage of the process rather than at a single point at the end, thereby offering a stronger and broader basis for validity (Wiggins, 1990). Further, authentic assessment involves instructional design that promotes active learning (Barr & Tagg, 1995), which research shows enhances learning outcomes (e.g., Christopher & Marek, 2002; Connor-Greene, 2000) and student satisfaction (e.g., Butler, Phillmann, & Smart, 2001; Hardy & Schaen, 2000). The true-to-life character of authentic assessment engages students effectively and encourages desired transfer to personal contexts.

Khattri and Sweet (1996) suggested that the growing enthusiasm for authentic assessment in curriculum reform could be attributed to three patterns that converged in higher education in the 1980s. First, employers stated publicly their substantial dissatisfaction with the quality of thinking skills of underprepared college graduates. Second, pressures for accountability prompted educators to find more meaningful ways to document the quality of their instruction than norm-referenced strategies. Third, the constructivist model became an impetus for student-centered learning strategies that promote enduring learning. Emerging from cognitive science, the constructivist model proposes that learners play an active role in their own cognitive and skill development by integrating new information with their prior learning and experience thereby creating their own ways of understanding (Von Glasersfeld, 1984).

The development of scientific reasoning has been cited as a crucial outcome in psychology education (Brewer et al., 1993). The Board of Educational Affairs of the American Psychological Association (APA) recently reaffirmed the critical role of science with the approval of the National Learning Goals and Outcomes for the Undergraduate Psychology Major (Halonen, 2002) that allocated half of the proposed goals to the enhancement of scientific training. Missing from the goals, however, is a description of how those goals and their related outcomes emerge as students progress through their training in psychology.

Halonen, Bosack, Clay, and McCarthy (2003) outlined developmental expectations for scientific reasoning based upon a collaborative effort that began in the APA Psychology Partnerships Project in June 1999. The collaboration identified eight critical domains of scientific reasoning and articulated developmental outcomes in each of these areas. Tables 8.1–8.8 display the dimensions of the rubric. The domains and skill areas include the following:

1. *Descriptive skills*: observation, interpretation, and measurement skills (see Table 8.1);
2. *Conceptualization skills* (the ability to use the concepts and theories of the discipline): recognition and application of con-

TABLE 8.1
Description of Proficiency Levels of the Descriptive Skills Domain

Components of Descriptive Skills	Levels of Proficiency				
	Before Training	Basic	Developing	Integrating	Professional
		Introductory Psychology	Advanced Undergraduate		Graduate and Beyond
Observation	Observes behavior superficially	Observes general patterns; tends to confuse observation and interpretation of behavior	Observes broadly and carefully; distinguishes observation from interpretation	Makes more subtle, sensitive observations that are distinct from interpretations	Uses sophisticated observational techniques appropriate to the circumstances
Measurement	Uses measurements in a limited or imprecise manner	Asks direction to measure critical elements but may resist demands for precision	Uses measurement as empirical strategy; complies with demands for precision	Actively pursues appropriate instrumentation; implements reasoned measurement strategy	Strives to produce optimal measurement strategy to reduce challenges to validity of conclusions
Interpretation	Relies on intuition that tends to focus on obvious and simplistic conclusions	Over-interprets behavioral events; forms judgment with limited regard to quality of evidence	Selectively combines data-based interpretations with personal experience	Relies upon data more systematically for interpretation; produces more complex interpretations	Interprets behavior at appropriate level of complexity that reflects contextual factors

Note. From "A Rubric for Learning, Teaching, and Assessing Scientific Inquiry in Psychology," by J. S. Halonen, T. N. Bosack, S. Clay, and M. McCarthy, 2003, *Teaching of Psychology, 30,* pp. 196–208. Copyright 2003 by Lawrence Erlbaum Associates, Inc. Reprinted with permission.

TABLE 8.2

Description of Proficiency Levels of the Conceptualization Skills Domain

Components of Conceptualization Skills	Levels of Proficiency				
		Basic	Developing	Integrating	Professional
	Before Training	Introductory Psychology	Advanced Undergraduate	Advanced Undergraduate	Graduate and Beyond
Concept skills: recognition and application	Explains and predicts behavior without reference to scientific concepts; tends to rely on pop psychology interpretation	Recognizes connection between psychological concepts and observed behavior	Can identify and apply concepts purposefully to explain a behavioral event when prompted	Identifies and applies concepts independently to explain and predict behavior	Uses psychological concepts fluently to explain and predict behavior; evaluates the validity of concepts as explanations; generates new concepts
Basic theory skills: recognition and application	Does not distinguish psychological theory from common sense	Can recognize theory elements in examples with guidance	Applies theory to explain and predict behavior but struggles when coping with counterintuitive conclusions from theory	Applies theory to explain and predict behavior and tolerates counterintuitive findings	Exploits discrepancy between intuitive findings and research as opportunity to explore new ideas

Advanced theory skills: evaluation, synthesis, and generation	Does not recognize or favor the use of psychological theory	Evaluates theory quality based on its goodness of fit with personal beliefs	Identifies some objective constraints in theory use; tests generalization of ideas by applying theory to new situations	Evaluates quality and fit of theory application objectively; compares and contrasts relative contributions of theories; integrates theoretical perspectives	Generates original theoretical explanations; assumes responsibility for criticizing and improving theory

Note. From "A Rubric for Learning, Teaching, and Assessing Scientific Inquiry in Psychology," by J. S. Halonen, T. N. Bosack, S. Clay, and M. McCarthy, 2003, *Teaching of Psychology, 30,* pp. 196–208. Copyright 2003 by Lawrence Erlbaum Associates, Inc. Reprinted with permission.

TABLE 8.3
Description of Proficiency Levels in the Problem Solving Skills Domain

Components of Problem Solving Skills	Levels of Proficiency				
	Before Training	Basic Introductory Psychology	Developing Advanced Undergraduate	Integrating	Professional Graduate and Beyond
Methods skills: recognition, evaluation, generation	Does not rely upon scientific method	Recites steps in conducting research; articulates basic knowledge of correlational and causal techniques; acknowledges value of controlled comparisons	Selects and applies appropriate method in simple projects; operationalizes and isolates variables; identifies influence of extraneous variables	Selects and applies appropriate method to maximize validity and reduce alternative explanations	Develops unique applications of research methods; establishes a research focus that identifies and builds on primary interests in behavior.
Statistical reasoning: recognition, application, evaluation, and generation	Tends to use the mathematical term "average" improperly, ignoring its literal meaning	Uses basic descriptive statistics; accepts inferential analysis without understanding statistical foundations	Selects and applies appropriate statistical processes to simple projects; evaluates success of projects in global sense	Selects and applies appropriate statistics with more independence; begins to use statistical reasoning as a basis for criticizing research results	Uses statistical reasoning routinely for evaluating research; develops unique applications of statistics

| Bias detection and management | Shows limited sensitivity to existence or effects of bias | Can recognize some potential sources of bias when prompted | Begins to recognize influence of bias and confounds in framing research questions | Identifies the potential influences of bias and confounds; recognizes personal, professional, and cultural interests influence problem and method selection | Implements and demands high standards for adherence to scientific method to minimize complications of bias and confounds |

Note. From "A Rubric for Learning, Teaching, and Assessing Scientific Inquiry in Psychology," by J. S. Halonen, T. N. Bosack, S. Clay, and M. McCarthy, 2003, *Teaching of Psychology, 30*, pp. 196–208. Copyright 2003 by Lawrence Erlbaum Associates, Inc. Reprinted with permission.

cepts; recognition and application of theory; and advanced theory skills (evaluation, synthesis, and generation; see Table 8.2).;

3. *Problem-solving skills* (the ability to conduct research and use research findings): recognition, evaluation, and generation of research methods; bias detection and management; and statistical reasoning (see Table 8.3);
4. *Ethical reasoning*: awareness, adherence (see Table 8.4);
5. *Scientific values and attitudes*: enthusiasm for research, objectivity/subjectivity, parsimony, skepticism, and tolerance of ambiguity (see Table 8.5);
6. *Communication skills*: resource-gathering skills, argumentation skills, and conventional expression (see Table 8.6);
7. *Collaboration skills*: project completion skills, process management, consensus-building skills, leadership, and brainstorming (see Table 8.7);
8. *Self-assessment*: self-regulation, self-reflection (see Table 8.8).

In addition to defining these eight domains, the collaboration introduced a developmental component that identifies five levels of increasing proficiency in scientific inquiry through which students pass as they progress through a psychology curriculum. These developmental levels, seen in each of Tables 8.1–8.8, consist of the following steps:

1. *Before training*: skill levels found prior to exposure to formal, curricular training or to practical experiences demanding scientific inquiry skills.
2. *Basic*: initial improvement in applying science to behavior that should emerge in the introduction to psychology course.
3. *Developing*: skills that students acquire as they move through a psychology curriculum or elect several additional courses in the field.
4. *Integrating*: behavioral expectations for psychology majors completing a capstone course and nearing the end of a psychology major.
5. *Professional*: target skills for persons completing graduate training in psychology and moving into early career settings.

The rubric proposed by Halonen, Bosack, Clay, and McCarthy (2003) also included one example of authentic assessment that illustrated how the rubric could promote improved teaching and learning strategies in a capstone course in the undergraduate major. The purpose of this chapter is to extend these applications in support of reform in psychology education based on principles of authentic assessment. We offer three additional examples of authentic assessment at different levels of sophistication, including begin-

TABLE 8.4

Description of Proficiency Levels of the Ethical Reasoning Domain

Components of Ethical Reasoning		Levels of Proficiency				
	Before Training	Basic Introductory Psychology	Developing Advanced Undergraduate	Integrating	Professional Graduate and Beyond	
Awareness of ethical standards	Shows limited awareness of or misconstrues general ethical practices in psychology	Recognizes existence of and rationale for ethical standards	Can identify how ethical standards apply to a given research example	Can identify how ethical standards enhance or constrain research	Monitors ethical practices in areas of research specialization	
Evaluation of ethical practices	May assume that psychologists generally tend to be ethically misguided	Can identify gross violations of ethical standards in practice	Can apply ethical standards to given examples to judge the quality of ethical practice	Recognizes more subtle ethical breeches and suggests alternatives	Routinely evaluates research from an ethical standpoint as an ongoing professional responsibility	
Adherence to ethical standards	Not applicable	Accepts ethical conditions required to participate in science but tends to question necessity	Accepts and adheres to prescribed ethical protocols when prompted	Executes appropriate ethical safeguards as a researcher's responsibility	Advocates for the best ethical practices to protect the public and improve the discipline	

Note. From "A Rubric for Learning, Teaching, and Assessing Scientific Inquiry in Psychology," by J. S. Halonen, T. N. Bosack, S. Clay, and M. McCarthy, 2003, *Teaching of Psychology, 30*, pp. 196–208. Copyright 2003 by Lawrence Erlbaum Associates, Inc. Reprinted with permission.

TABLE 8.5

Description of Proficiency Levels of the Scientific Attitudes and Values Domain

Components of Scientific Attitudes and Values	Levels of Proficiency				
	Before Training	Basic Introductory Psychology	Developing Advanced Undergraduate	Integrating Advanced Undergraduate	Professional Graduate and Beyond
Enthusiasm for research	Does not think about research findings	Accepts research findings that confirm personal experience; rejects disconfirming results	Allows selected scientific results to clarify personal experience	Views scientific method as valuable for personal and professional discovery	Practices scientific method and accepts its limitations
Objectivity/ subjectivity	Relies solely on subjective/personal reality	Recognizes the difference between objective and subjective realities in limited, controlled, directed circumstances	Distinguishes objective and subjective reality; recognizes that perceptions of reality vary between individuals	Shows greater vigilance about avoiding negative outcomes of subjective influences	Guards against subjective influences
Parsimony	Shows little or no preference for a given explanation from a range of explanations	Recognizes that precise explanations tend to be better than imprecise ones	Attends to precision as an important aspect of research design	Uses precision as a criterion to determine quality of explanation	Seeks the most precise explanation

Skepticism	Accepts or fails to question the status quo	Tends to resist asking questions to avoid making situations too messy or too complex	Practices limited skepticism as externally, hedonistically driven (e.g., it's what the professor wants)	Practices skepticism selectively to improve evaluation skills	Uses skepticism consistently as an evaluative tool
Tolerance of ambiguity	Expects and accepts simple or easy behavioral explanations	Resists, protests, ambiguity	Begins to seek clarity in understanding behavior, but prefers simple/easy explanations over complex ones	Assumes behavioral explanations will be complex, and begins to tolerate ambiguity	Enjoys complexity during the search for clarifying behavioral explanations

Note. From "A Rubric for Learning, Teaching, and Assessing Scientific Inquiry in Psychology," by J. S. Halonen, T. N. Bosack, S. Clay, and M. McCarthy, 2003, *Teaching of Psychology, 30,* pp. 196–208. Copyright 2003 by Lawrence Erlbaum Associates, Inc. Reprinted with permission.

TABLE 8.6
Description of Proficiency Levels of the Communication Skills Domain

Components of Communication Skills	Levels of Proficiency				
	Basic		Developing	Integrating	Professional
	Before Training	Introductory Psychology	Advanced Undergraduate	Advanced Undergraduate	Graduate and Beyond
Resource-gathering skills: selectivity, relevance, currency, quality of evidence	Relies upon popular press reports of psychology and anecdotal evidence; selects sources based upon personal bias	Reproduces simplistic, textbook capsules of information about behavior; conducts limited, expedient literature search; relies on secondary sources	Relates content from several sources, but tends to include resources nonselectively; shows limited use of formal literature	Integrates content from multiple sources, acknowledging contradictory information; uses resources selectively	Evaluates relevant content from broader range of available sources; reflects how context influences judgment; shows refined and flexible use of published research
Argumentation skills: organization, awareness of audience, persuasiveness	Argues based upon common sense; accepts personal experience as conclusive	Uses basic concepts to develop simple arguments; shows limited awareness of engaging audience; tends to argue from personal experience rather than from research evidence	Develops plausible arguments; demonstrates some awareness of audience by using engaging language and examples, but presumes audience knowledge is consistent with own	Creates coherent and integrated arguments based upon research evidence; engages audience by refined use of language, examples, and supports	Creates compelling arguments with attention to subtle meanings of content; anticipates and defends against criticism; adapts arguments for wide range of audiences

Conventional expression: use of APA format; grammar; appropriate supportive visuals	Not relevant	Recognizes existence of APA format but questions its value and rigor; applies APA format with serious flaws; expresses ideas in informal language	Uses APA style inconsistently; shows increasing formality and professionalism in expression	Uses APA format more consistently; practices professional, formal expression to improve communication appeal	Uses APA format expertly with minimal errors; demonstrates sophisticated conventional expression

Note. From "A Rubric for Learning, Teaching, and Assessing Scientific Inquiry in Psychology," by J. S. Halonen, T. N. Bosack, S. Clay, and M. McCarthy, 2003, *Teaching of Psychology, 30,* pp. 196–208. Copyright 2003 by Lawrence Erlbaum Associates, Inc. Reprinted with permission.

TABLE 8.7

Description of Proficiency Levels of the Collaboration Skills Domain

Components of Collaboration Skills	Levels of Proficiency				
	Before Training	Basic	Developing	Integrating	Professional
		Introductory Psychology	Advanced Undergraduate		Graduate and Beyond
Project completion skills	Not relevant	Can complete simple projects with direction	Completes more complex projects with reduced direction	Completes more complex projects that may require collaboration over time with minimal direction	Independently completes sophisticated group projects that may require collaboration over time
Process management		Adheres closely to directions provided by authority figure; tends not to attend to quality of group process	Expects group members to contribute equal work to accomplish goal; begins to monitor group process to manage process more effectively	Collaborates to assign roles and responsibilities more strategically to achieve completion; evaluates quality of thinking produced by the group to improve process	Systematically plans project completion strategy, including back-up plans to overcome likely obstacles
Leadership		Expects and complies with leadership from appointed group leaders	Shares leadership or fulfills assigned responsibilities to help group achieve success	Exercises some leadership to contribute to positive working climate	Convenes colleagues to improve quality of projects and programs

Consensus-building skills	Expects agreement; may be unable to function in conflict	Tends to stress value of own position ahead of others but recognizes that other positions may have merit	Can integrate diverse viewpoints to improve quality of group process and outcome	Conscientiously seeks expression of broad opinions and productive conflict resolution
Brainstorming	May not spontaneously generate creative alternatives in a structured situation	Can develop creative solutions/ alternatives when encouraged	Contributes to building safe climate to reduce risk in generating creative alternatives	Actively promotes and enjoys group creativity

Note. From "A Rubric for Learning, Teaching, and Assessing Scientific Inquiry in Psychology," by J. S. Halonen, T. N. Bosack, S. Clay, and M. McCarthy, 2003, *Teaching of Psychology, 30,* pp. 196–208. Copyright 2003 by Lawrence Erlbaum Associates, Inc. Reprinted with permission.

TABLE 8.8
Description of Proficiency Levels of the Self-Assessment Skills Domain

Components of Self-Assessment Skills	Levels of Proficiency				
	Before Training	Basic Introductory Psychology	Developing Advanced Undergraduate	Integrating Advanced Undergraduate	Professional Graduate and Beyond
Self-regulation: work completion skills	Works reactively in response to task demands without careful planning	Acknowledges role of planning to complete tasks appropriately but may not always be successful	Plans priorities reasonably to accomplish tasks	Executes complex projects properly, taking into account personal characteristics and challenges	Formulates backup plans to anticipate and overcome obstacles
Self-reflection: thinking about thinking	Tends not to reflect on own thinking or engage in self-reflection	Can make global self-assessments about quality of own work	Applies criteria to judge own performance with some consistency and accuracy; demonstrates some preference for shallow rather than deep critique	Makes refined, accurate judgments about quality of own work; prefers deep criticism to improve quality of future work	Uses self-assessments to establish realistic goals

Note. From "A Rubric for Learning, Teaching, and Assessing Scientific Inquiry in Psychology," by J. S. Halonen, T. N. Bosack, S. Clay, and M. McCarthy, 2003, *Teaching of Psychology, 30,* pp. 196–208. Copyright 2003 by Lawrence Erlbaum Associates, Inc. Reprinted with permission.

ning, developing, and advanced. We conclude the discussion with an exploration of the intersection of grading practices and authentic assessment.

USING THE DEVELOPMENTAL RUBRIC

The rubric may be used in a variety of contexts for several purposes. First, as may be seen in the examples provided, the rubric is useful for defining expectations and establishing criteria for grading of assignments in single courses in which goals include the development of scientific inquiry skills. Second, psychology departments with well-defined sequential curricula that seek progressively greater mastery of these skills may use the rubric to assess the effectiveness of courses at each point in the program for moving students through the increasing levels of sophistication of the rubric. Third, departments engaged in curriculum review may use the developmental rubric to guide course sequencing and content to encourage progress toward their stated goals. Fourth, instructors may use student performance patterns to pinpoint common areas of substandard mastery in order to focus more teaching resources in these areas. Finally, the rubric can be useful in preparing letters of reference for graduate study or employment by enabling the writer to document concrete examples of performance applicable to that next context.

Since the rubric consists of behavioral descriptors in developmental progression, it is applicable to evaluating student performance on any task that results in a product or activity that produces a behavior sample. Products may include term papers, reports of empirical research, informational and editorial essays, journals, essay examinations, reports of psychological evaluations, descriptions of group processes, and electronic media. Behavior samples may include oral reports, role-play, debates, lectures, or even class discussions. In this regard, the rubric is sufficiently flexible that it applies to nearly all assignments typical of psychology courses.

Course Considerations

The developmental rubric is most useful for evaluating performance when used in the context of a course that has well designed goals. Therefore, goals and outcomes of the course must be conceptualized in advance, and each performance-based assignment should contribute to progress toward the learning goals. Many considerations may contribute to course goals, including specific content, needed skill development, departmental and institutional missions and curricular demands, level of the course, and the broad domains of scientific inquiry. In psychology courses, understanding of the principles of scientific inquiry is likely to be among the major goals because standards for instruction and outcomes have repeatedly emphasized their integral position in the discipline (APA, 2002; Brewer et al., 1993; Halonen et al., 2002).

Application to Assignments

Having designed an assignment well suited to course goals, teachers can use the developmental rubric to identify the proficiency level appropriate to the course and the students involved. Because most assignments will not incorporate all eight domains of scientific inquiry, teachers should select the most relevant domains and the specific components. Although the rubric identifies expectations in behavioral terms, the scheme uses general language that is not specific to any particular student project. Therefore, instructors must craft the behavioral language of the rubric into specific expectations that capture the unique behavior samples required in their assignments. For example, expectations for Adherence to Ethical Standards (see Table 8.4) in a senior undergraduate research project with human participants (Integrating Level), might refer to attaining Institutional Review Board approval or its equivalent, obtaining proper informed consent, and incorporating appropriate safeguards for confidentiality. The same standard for an Integrating Level animal research study might focus explicitly on Institutional Animal Care and Use Committee regulations. Behavioral expectations in an undergraduate clinical internship might highlight the safeguards established in the course and by the placement facility. The three examples provided below offer concrete instances of translating the rubric language into behavioral expectations of assignments that are specific to the context.

SAMPLE APPLICATIONS OF THE RUBRIC

To help teachers use the rubric in their own assignments, we present three examples designed for different levels of proficiency. These include an introductory psychology course at a community college at the Basic Level, a survey course in child psychology at a four-year college at the Developing Level, and an assessment course in a university graduate program at the Professional Level. Each example identifies the developmental and situational context of its application and states the goals or purpose for its use. The assignments include a brief summary of the directions provided to students and then identify the domains of scientific inquiry tapped by the tasks, the component skills within each domain, and the specific behaviors exemplifying each component skill. Finally, the examples provide explanation of the criteria used to assign grades to student performance.

Example One: Basic Level

The Behavior Self-Modification Project appears in Appendix 8.1. This project, which incorporates seven of the eight domains of scientific inquiry in the developmental rubric, requires students to generate a plan grounded in operant conditioning to produce a change in an aspect of their own behavior. As seen in Appendix 8.1, for each component skill within domains there is an articulation of the language of the rubric with the particular expectations of the assignment. For example, the goal for Methods Skills within the Problem Solving Domain translates the language of the rubric template from "recites steps in conducting research" to the behavior appropriate to this particular assignment: "plans appropriate schedule and steps to produce change."

Example Two: Developing Level

Appendix 8.2 describes an assignment in a survey child psychology course requiring students to review the psychology research literature on a topic pertaining to children's well-being and to devise an initiative from that literature that may contribute to improving conditions for children. The students then incorporate the research and their reasoning about it into a letter to someone in a position to influence implementation of the initiative. Campbell (1996) originally reported this assignment, and our example adapts it for use with the rubric for scientific inquiry. As seen in Appendix 8.2, the major focuses of the adapted assignment include compiling a research literature base, developing an argument from that base, and expressing the argument in compelling and appropriate language. These skills fall largely within the Communication Skills Domain, relating to Resource Gathering, Argumentation Skills, and Conventional Expression.

Example Three: Professional Level

An entry-level graduate course in psychological assessment uses the rubric to evaluate student performance in critiquing a published psychological instrument according to principles taught in the course. The assignment places emphasis on achieving a high level of understanding of well-defined factual content (the instrument selected), and on demonstrating the complexity of the psychometric characteristics of the test in written and oral presentation. As seen in Appendix 8.3, this example targets the domains of Communication Skills, Scientific Attitude, Conceptualization Skills, and Ethical Reasoning.

GRADING AUTHENTIC ASSESSMENTS

Norm-referenced strategies rely on quantitative approaches that capture expert faculty judgment about student learning (Trice, 2000). As such, norm-referenced strategies offer a comfortable perch from which to make comparisons about students' learning achievements and have become standard in the majority of institutions of higher education. However, traditional course grades have come under attack for a variety of reasons. Milton, Pollio, and Eison (1986) summarized the problematic nature of grading practices with Dressel's (1983) definition of a grade: "An inadequate report of an inaccurate judgment by a biased and variable judge of the extent to which a student has attained an undefined level of mastery of an unknown proportion of an indefinite material" (p. 12).

Baron and Boschee (1995) suggested that educational reform relying on authentic assessment transforms the individualistic emphasis of the teacher-centered testing culture to a "collaborative assessment culture" that appropriately blurs the distinction between learning and assessment. As such, authentic assessment offers an alternative that provides more defensible evaluation strategies. The public nature of performance criteria creates a stronger sense of partnership between teacher and learner. Students do not need to guess what the instructor wants from them on an assignment when criteria make expectations explicit.

Baron and Boschee (1995) offered a generic rubric that can provide a foundation for grading judgment. For example, they suggested the following four-part rubric:

4   Exceeded established criteria for outcome
3   Met established criteria for outcome
2   Minimally met established criteria for outcome
1   Failed to meet established criteria for outcome

Faculty may be reluctant to embrace authentic assessment because they question how their grading strategies can be retrofitted to accommodate a criterion-based approach. However, any instructor who has designed an assignment for students to complete a project can translate the instructions for the project into a rubric that specifies performance expectations.

Adopting the rubric for scientific reasoning as the basis for curriculum design promotes the articulation of appropriate criteria in assignment design. Adhering to the expectations outlined in the rubric can suggest different kinds of assignment design that reflect the level of development expected in any particular course context. For example, each of the assignments detailed in this chapter targeted a particular level of development and incorporated relevant criteria both in the instructions and the assessment rubrics used to evaluate student performance. Students are able to achieve excellence by exceeding the criteria corresponding to their expected level of development.

Although the Baron and Boschee (1995) generic rubric could be used within a traditional grading framework, the authors advocated exploring other avenues for reporting student progress that would keep greater student attention on the skill levels attained rather than on the competitiveness of their GPAs. Indeed, several colleges have abandoned traditional grades, citing the potential that grades demonstrate for undermining learning. Mentkowski et al. (2000) suggested that criterion-based approaches facilitate students' abilities to become independent learners because they can develop habitual self-reflective processes that use criteria to judge the quality of their own work.

CONCLUSION

In addition to discussing the value to teaching, learning, and assessment of our developmental rubric for scientific inquiry, this chapter offered three practical applications designed for different levels of psychology education and considered ways of scoring these authentic assessments. The spirit of this approach and the multilevel character of the examples reflect several of the points elaborated by Halpern in chapter 1 of this volume as important elements of assessment. The focus of the rubric is upon student learning and skill acquisition. Assignments using the rubric require clear articulation of goals and desired outcomes. Its developmental nature is consistent with Halpern's call to recognize the linkages among the different segments of psychology education from high school through graduate study, to facilitate partnerships among these segments, and to construe student progress in terms of skill and knowledge acquisition rather than courses completed. Furthermore, use of the rubric throughout a sequenced curriculum provides for measures of student advancement at each step in the curriculum and a determination of the effectiveness of each of the steps. Through this application, teachers and programs can proceed to improve their teaching and learning. Therefore, we are hopeful that this proposal for authentic teaching, learning, and assessment will, in conjunction with other practices elaborated in this volume, contribute to further advances in psychology education.

REFERENCES

American Psychological Association. (2002). *American Psychological Association Task Force for the Development of National High School Psychology Standards*. Retrieved January 1, 2004, from http://www.apa.org/ed/pcue/reports.html

Baker, E. L., O'Neil, H. F., & Linn, R. L. (1993). Policy and validity prospects for performance-based assessment. *American Psychologist, 48,* 1210–1218.

Baron, M. A., & Boschee, F. (1995). *Authentic assessment: The key to unlocking student success.* Basil, Switzerland: Technomic Publishing.

Barr, R. B., & Tagg, J. (1995). From teaching to learning: A new paradigm for undergraduate education. *Change, 27,* 6, 12–25.

Brewer, C. L., Hopkins, J. R., Kimble, G. A., Matlin, M. W., McCann, L. I., McNeil, O. V., et al. (1993). Curriculum. In T. V. McGovern (Ed.), *Handbook for en-*

hancing undergraduate education in psychology (pp. 161–182). Washington, DC: American Psychological Association.

Butler, A., Phillmann, K., & Smart, L. (2001). Active learning within a lecture: Assessing the impact of short, in-class writing exercises. *Teaching of Psychology, 28,* 257–259.

Campbell, J. F. (1996). Psychology student as advocate: Public policy in the classroom. *Teaching of Psychology, 23,* 116–118.

Christopher, A. N., & Marek, P. (2002). A sweet-tasting demonstration of random occurrences. *Teaching of Psychology, 29,* 122–125.

Connor-Greene, P. A. (2000). Making connections: Evaluating the effectiveness of journal writing in enhancing student learning. *Teaching of Psychology, 27,* 44–46.

Dressel, P. (1983, December). Grades: One more tilt at the windmill. In A. W. Chickering (Ed.), *Bulletin,* Center for the Study of Higher Education. Memphis, TN: Memphis State University.

Halonen, J. S. (Ed.). (2002). *Suggested learning outcomes and goals for the psychology undergraduate major.* Washington, DC: American Psychological Association. Retrieved January 1, 2004, from http://www.apa.org/ed/pcue/taskforcereport2.pdf

Halonen, J. S., Bosack, T., Clay, S., & McCarthy, M. (with Dunn, D. S., Hill IV, G. W., McEntarffer, R., Mehrota, C., Nesmith, R., Weaver, K., & Whitlock, K.). (2003). A rubric for learning, teaching, and assessing scientific inquiry in psychology. *Teaching of Psychology, 30,* 196–208.

Hardy, M. S., & Schaen, E. B. (2000). Active learning within a lecture: Assessing the impact of short, in-class writing exercises. *Teaching of Psychology, 27,* 47–49.

Khattri, N., & Sweet, D. (1996). Assessment reform: Promises and challenges. In M. B. Kane & R. Mitchell (Eds.), *Implementing performance assessment: Promises, problems, and challenges* (pp. 1–22). Mahwah, NJ: Lawrence Erlbaum.

Mentkowski, M., Rogers, G., Doherty, A., Loacker, G., Hart, J. R., Richards, W., et al. (2000). *Learning that lasts: Integrating learning, development, and performance in college and beyond.* San Francisco: Jossey-Bass.

Milton, O., Pollio, H. R., & Eison, J. A. (1986). *Making sense of college grades: Why the grading system does not work and what can be done about it.* San Francisco: Jossey-Bass.

Resnick, D. P., & Resnick, L. B. (1996). Performance assessment and the multiple functions of educational measurement. In M. B. Kane & R. Mitchell (Eds.), *Implementing performance assessment: Promises, problems, and challenges* (pp. 23–38). Mahwah, NJ: Lawrence Erlbaum.

Trice, A. D. (2000). *A handbook of classroom assessment.* New York: Longman.

Von Glasersfeld, E. (1984). An introduction to radical constructivism. In P. Waltzlawick (Ed.), *The invented reality* (pp. 17–40). New York: Norton.

Wiggins, G. (1990). *The case for authentic assessment. ERIC digest* (Report No. EDO-TM-90-10). Washington, DC: Office of Educational Research and Improvement. (ERIC document reproduction Service No. ED 328611)

APPENDIX 8.1

BASIC LEVEL

INTRODUCTORY PSYCHOLOGY ASSIGNMENT: BEHAVIOR
SELF-MODIFICATION PROJECT

Context

This assignment exemplifies behavioral expectations for students who
are just beginning their studies in psychology. Taught as Online Introductory Psychology, the course strives to develop psychology as an empirical
discipline that has developed applications useful in students' daily living. An
element of this empirical approach is to show how practical applications
emerge from earlier empirical work and theory and that careful planning and
recording of behavioral observations are at the heart of scientific inquiry.

The assignment follows the chapter on learning that emphasizes classical conditioning and operant conditioning, the theoretical and empirical
foundations of the activity. Class notes on this topic highlight the principles
and process of reinforcement as well as how they apply to life. Some components of nearly all domains of the rubric are tapped by the exercise as indicated below.

Purpose of the Assignment

To apply behavior modification principles to promote personal change
and understand the principles underlying reinforcement. Students often want
to make changes in their lives and lack the strategies to succeed. This activity allows students to get practical experience with the process and promotes
these strategies as solutions to future problems.

Directions

Complete the assignment in three parts and submit online privately to
instructor.

Part I: Design the Behavior Self-Modification Plan

1. Describe the target behavior you wish to change.
2. Describe the situations/context in which the behavior occurs
   or does not occur.
3. Describe what reinforcement principle you will use. Choose
   from negative reinforcement, positive reinforcement, punish-
   ment, or extinction.
4. Design the reinforcement schedule and describe how it should
   change over time to produce an enduring change in your
   behavior.

5. Predict how long it will take for a change in your selected behavior to be apparent and explain your prediction.
6. Justify your design ethically.

Part II: Implementation of Plan: Try out your plan and observe the results carefully.

Part III: Outcome

1. Describe the outcome of the behavior modification.
2. Evaluate whether the plan was successful.
3. Describe any insights you may have about the behavior after measuring and attempting to change the behavior.
4. Describe other questions or problems that you encountered in implementing your plan.
5. Outline what you would do differently next time, if anything.

Grading Rubric for Part I: Design of the Behavior Modification Plan

Descriptive Skills: Observation

____ Provides sufficient detail about target behavior
____ Describes behavior accurately

Conceptualization Skills: Concept Recognition and Application

____ Selects appropriate reinforcer and reinforcement principle
____ Predicts logical outcome from plan

Problem Solving Skills: Methods Skills

____ Plans appropriate schedule and steps to produce change
____ Produces measurement strategy

Ethical Reasoning: Awareness

____ Discusses relevant ethical concerns

Rubric for Parts II and III: Implementation of the Plan and Outcome

Descriptive Skills: Measurement

____ Reports reasonable behavior measurement

Conceptualization Skills: Application

____ Describes how reinforcement principles work in relation to results
____ Demonstrates how learning principles might generalize

Values and Attitudes: Enthusiasm for Research, Objectivity/Subjectivity

____ Discusses insights about objective measurement of behavior

Communication Skills: Conventional Expression

___ Expresses ideas with appropriate grammar and word choice

Self-Assessment: Self-Reflection

___ Accurately self-assesses quality of work

Grading Criteria

A   requires satisfactory completion of all assignment criteria

B   achieves nearly all criteria but responses reflect minor difficulties with concept accuracy or application and evaluation
of relevant principles

C   demonstrates limited ability to apply and evaluate reinforcement principles

D   achieves success on only a few criteria in the assignment

F   fails to demonstrate knowledge of reinforcement principles
or how to apply them to personal goal

APPENDIX 8.2

DEVELOPING LEVEL

UNDERGRADUATE CHILD PSYCHOLOGY COURSE: LETTER
ADVOCATING CHILD-FRIENDLY INITIATIVE

Context

This is a second-level, traditional course in child behavior, for which
an introductory course is usually a prerequisite. In addition to emphasizing
the importance of applying careful science to expanding the understanding
of children, the course stresses that pat answers to all questions that one
might encounter in working with or raising children are not realistic. Therefore, students develop data collection and library research skills that will
help them search for answers to questions they encounter in the future. This
assignment requires students to become familiar with searching literature
databases and to apply empirically gathered data to a practical problem related to children. In doing so, it provides an opportunity to develop and
demonstrate these Developing Level skills found in the rubric. In addition, the
psychology and education majors who primarily elect this course will probably
need to articulate reasoned programs of intervention for children who will
later come under their care. This assignment provides training and experience
in making an empirically based argument in an area of child welfare.

Purpose of the Assignment

This assignment requires a literature search on a topic relating to the well-being of children and development of an initiative that could benefit children based upon that literature review. The product is a business letter presenting a sound, research-based argument in favor of the initiative to an individual having some sway in the area addressed. Goals include effective use of library databases, selection of several appropriate primary sources on the topic, accurate description of the sources, and integration of the sources into a logical argument for the initiative.

Directions

Based upon experience gained in the course or elsewhere, propose an initiative or policy that you think will contribute positively to children's well-being or development. Using electronic databases such as PsycINFO, search the psychology literature relevant to the initiative and its behavioral domain, and determine the degree of support for your position. Write a logical, research-based argument to someone who is in a position to advance your initiative urging that person to support its implementation.

Rubric for Assessing the Letter

Communication Skills: Argumentation Skills

_____ Clearly defines and explains the problem area
_____ Is related to child behavior and children's well-being
_____ Proposes an initiative to resolve the problem
_____ Clearly explains the initiative
_____ Explains how the initiative will resolve the problem
_____ Clearly relates each source to the problem and initiative
_____ Presents a logical, well-integrated, research-based argument
_____ Does not torture the facts to support the initiative
_____ Is sensitive to the intended audience
_____ Asks for the appropriate form of support or action from the recipient
_____ Explains why the recipient was chosen to receive the letter

Communication Skills: Resource-Gathering Skills

_____ Uses at least three primary research articles from psychology sources
_____ Uses articles from the psychology literature as the major sources to develop and support the initiative
_____ Limits use of secondary sources to providing background information

Communication Skills: Conventional Expression

_____ Is typed in grammatical and properly spelled English
_____ Follows proper business letter format

_____ Includes topic sentences in paragraphs and remains on topic
_____ Uses transitional words to guide the reader through the writer's reasoning
_____ Uses proper APA style in body of text
_____ Includes reference list in proper APA style
_____ Incorporates all and only citations in the text in the reference list

Scientific Attitudes and Values: Tolerance of Ambiguity

_____ Acknowledges interpretations when appropriate

Problem Solving Skills: Methods Skills

_____ Explains concisely the method, results, and conclusions of at least three primary research articles from the psychology literature
_____ Provides sufficient detail to show understanding and mastery and to inform the reader

Collaboration Skills: Project Completion Skills

_____ Provides two copies of the letter with one signed
_____ Provides a typed, 9.5 x 4 in. #10 stamped envelope with proper address and return address
_____ Appears to be a serious effort to produce a high quality presentation consistent with the assignment
_____ Submits the assignment on time

Self Assessment Skills

_____ Applies the components of this rubric in completing the assignment

Grading Criteria

A   reflects satisfactory completion of all stated criteria
B   reflects satisfactory demonstration of all criteria for Argumentation and Resource-Gathering Skills and minor lapses in other areas
C   reflects failure to display adequate Argumentation and Resource-Gathering Skills
D   reflects deficiencies in all domains
F   reflects serious deficiencies in all domains

APPENDIX 8.3

PROFESSIONAL LEVEL

GRADUATE ASSESSMENT COURSE: REVIEW OF A PSYCHOLOGICAL INSTRUMENT

Context

This course provides an introduction and overview of psychological assessment. In addition to a basic introduction to psychometric principles, students learn basic skills pertaining to psychological assessment. Students who enroll in this course anticipate a career in an applied area of psychology, such as clinical or school psychology, in which they will need to select, evaluate, and interpret psychological tests for clients and agencies. Competencies obtained from this course should include an ability to evaluate a standardized instrument with respect to reliability, validity, norming, and applicability. This assignment introduces these issues in very much the manner that a professional psychologist would employ to arrive at evaluation of an instrument using principles of scientific inquiry.

Purpose of the Assignment

Students are required to obtain empirical support for a thorough evaluation of a standardized instrument. A professionally written report using APA style is the product of this exercise. This assignment is structured as an authentic assessment because students are asked to provide evaluative information in a professional context.

Directions

Select a standardized psychological instrument from the literature and conduct a critical analysis of the instrument. Particular attention should be placed on analysis of basic psychometric properties, practical applications, and utility of the instrument in the context of practice in the discipline of psychology

Rubric for Review of a Psychological Instrument: Assessment of the Product

Communication Skills: Resource Gathering (Selectivity, Relevance, Currency, Quality)

____ Identifies a standardized instrument appropriate for evaluation
____ Uses appropriate testing reference materials (MMY, Tests in Print)
____ Uses Web-based testing sites
____ Obtains appropriate reference materials
____ Cites professional journal articles

___ Uses relevant text materials
___ Describes the instrument in a sophisticated manner
___ Integrates literature throughout the paper
___ Follows APA format

Scientific Attitude: Skepticism

___ Evaluates quality of data for review
___ Evaluates appropriateness of instrument for use in psychology
___ Evaluates objectively, avoiding personal bias and demand characteristics
___ Provides sufficient level of complexity and precision in the argument
___ Sufficiently evaluates limitations of empirically referenced material

Conceptualization Skills Recognition and Application

___ Evaluates the components of psychometric theory with respect to the test reviewed
___ Accurately considers discrepancies between principles and application
___ Offers recommendations for improving the instrument
___ Offers recommendations for practice

Ethical Reasoning: Adherence to Ethical Standards

___ Evaluates ethical considerations of the instrument noted
___ Identifies multicultural issues associated with the instrument
___ Proposes remedies for multicultural problems

Grading Criteria

Four broad components of the rubric are used to evaluate the paper that the student writes. First, students are evaluated on their ability to obtain relevant empirical materials and to integrate them into the assignment. Use of scientific skepticism is evaluated through an examination of the student's presentation of empirical data in an objective framework. Additionally, students must apply their understanding of psychometric principles by integrating the information into their papers. Finally, students are evaluated on their ability to consider ethical practice within the context of using standardized assessments.

Broader Scope of This Assignment

Use of psychological principles in an applied setting represents a specific outcome that benefits from authentic assessment. This example may be used for similar assignments which require graduate students to apply a particular construct in an applied setting.

9

EMPOWERING PSYCHOLOGY STUDENTS THROUGH SELF-ASSESSMENT

DANA S. DUNN, ROB McENTARFFER, AND JANE S. HALONEN

A hallmark of an educated person is the capacity to reflect on and learn from experiences such that the learning yields meaningful interpretations of life occurrences and informs future action.
—Catherine Marienau (1999)

And when is there time to remember to sift, to weight, to estimate, to total?
—Tillie Olsen (1995)

"Now that you are nearly finished with your undergraduate degree, tell me what you have learned to do?" This question is typical of an interview protocol conducted during a departmental review, in which a consultant explores the nature and quality of senior students' experiences in the psychology program. Surprisingly, this question often befuddles students and, sadly, many come up empty-handed. They are accustomed to "seat time" in specified courses as the currency of their education (cf. Halpern, chap. 1, this volume). The students have not given much thought to how their course work has changed how they think and who they have become. In other words, they have not reflected on, let alone evaluated, their own intellectual development in the discipline (e.g., MacGregor, 1993b). They have not considered what characteristics mark a truly educated person.

We are grateful to our colleagues, the Assessment All-Stars, whose efforts and ideas are reflected in this chapter. Members of the Moravian College Faculty Writers Group, Ted Bosack, and Kristen Whitlock provided helpful comments on an earlier version of this chapter.

Among the litany of criticisms that has surfaced in relation to the quality of higher education is the concern that students show limited ability to judge the quality of their own work and may have insufficiently developed work habits to help them with life after education. Students often report that higher education feels like an obstacle course comprised of one grade goal after another with limited time to reflect on the meaning of what they have learned or to assay the learning's impact. In turn, faculty find themselves distressed by students' quest for the grade rather than for the learning; knowledge rarely seems to be pursued for its own sake.

Barr and Tagg (1995) suggested that higher education needed to make a critical paradigm shift from teacher-centered strategies in the classroom to learning-centered approaches focused on students. Many scholars have begun to advocate the critical role that systematic self-assessment by students could play in improving the quality of educational experience and to explore specific strategies for promoting self-awareness to achieve those ends (e.g., Lipman, 1988; MacGregor, 1993a). For example, many departments have adopted portfolio strategies to promote the student-as-learner approach and to address the accountability issues that fuel the assessment movement (see Keller, Craig, Launius, Loher, & Cooledge, chap. 10, this volume). Implicit in this view of self-assessment is the assumption that, rather than being biased or psychologically suspect, some forms of self-report data and self-observation can actually demonstrate student learning and achievement in educational contexts.

In this chapter, we clarify the meaning of student self-assessment and advocate for its broader use in psychology curriculum reform. We offer suggestions that teachers can use to empower their students to learn self-assessment skills. We invoke the work completed by the Assessment Group of the American Psychological Association sponsored Psychology Partnerships Project to provide some developmental expectations about how self-assessment can be incorporated into psychology curricula at all levels (Halonen, Bosack, Clay, & McCarthy, 2003). We also comment on the challenges that are inevitable when reformers advocate redirecting time away from content coverage.

THE MEANING OF SELF-ASSESSMENT

Self-assessment entails moving away from the general assessment question posed by instructors ("What has a student learned?") to a self-generated, inward search carried out by each student ("What have I learned, and how well can I demonstrate what I know?"). Broad assessment becomes self-assessment, where instructors are responsible for teaching students how to evaluate their educational programs actively. *Self-assessment* refers to a conscious process of observing, analyzing, and judging one's performance against established standards while identifying ways to improve it (Loacker, 2000). As an activity—really, a collection of activities—self-assessment entails product as well as process, outcomes as well as outputs. Self-assessment activities have four qualities that promote skill acquisition and development in students: observing, interpreting or analyzing, judging, and planning (Loacker, 2000). The experience and performance-based nature of these skills is beneficial to students and teachers alike.

In our view, student self-assessment is comprised of two related skills: self-regulation and self-reflection. *Self-regulation* skills are the observable, public actions students take to learn about psychology. Self-regulated actions are organized and planful, as students are learning to control and coordinate what they do in disciplinary courses. In concrete terms, students compare their performance against existing criteria. Self-regulation skills are needed to effectively search the psychological literature to locate appropriate research concerning a topic. To do so, for example, a student must follow the search guidelines required by an instructor, outlined in a psychology text, or described in the available database. In contrast, *self-reflection* skills are more private, where students actively think about what they are learning and how it relates to what they already know. For instance, a student engages in self-reflection when evaluating whether codified ethics from psychology inform how she relates to peers' confidences or evaluates a published experiment's procedure. Students' thoughts need not be publicly shared, however, or even necessarily follow established standards (Loacker, 2000). The important point is that reflecting on what one has learned (or for that matter, failed to learn) provides a link between existing knowledge and future action.

Acquiring and refining regulatory and reflective self-assessment skills also involves receiving feedback, such as questions, comments, and constructive criticism, from instructors and student peers. With time and experience, students who actively and thoughtfully engage in self-assessment should be capable of generating personal performance standards that are in line with disciplinary and education-based standards. Indeed, the goal of self-assessment is to encourage students to learn actively, assess, reflect, and perform self-evaluative activities responsively on their own as they encounter both familiar and unfamiliar educational challenges.

High quality self-assessment should also reflect psychological consequences attributed to self-efficacy theory (Bandura, 1997). Self-efficacy theory bridges the gap between performance knowledge and execution by examining people's efficacy-related beliefs. In other words, besides knowing what to do with respect to some task, do individuals also believe that they can actually accomplish what needs to be done? Student self-efficacy beliefs and goal setting, for example, have been linked to academic achievement (Zimmerman, Bandura, & Martinez-Pons, 1992).

SELF-ASSESSMENT OF SCIENTIFIC INQUIRY
AS A DEVELOPMENTAL PROCESS

How can faculty most effectively assist students in becoming accurate judges of the quality of their own work in psychology? We need to articulate what skills comprise effective self-assessment and to make explicit how those skills should evolve over the course of psychological training. Our Assessment Group undertook that task in the development of a "rubric for scientific inquiry" (Halonen, Bosack, Clay, & McCarthy, 2003), which is detailed in chapter 8, this volume.

A quality educational rubric provides a clear system for assessing—measuring and comparing to some standard—students' comprehensive activities within some domain (Trice, 2000). The Halonen, Bosack, Clay, & McCarthy (2003) rubric addressed self-assessment as the final and integrative domain of skills relevant to the development of scientific inquiry skills. Further, the rubric addresses the two skills within the domain of self-assessment: the development of self-regulation for goal planning, management, and achievement and self-reflection to enhance accuracy in self-judgment. Echoing the four qualities of self-assessment (Loacker, 2000), the rubric outlines ways in which students' ability to examine and interpret behavior should develop in self-reflection and self-regulation—from novice to professional—in the course of their disciplinary education (see Table 9.1).

In the examples that follow, we offer illustrations of ways in which self-assessment strategies can enhance self-regulation and self-reflection before training, and then at the basic, developing, integrating, and professional levels of education in psychology. These levels portray students' cognitive development in an orderly, progressive manner. In reality, of course, students mature at different rates; some beginning students, for example, will demonstrate the characteristics of developing or integrating students (and vice versa). Thus, students' cognitive development is apt to be only loosely associated with the educational contexts we describe. Nonetheless, we believe that there is heuristic value in describing self-regulation and self-reflection skills through interplay of developmental and contextual considerations.

All of the examples have in common the use of explicit benchmarks for self-regulation and self-reflection related to the self-assessment domain that we have based on the rubric. We conclude each example with a brief discussion of the distinctive challenges of self-assessment within a given context.

Self-Assessment Skills Before Training

Many students enter their first psychology class with excitement, interest, and misconceptions about psychology. Psychology is presented in popular magazines and on television as primarily consisting of talk therapy, with all-too-rare glimpses of the world of psychological research. Students who primarily know about psychology through talk shows need accurate informa-

TABLE 9.1
Self-Assessment Domain of the Rubric for Scientific Inquiry

	Self-Regulation Skills	Self-Reflection Skills
Before training	Works reactively in response to task demands without careful planning.	Tends not to reflect on own thinking or engage in self-reflection.
Basic level (introductory psychology)	Acknowledges the role of planning to complete tasks appropriately but is not always successful.	Can make global self-assessments about quality of own work.
Developing	Plans priorities reasonably to accomplish tasks.	Applies criteria to judge own performance with some consistency and accuracy; demonstrates some preference for shallow rather than deep critique.
Integrating (advanced undergraduate)	Executes complex projects properly, taking into account personal characteristics and challenges.	Makes refined, accurate judgments about quality of work; prefers deep criticisms to improve quality of future work.
Professional (graduate)	Formulates backup plans to anticipate and overcome obstacles.	Uses self-assessment to establish goals.

Note. From "A Rubric for Authentically Learning, Teaching, and Assessing Scientific Reasoning in Psychology," by J. S. Halonen, T. Bosack, S. Clay, and M. McCarthy, 2003, *Teaching of Psychology, 30,* p. 202. Copyright 2003 by Lawrence Erlbaum Associates, Inc. Adapted with permission.

tion about the science of psychology before they can begin to self-regulate and self-reflect in meaningful ways. During their first psychology courses, students should be encouraged to reflect on their new knowledge and learn how to demonstrate, use, and apply this knowledge to their lives.

Self-Regulation

When first exposed to psychology—possibly in secondary school settings—students' self-regulatory skills are very limited. Before training in the discipline, they work reactively by doing assignments without careful planning (see row 1 in Table 9.1). Before training, students lack accurate information about how psychologists conceive and execute research. Without examples or background knowledge, they are unlikely to plan their work carefully. In a high school classroom, for example, a teacher may ask students to select some interesting theory from a textbook before developing a related research project. Mere choice is often very difficult for beginning students because they do not know enough about psychology yet to make an informed decision. Once they learn the history of psychology and discuss the various psychological perspectives, students are capable of choosing a theory that matches their interests. Teachers must be sure to provide the background knowledge students need to begin to make informed choices and to begin their own work in psychology.

Prior to training, students often display an overconfidence that is actually related to their lack of familiarity with the discipline. Before realizing the level of sophistication involved in psychological theories and concepts, students cannot accurately judge how much work is involved in completing most assignments. Because they lack time-management skills, they are incapable of discerning how much time it takes to research and write papers for psychology classes. Teachers can help students acquire self-regulation skills by providing information (e.g., concrete paper guidelines) about the level of sophistication expected in assignments and by setting incremental deadlines for separate parts of the assignment. An in-depth examination of any psychological question can be broken down into individual parts. Each part of a project can then be explained to the students, giving them a more accurate picture of what is expected in the final product. Finally, instructors can also share successful examples of past student projects with a current class.

Self-Reflection

Beginning psychology students encounter similar problems in their own reflections about what they are learning. During their first encounter with psychology, students tend to be passive learners. Many students have the impression that all they need to do is parrot back information garnered from their textbook and instructor, and that they then "know" psychology. This mistaken impression discourages any attempt at self-reflection about what they are learning. Students cannot compare what they are learning against existing criteria if they do not understand what criteria to use to perform a comparison. Instructors must encourage students to reflect on how personal experiences, family backgrounds, even past jobs, can be related to course material. In a high school psychology class, for example, students could choose a personal hobby or sport and then examine it through the lens of some psychological theory (e.g., operant conditioning). Thus, students can use what they already know to reflect on how well or poorly a psychological theory accounts for their interest.

Another obstacle to self-reflection is linguistic. Before training, students are not familiar with the vocabulary of psychology. They need to gain familiarity with disciplinary terminology in order to be able to think about what they are doing in their classes or to question the validity of the psychological conclusions they are making. Teachers must spend adequate time defining common psychological terms and explaining how to correctly apply them.

Basic Level Self-Assessment Skills

Following their first exposure to psychology, students are better able to assess their own learning. This ability, however, is still limited because of gaps in their disciplinary knowledge. Students at the basic level know they need to plan their work in order to complete tasks—the problem is that they still do not plan to an appropriate level of detail. Students, too, often remain overconfident of what they know after their basic exposure to psychology. They perceive many psychological concepts to be "easy" or "common sense," possibly because the material presented in introductory classes summarizes theory simplistically. More detailed, sophisticated portrayals of theories and supporting evidence are rare. Students do not understand that a theory is not a simple statement about cause and effect. One problem is that overconfidence about their level of understanding can lead students to consider doing unrealistic psychology projects. For example, students routinely underestimate the complex chain of reasoning involved in accounting for the incidence and treatment of addictive behaviors (e.g., smoking, drug use).

Self-Regulation

In some ways, basic level psychology students know just enough about the field to misjudge significantly critical aspects of self-regulation. Although introductory students know basic information about research methodology, their actual understanding of how to apply it is limited and can lead to poor planning. When introductory students design research projects, their initial plans are usually unrealistically ambitious, possibly involving the gathering of experimental data from hundreds of participants or surveying thousands of respondents. Lack of practical knowledge about available time and resources is most often the culprit. Teachers must be sure to explain that overcomplex, even grandiose, research plans can adversely affect the quality of student work.

Self-Reflection

Basic level psychology students are capable of making global self-assessments about the quality of their psychological thinking. Students at this level can reflect on how their thinking fits into the bigger picture of psychology as a science. Introductory students understand the major perspectives of psychology and historical schools of thought. They can use this information to consider how an answer to a psychological question might be different if examined from a different perspective. For example, students can evaluate whether a certain behavior (e.g., procrastination, gambling, altruism) might be best explained in a learning, cognitive, neuroscience, evolutionary, or cultural context. Introductory students are also aware that there are different types of psychologists and, with instructor guidance, can appreciate the difference between clinical psychologists and other mental health care providers.

Introductory students understand research methodology well enough to begin critical evaluation of research studies, including research designs. Understanding the basic concepts underlying theories, hypotheses, populations, sampling, random assignment or selection, operational definitions, and simple data analysis helps students to identify the limitations of certain studies and what can reasonably be concluded from any piece of research. This growing ability allows introductory students to begin a critical examination of the psychological research presented in the popular media. Introductory students can become adept at spotting causal claims (e.g., "Good students have high self-esteem") that are inappropriately based on correlational research (e.g., self-esteem and academic achievement), a first step in avoiding similar faulty inference in their daily lives. Basic level students can also read straightforward journal articles intelligently, reflect on researchers' conclusions, and then discuss them with peers or teachers. These students do not yet have the advanced data analysis skills that are usually necessary for deciphering the statistical analyses described in the results sections of most journal articles. They do know enough, however, to criticize some elements of a research design and to evaluate an author's conclusions critically.

Developing Level Self-Assessment Skills

Self-assessment of skill domains at this third level of scientific inquiry assumes that students have completed a basic experience in psychology (see row 3 in Table 9.1). Practically speaking, most second-level students are undergraduates who elect more courses to satisfy the demands of their chosen major, including those who choose psychology.

Developing skills in psychology are those that gradually emerge with experience and education typically available at the undergraduate level. Students' course experiences lead them to appreciate that psychology is concerned with myriad aspects of behavior, not simply those associated with a few salient or popular domains, such as abnormal, developmental, or social psychology. Students learning at this level realize that not all psychologists are practitioners, that many are researchers and educators. At the same time, students understand that psychologists use empirically oriented strategies as the primary methods for investigating and testing theories about behavior. Developing skills are marked by students' awareness that controlled experimentation and careful, incremental inference are necessary tools for scientific reasoning.

Self-Regulation

The self-regulation of developing skills entails actions that enable students to work toward the completion of discipline-related efforts, such as reading and understanding a primary source, conceiving and writing a research paper, or carrying out a simple experiment (i.e., one dependent variable, no more than two independent variables) from the design through the analysis phases. Developing students are in the process of learning to identify priorities for accomplishing project tasks. When writing a research paper for a psychology course, for example, a student at a developing level of proficiency has a realistic sense of how long it will take to identify a sufficiently narrow topic, do an online literature search, analyze selected sources, and construct and revise a paper. Developing students recognize that being conscious of time demands and the need to balance other academic responsibilities are valid concerns. Teachers must go beyond exhorting students to work ahead—they must actually give them practical advice about how to study efficiently and effectively, as well as to organize projects from start to finish.

This is easier said than done, of course, and these novice researchers are often overwhelmed by the amount of necessary detail required. For this reason, instructors play a crucial role in developing self-regulatory skills. Instructors must introduce the research process, outline the sequence of stages involved, and link specific concepts drawn from research methods in psychology to the context of actually doing research. Otherwise, students are apt to fall back on familiar ways of juggling responsibilities—for instance, tackling them serially instead of in tandem—just as they are likely to underestimate the time needed to run even the most rudimentary observational study.

Modest struggle with developing skills is normative, as most students learn that any one task requires completing several related chores. Instructors must explain this reality but developing students must nonetheless learn by doing. Consider, for example, what happens after students finally organize and execute a basic experiment. Work begins, not ends, once data are collected. The data must be coded into numerical form, checked, entered into a spreadsheet, and re-checked—only then can the statistical analyses begin. Data analysis, in turn, requires knowledge of how to use available software and the ability to choose the appropriate statistical test from an array of possibilities. Finally, students must know how to interpret results and convey any meaning in lay terms as well as statistical prose. Instructors introduce most of these skills individually in research methods or statistics courses, but students are not accustomed to the necessity of tying them all together while doing a research project or writing a paper. More to the point, they will not learn them effectively or retain them for the future without close and frequent evaluative feedback from instructors.

Self-Reflection

The self-reflective side of self-assessment among developing students is marked by both virtues and shortcomings. The chief virtue is that students can use available criteria to judge their own research performance with a fair degree of consistency and accuracy. The key factor is the availability of evaluative criteria, which is largely dependent on instructor vigilance. Seasoned instructors of experimental psychology, for example, will require that the entire class of students conduct an experiment together or in small groups before encouraging solo research efforts. Instructors will explain each stage of a project and every step within it. The experience of conducting a project in common is eye-opening, and it does make subsequent, independent work more manageable. Students learn to balance multiple concerns, such as predicting time demands (e.g., Do I need two weeks or can I perform the experiment in just one?), assessing progress (e.g., Are five sources enough for my paper?), and meeting deadlines (e.g., Can I finish a complete rough draft before next class?).

When it comes to sharing results in written form, instructors traditionally introduce APA style in research methods courses. Within psychology, there may be no better exemplar where students can compare their fledgling efforts against clearly specified criteria. Besides receiving evaluative feedback from instructors on how well their work adheres to the constraints imposed by APA style, students can learn by emulating examples found in scholarly journals, the *Publication Manual* (American Psychological Association, 2001), and numerous books devoted to teaching and improving writing in the discipline. Conscientious or motivated but still developing students need only follow rules that, with practice, become habitual. Besides providing detailed comments on all papers, teachers should require students to turn in multiple drafts of their work. By responding to the same paper as it takes shape, instructors can teach students invaluable writing, revising, and editing skills while actually demonstrating that scholarly writing is as much about process as product.

The shortcoming in developing students' self-reflective skills is a marked preference for surface rather than deep critiques of their work. In practice, for example, a student at this stage will prefer merely to correct surface errors in a paper draft, including problems in grammar, punctuation, and spelling, and obvious departures from APA style. Developing students are less likely to tackle major conceptual revisions or integrate additional material, however, even when such changes would improve their work and, consequently, a final grade. Similarly, developing students are likely to report research findings by highlighting statistical significance (or the lack thereof) without any accompanying behavioral description, although both are essential to convey accurate meaning to readers. Developing students, too, routinely forget to report condition or group averages in their papers, despite the fact that their analyses frequently involve mean comparisons. Thus, the self-reflective practices at this level have a "good enough" quality rather than one oriented toward continually refining and improving conclusions. Students at this level tend to accept criticism defensively even when their instructors deliver it in a positive, constructive manner.

Integrating Level Self-Assessment Skills

Following additional course work and (ideally) experience with empirical investigation, students gradually develop integrating skills (see row 4 in

Table 9.1). Advanced students realize that adequate explanations for behavior are both subtle and complex, that subjective judgments are no substitute for rigorous, theoretically based predictions and empirical demonstrations. When students meet experimental expectations, they realize that their results are by no means definitive. Rigorous practice demands independent verification and replication and, in any case, good results only produce more questions for future research efforts, not final answers. When predictions go awry, students possessing integrating skills try to learn why by revisiting theory and hypotheses, as well as research design and analysis issues. Students exhibiting integrative self-assessment do not think exclusively in terms of educational "success" or "failure," rather they realize that learning occurs independent of whether they meet expectations or produce predicted outcomes. Increasingly, self-assessment becomes an intrinsically rather extrinsically focused activity.

Self-Regulation

An undergraduate student engaging in self-regulation at the integrating level demonstrates a greater degree of control over the various demands of the process. An integrating student is capable of carrying out complex projects both properly and promptly. He or she is aware of time constraints and how to manage them successfully, enhanced by awareness of the potential for personal strengths and shortcomings to influence the success of the project. Thus, a student prone to procrastinate will know to begin a project on the early side; another who struggles to create clear prose will share preliminary paper drafts with an instructor. In essence, a student will not only apply his or her best qualities to a project but also will dutifully and effectively compensate for potential deficits that could threaten a project's success.

Self-Reflection

Self-reflection in the integrative stage involves a higher degree of metacognition, thinking about one's own thoughts with respect to disciplinary learning in psychology. A developing student is capable of applying established criteria to his or her own intellectual performance, recognizing, for example, that standards can differ for achieving a high or an average grade on a course assignment. Moreover, the developing student uses the available performance criteria with a fair degree of consistency and accuracy, recognizing, too, that one person's work can be superior to another's on a variety of dimensions (e.g., quality of idea, operationalization, oral or written presentation).

In contrast to a student working reactively at the developing skill level, the self-reflective practices of the integrating student at the undergraduate level are anticipatory. Working on and thinking about a project's progress, he or she actively anticipates problems, questions, or concerns that could reasonably be offered by peers or an instructor. Thus, an integrating student will embrace and adhere to criteria. Self-reflective students are entirely capable of making refined and accurate judgments about the quality of what they produce (Halonen, Bosack, Clay, & McCarthy, 2003), however, they may not yet have embraced self-reflective practices as part of their professional skill repertoire.

Beyond evaluating the quality of their own thoughts and reactions to their progress, integrating students actively seek feedback from others about their work. To that end, students will approach instructors, mentors, and knowledgeable peers who are also working in psychology. When doing so, students at this level welcome deep criticism, that is, candid, detailed assessments of their work. Such assessments are welcome not only because they improve the quality of the current work but also because they will influence how a student approaches similar tasks in the future. In other words, integrating students realize that learning and performance can always be improved, that intellectual satisfaction comes not necessarily from a finished product, but from doing the work.

Having students at the developing and integrating levels of proficiency engage in self-assessment using the rubric for scientific reasoning in psychology leads to two practical benefits. First, undergraduate students have a set of defined descriptive skills they can review at any point while enrolled in a course or when conducting a research project. They are able to compare and assess their own ongoing performance with established criteria. Of course, as Halonen and colleagues (2003) caution, even integrating students should not routinely receive the entire rubric for scientific reasoning in psychology as the foundation for any given assignment. To introduce the full rubric too early in their undergraduate experience could be daunting. Saving the complete rubric for students enrolled in methodology or theory-based courses makes greater pedagogical sense.

Second, availability of the rubric allows them to discuss what they have learned with peers and teachers, as well as to identify those educational issues in psychology that continue to pose individual challenges. Comfort and sophistication with data analysis, for instance, generally requires more than one statistics course, as well as actual experience working with the data collected during a research project.

Professional Level Self-Assessment Skills

Faculty hope, and sometimes inappropriately assume that, when students enter graduate school or the workforce following graduation, they will have mastered the self-assessment goals at the Integrating Level. That is, students will be able to "execute complex projects properly, taking into account personal characteristics and challenges" (Halonen, Bosack, & McCarthy, 2003, p. 202). Students should have developed a preference for deep criticism to improve their work quality, and they should be able to judge their own work quality accurately. Without systematic self-assessment practice, however, the reality is that many graduate students and new psychology professionals may be relatively unsophisticated in their ability to self-assess. As such, they may exhibit unwelcome dependence on whatever authorities inhabit the respective professional context for guidance and feedback regarding whether their performance is "good enough." The goal at the professional level is to smooth the progress of self-directed learning in which task management and performance evaluation skills effectively support students' career objectives.

To refine self-assessment skill development at the professional level, graduate educators and professional trainers would do best to evaluate the level of students' skills rather than assuming that their students simply need professional polish. Graduate instructors should verify this assumption by actually determining what skills students already possess through focused in-class assessment (for suggestions, see Angelo & Cross, 1993). Typically, graduate courses involve students in complex projects to develop their thinking skills; the process of completing the project is as important as the high quality product itself. How can we exploit the graduate learning context to refine self-assessment to professional levels?

Self-Regulation

Prospective graduate students typically demonstrate a high degree of success in self-regulation in the evidence (e.g., grades, objective test scores, letters of recommendation, prior research experience, employment) they submit in their graduate applications. However, the intensity of graduate program requirements may escalate the self-management challenges they will confront, in part because the depth and complexity of their project work will be more demanding. Graduate students may have new difficulties balancing complex academic deadlines with graduate assistantships, teaching and research opportunities, and family responsibilities. Natural events will often force the development of "Plan B" skills; however, an explicit self-assessment focus incorporates alternative path planning. For example, at least some students in any given class will encounter problems related to computer malfunctions, health, and social emergencies. Less sophisticated students do not plan with contingencies in mind. Instructors can require students to identify potential obstacles explicitly as part of their planning. Talking about the impact of possible threats to the process and quality of students' work can be an important addition to instructions for complex projects to facilitate "Plan B" skills. Instructors should promote a "what if?" perspective in helping students more routinely develop contingency planning.

Self-Reflection

One of the failings of traditional grading systems is the tendency for students, even at the graduate level, to check the grade and ignore the feedback on which faculty may have labored to promote the development of students. At the professional level, self-assessment activities should concentrate on helping the student contribute to the establishment of reasonable performance standards and then strive to meet those expectations.

Instructors can promote the use of self-assessment for professional goal-setting using some remarkably simple techniques. For example, ask the students to address, orally or in writing, the question, "Is this your best work" when they submit their final version. This challenge can be startling for students who have not regulated their work properly. The question holds them accountable for being willing to submit subpar performance just to get the work off of their desks. Follow-up questions that support self-assessment growth emphasize their explanation of why it is or is not solid professional performance. If the work is not up to standard, students should determine what steps to take to prevent this from happening again. As a consequence, students aspiring to professional levels might embrace the work ethic of managing their efforts so they will not submit subpar work.

A second strategy that promotes professional goal setting involves asking students to grade themselves using criteria that have been supplied for the project. This strategy can be employed summatively at the end of the project so that the students' views can influence grade determination. Alternatively, the challenge can occur at other critical points in the process, which can produce formative feedback and a course correction. When students' self-assessment comes up short, the instructor can require an explanation about the shortcoming. Again, a follow-up question prompting students to explore what this might mean for future work should promote more habitual self-reflective strategies.

The third strategy to promote professional self-assessment skills is the most demanding. Students themselves should assist in the construction of evaluative criteria for a complex project. This practice increases the stake that students feel in successful completion of the work and models the importance of creating personal standards to guide your work when graders no longer provide regular feedback on the work professionals perform.

Our students often report surprise at the range and forms of criticism that will shape their professional lives. Many of the critics they face will not be student-centered or developmental in their approaches. The outcome of professional performance evaluation can be high-stakes as well, including the loss of a job or rejection of a scholarly plan or project proposal. As such, perhaps another element of self-assessment not addressed in the rubric is the development of resilience. Accurate self-assessment based on evidence can provide a safe harbor if evaluative processes are not accurate, favorable, or fair.

CONCLUSION

Self-assessment—regulatory and reflective practice aimed at enhancing individual performance—is by no means limited to student learning. As other chapters in this volume attest, teachers, department chairs, other administrators, even entire psychology departments, can hone their respective skills by engaging in some degree of self-assessment (see, e.g., chaps. 2, 4, and 5, this volume). Certainly, successful individuals who work in psychology can be assumed to have mastered some degree of self-assessment. In any case, our focus on developing self-assessment among psychology students is not meant to limit the applicability of regulatory or reflective practices for other educational ends.

Nonetheless, we believe that empowering students is the proper beginning for thinking about and engaging in self-assessment. If we take seriously the shift from teacher-centered to learning-centered strategies argued by Barr and Tagg (1995), we must incorporate educational practices that develop self-assessment skills. In this chapter we have advocated for the formal use of the rubric for scientific inquiry by both faculty and students to empower students as self-assessors. The advantage from a self-assessment perspective, of course, is that, as learners and budding researchers, students can compare their actions with those recommended by the rubric. In this conceptualization, the domain of self-assessment is the capstone set of skills, one that routinely invokes aspects of all of the others. More to the point, as students progress in their disciplinary course work over time, frequent reference to and use of the rubric will lead them to reflexively rely on it when doing reading and writing assignments, thinking about research, or actually designing and conducting it. Empowered self-assessment leads to self-directed learning (Kusnic & Finley, 1993).

Although we have argued for the formal use of the rubric in promoting self-assessment skills in psychology contexts, we also recognize that the rubric itself may not be essential to the process. More important is developing commitment to the position that "time to remember, to sift, to weight, to estimate, to total" are essential to creating empowered learners. To produce truly educated people, in the sense that Marienau (1999) described, will require changes in how we design course activities and performance feedback. Critics of this position are likely to decry that such attention inevitably will lead to the sacrifice of course content. We agree that this emphasis will entail such a cost. However, we think time invested in promoting self-directed learning warrants the sacrifice. Indeed, instructors should consider that successful self-assessment—sustained self-regulation and self-reflection—imparts what most good teachers want in the first place: an outlook of open inquiry.

REFERENCES

American Psychological Association. (2001). *Publication manual of the American Psychological Association* (5th ed.). Washington, DC: Author.

Angelo, T. A., & Cross, P. K. (1993). *Classroom assessment techniques* (2nd ed.). San Francisco: Jossey-Bass.

Bandura, A. (1997). *Self-efficacy: The exercise of control.* New York: W. H. Freeman.

Barr, R. B., & Tagg, J. (1995, November/December). From teaching to learning—A new paradigm for undergraduate education. *Change, 27,* 12–25.

Halonen, J. S., Bosack, T., Clay, S., & McCarthy, M. (with Dunn, D. S., Hill, IV, G. W., McEntarffer, R., Mehrotra, C., Nesmith, R., Weaver, K., & Whitlock, K.). (2003). A rubric for authentically learning, teaching, and assessing scientific reasoning in psychology. *Teaching of Psychology, 30,* 196–208.

Kusnic, E., & Finley, M. L. (1993). Student self-evaluation: An introduction and rationale. In J. MacGregor (Ed.), *Student self-evaluation: Fostering reflective learning* (pp. 5–14). San Francisco: Jossey-Bass.

Lipman, M. (1988). Critical thinking—what can it be? *Educational Leadership, 46,* 38–43.

Loacker, G. (Ed.) (2000). *Self-assessment at Alverno College.* Milwaukee, WI: Alverno College Institute.

Marienau, C. (1999). Self-assessment at work: Outcomes of adult learners' reflections on practice. *Adult Education Quarterly, 49,* 135–146.

MacGregor, J. (Ed.) (1993a). *Student self-evaluation: Fostering reflective learning.* San Francisco: Jossey-Bass.

MacGregor, J. (1993b). Learning self-evaluation: Challenges for students. In J. MacGregor (Ed.), *Student self-evaluation: Fostering reflective learning* (pp. 35–46). San Francisco: Jossey-Bass.

Olsen, T. (1995). *Tell me a riddle.* New Brunswick, NJ: Rutgers University Press.

Trice, A. (2000). *A handbook of classroom assessment.* New York: Addison-Wesley-Longman.

Zimmerman, B. J., Bandura, A., & Martinez-Pons, M. (1992). Self-motivation for academic achievement: The role of self-efficacy beliefs and personal goal setting. *American Educational Research Journal, 29,* 663–676.

10

USING STUDENT PORTFOLIOS TO ASSESS PROGRAM LEARNING OUTCOMES

PETER A. KELLER, FRANCIS W. CRAIG, MARGARET H. LAUNIUS, BRIAN T. LOHER, AND NANCY J. COOLEDGE

In this chapter we describe the experience of an undergraduate psychology department at a small state university in developing a comprehensive portfolio for assessing student learning and identifying needs for program improvement. Our psychology curriculum is similar to that of many other institutions with the exception of an option in human resource management that allows students to merge their interests in business and psychology. About 80% of our 150 majors choose the more traditional psychology option. Our efforts to understand more deeply the learning experiences of our students as well as the effectiveness of our teaching began well over a decade ago and are facilitated by faculty retreats at the end of each semester. The development of our varied assessment efforts is one of the more important outcomes of our retreat discussions.

We collected our first student portfolios in 1993 and have been making improvements in this process each year since then. The portfolios contain examples of students' best written work and related documents that demonstrate specific learning outcomes. Our department is committed to using portfolios as one of its primary vehicles for assessment because of: (a) the important discussions about student learning and program effectiveness that result from the process; (b) the ways in which the process supports an integrated curriculum based on desired learning outcomes; and (c) the perceived value of portfolios for our students. We anticipate that our process will continue to evolve as we reflect on the role of portfolios as an assessment tool.

STUDENT PORTFOLIOS AS A TOOL FOR ASSESSING STUDENT LEARNING AND PROGRAM EFFECTIVENESS

The potential of student portfolios for assessing learning outcomes has been recognized for well over a decade, but the focus has largely been on applications in primary and secondary school settings (e.g., Johnson & Rose, 1997; Paris & Ayres, 1994; Shaklee, Barbour, Ambrose, & Hansford, 1997). Little attention has been given to the potential of portfolios either to enhance learning or assess outcomes of undergraduate psychology programs within the formal literature of our discipline. The contents of portfolios are referred to as "artifacts," and the process often involves "authentic assessment" (Wiggins, 1990). Authentic assessment focuses on the direct observation or inspection of students' work, as opposed to traditional examinations, which are viewed as proxy measures of students' actual learning. This form of assessment typically relies on publicly observable outcomes of learning. Our experience suggests that a program's readiness for initiating portfolio-based assessment is critical to the success of this process.

ESTABLISHING A PROGRAM CLIMATE CONDUCIVE TO IMPLEMENTING PORTFOLIOS

Our faculty unintentionally began to build an important part of the foundation for our portfolio process in 1985 when we began day-long, off-campus faculty retreats at the end of each semester. We initiated the retreat process because we recognized that deeper discussions about program planning and development, as well as the relationship building necessary for collaborative efforts, required more extended time than could be provided by our biweekly meetings during the academic year. With increased time together, we gradually established the group climate necessary to discuss some of the more sensitive issues or tensions that are likely to exist in any academic department.

To address program assessment successfully, faculty need: (a) reasonably high levels of trust in each other; (b) a genuine commitment to improving student learning across the program; (c) the capacity to establish a shared mission and goals for the program or department, as well as desired outcomes for student learning; (d) the ability to accept and respectfully work through differences of opinion; (e) the willingness to have the outcomes of courses scrutinized in a team environment; and (f) the persistence to follow through on a long-term process of discovery and improvement. Lucas (1994, 2000) offers a valuable perspective on building the teamwork necessary for departments to move forward with the kinds of collaborative processes that, we believe, facilitate the accomplishment of such tasks.

The retreats we hold at the end of each semester provide the time needed to (a) understand some of our shared frustrations as faculty, (b) discuss important aspects of our teaching, (c) build shared visions about the future of our program, and (d) develop action plans for improving our teaching as well as our students' opportunities to learn. Our initial thinking about assessment was spurred when one of our faculty members visited Alverno College, which was an early innovator in assessing learning across its curriculum with portfolios (Alverno College, 2002). We noted that not only were Alverno students producing tangible evidence of their learning, but that they seemed to be deeply involved in both self-assessment and the assumption of responsibility for their learning.

Our early deliberations identified concerns about the ability of our students to retain and apply basic concepts, principles, and methodologies of psychology across our four-year curriculum. We struggled to determine if the problems we noted were a consequence of our teaching failures or our students' failures to assume responsibility for their learning. In the end, we concluded that we needed to address both issues.

At the time we initiated this process, we found little literature that directly addressed our needs as a psychology department. (A few departmental Web sites, including the Meredith College Psychology Department [2003] and the University of North Carolina Greensboro Psychology Department [2003], now contain models for using portfolios as a means of assessing student learning outcomes.) We choose to approach the challenge by: (a) identifying a set of common learning outcomes for our curriculum; (b) agreeing to teach to the outcomes with more consistency across our courses in the major; (c) using the outcomes to link our courses across the curriculum, beginning with an orientation to the major course and culminating in a capstone senior seminar; and (d) using a program portfolio to demonstrate and assess the learning outcomes.

Figure 10.1 describes our model schematically. Based on our institutional mission, expectations of the discipline (McGovern, Furumoto, Halpern, Kimble, & McKeachie, 1991), our own faculty expertise, our students' expectations and backgrounds, and other program models (e.g., Kennesaw State University outcomes for psychology majors; Kennesaw State University, 1999), we identified the specific outcomes we wanted for our psychology majors. The definition of outcomes and methods for demonstrating learning was, at first, one of the more challenging matters on which to reach agree-

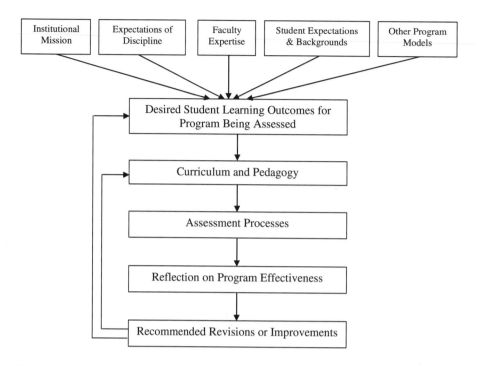

Figure 10.1. Schematic of the context for implementing portfolio assessment.

ment. Once this was accomplished, we examined our curriculum to identify the ways in which our existing courses and their sequence supported the outcomes we had defined. We then identified measures that would allow us to assess the ways in which student learning was consistent or inconsistent with our desired outcomes. The student portfolio, which contains artifacts representing learning outcomes collected from key courses in our major programs, became a primary focus of our efforts for a number of reasons. Portfolios provide us with evidence of student learning, which then forms the basis for reflection on the strengths and weaknesses of our program. The reflection process leads to important discussions about opportunities for program improvement. The sections that follow provide a practical perspective on how our portfolio process has evolved.

DEVELOPING AND REFINING THE PORTFOLIO PROCESS

We defined nine general outcomes (e.g., understanding of conceptual bases, information literacy, critical thinking skills) and identified a variety of methods (e.g., examinations, written papers, oral presentations, video tapes of peer counseling sessions) that students could use to demonstrate their learning and or skills. Table 10.1 describes the general outcomes in column one,

TABLE 10.1
Summary of Psychology Learning Outcomes and
Methods of Demonstration

General Outcome	Demonstration Methods
An understanding of the conceptual bases of psychology	Successful performance on a senior-level exit examination that demonstrates an understanding of critical facts, theories, and issues in psychology
The ability to skillfully and systematically gather *and assess* library and computerized information about issues addressed by the discipline	Library research and paper assignments in required major courses
The ability to think critically about important issues addressed by the discipline	Monitored group discussions, reaction papers, other paper assignments, and writing projects in required major courses
The ability to use the language of the discipline with clarity and understanding	Monitored group discussions, reaction papers, other paper assignments, and writing projects in required major courses
An understanding of research methods and basic statistical skills in the discipline	Successful completion and public presentation of reports based on the student's own or a group research project
The ability to communicate clearly, skillfully, and sensitively with others in a variety of settings where graduates might work	Monitored group discussions, demonstration in classes that require interviewing and discussion skills, and reports from internship supervisors
An understanding of the roles psychologists fill and settings in which psychologists and related professionals work	Topic papers, appropriate discussion in required major courses, and discussions with advisors
An appreciation of individual differences and diversity among people from different genders, races, ethnic, and cultural backgrounds	Topic papers, monitored group discussions, participation in department events that address diversity, and examinations in required major courses
An understanding of the critical ethical issues related to research and applications of psychology	Reaction papers, guided and monitored group discussions, and examinations in required major courses

Note. Portions of this table were adapted from materials developed by the Psychology Department at Kennesaw State University and revised by Mansfield University psychology faculty.

followed by the methods used to demonstrate the outcomes in column two. As we write this chapter, the outcomes are under revision to make them more consistent with the current APA learning goals and outcomes (Halonen et al., 2002; see Appendix 10.1, this volume).

Next, we identified the outcomes and demonstration methods applicable to each of the students' required courses and primary electives in the psychology major. We combined the results into a single document that identified each outcome, the demonstration methods utilized, and the specific courses where students could expect this learning or experience to occur. For example, the outcome "understanding of research methods and statistical skills" might be demonstrated by correct answers to specific items on examinations in introductory psychology and research methods courses, a paper from a laboratory course, and a formal research presentation resulting from an experimental design course. Developing a table that tracked program outcomes and demonstration methods in specific courses was a crucial part of our team approach to program assessment. Courses and related assignments now appeared as parts of a larger whole integrated more clearly with our department's overall learning goals.

Departments interested in pursuing our integrated strategy will need to set aside a significant amount of time to discuss the overall goals of the portfolio in relation to the program's mission as well as the "nuts and bolts" of the portfolio, including how to integrate the portfolios into the curriculum; whether to review all student portfolios or only a sample; how to adequately assess the portfolios collected; and how to use the information obtained from the process for improvement of the learning process.

At present, our student portfolios are comprised primarily of written work that is compiled into a binder. Appendix 10.1 contains the current portfolio content guide, which includes sections for students to demonstrate their knowledge and competencies in areas associated with the desired program outcomes. Major sections include evidence of career or graduate school preparation, critical thinking papers, research papers, and community service. We also expect evidence of understanding the general knowledge base of psychology, which is currently assessed partly by an objective examination created by the department and administered in the Senior Seminar.

We decided to have students select only their best papers, presentations, and other outcomes for inclusion in the portfolio. Because we also determined that the portfolio would be something students might want to share with prospective employers or graduate programs to which they were applying, we decided against including graded work containing faculty corrections. Students revise and have their final papers "signed off" by the course instructor prior to inclusion in the portfolio.

ASSESSMENT OF THE PORTFOLIO

A committee of three faculty members independently reviews the sample of portfolios randomly selected by the Senior Seminar instructor. The sample

TABLE 10.2
Steps to Improve Reliability and Validity of Portfolios

What To Do	What It Improves
Determine the programmatic learning goals.	Construct validity
Create a list of activities or assignments and a table of artifacts for each.	Content validity
Establish criteria standards and rubrics.	Reliability
Obtain multiple measures of each goal or outcome.	Reliability and validity
Train portfolio raters using criteria.	Reliability

Note. Data from "Thorny Issues of Reliability, Validity, and Fairness When Evaluating Portfolio Assessment," by N. Cooledge, J. Cooledge, and K. Weihe, October 2000, Proceedings from the Annual Alliance/ACE Conference, Chicago, IL.

size is typically six to seven portfolios, or about 25 to 30% of the students in the capstone course. We use a rudimentary scoring rubric to help guide the review process. Portfolios are rated on a five-point Likert scale for six specific dimensions, as well as a global rating of the portfolio (see Appendix 10.2). Reviewers also add comments, and the summary data are reported as part of the department's annual outcomes report for the university.

Reliability and validity of portfolio assessment processes are important considerations (Koretz, 1998). Moskal (2000) and Moskal and Leydens (2000) provide useful discussions of both rubric development and scoring validity and reliability that interested readers may wish to consult. A detailed discussion of reliability and validity issues is beyond the scope of this chapter, but Table 10.2 summarizes basic steps that should be considered to establish reliability of validity of this process.

The overall mean rating for recent portfolios was 3.59 on a 5-point scale. An analysis of the specific dimensions consistently found that understanding research methods and statistics received the least satisfactory rating by our reviewers. Comments by raters also indicated that faculty have differing expectations regarding students' use of APA style in written work. Other frequent comments refer to the absence of *specific evidence* of outcomes, most commonly those related to understanding ethics and appreciation of diversity.

Consistent with other studies of portfolio rater reliability, our interrater reliability correlations are low to moderate (Baume & Yorke, 2000; Koretz, 1998). In 1998, the mean Pearson correlation based on three raters was .36. In 2000, we found better agreement between raters (following a decision by the Senior Seminar instructor to be more directive in the portfolio completion process) with a mean Pearson correlation of .46. In general, good portfolios were rated consistently high by raters, while the ratings of portfolios created by generally less able or less motivated students were more variable. We believe collaborative training on the rating process could substantially increase our reliability in the future.

INTRODUCING THE PORTFOLIO TO STUDENTS

The portfolio has evolved into an important part of the department's culture. We introduce students to the department's outcomes and the portfolio system as part of an orientation to the major course. Students purchase the portfolio binder as part of their required materials for this course. Enclosed in the three-ring binder are printed copies of the department's general manual for majors, manuals for the independent study and internship experiences, summary guides to APA writing style and writing tips, most of the learning exercises for the orientation course itself, and portfolio instructions and examples. Manuals and other materials are organized with color-coded index tabs so that students can easily locate items. The portfolio binder also includes a 3.5-inch, 1.44 MB diskette on which students store backup copies of portfolio-related papers.

Students in both psychology and human resource management emphases are required to take the orientation course following declaration of the major. The orientation course introduces the APA's goals for undergraduate psychology majors (Appendix 10.1; Halonen et al., 2002; McGovern et al.,1991) to provide a context for understanding class-specific exercises and the categories in the portfolio. Our general outcomes and demonstration methods (see Table 10.1) are subsequently described. As a result of this process, students seem to have a greater understanding of the rationales for the portfolio categories and expectations.

A simple assignment completed in the orientation course helps to focus students on the portfolio process. The exercise begins by reviewing the default cover page, current categories for the portfolio (see Appendix 10.1), and simulated "table of contents" and "community service" pages. Instruction includes guidance concerning the specific courses that produce category-appropriate materials. We also describe the mechanics of the portfolio at this time. With author permission, we circulate sample final versions of the portfolio from seniors or alumni among the orientation students so that they have a clearer understanding of the department's expectations for this product.

At the conclusion of this assignment, students present an initial portfolio for inspection by the instructor. Products from two completed assignments in the orientation course (a personal goals statement form and a résumé) must also be included under the "goals and career planning" category to document that the student understands how specific course materials fit within the broader outcomes demonstrated in the portfolio.

To emphasize that the portfolio is a significant part of program expectations, the due date for this assignment is explicitly linked to the beginning of the advising and registration period for the next semester. We tell students that their psychology faculty will review portfolios during academic advising sessions. Students complete the orientation course with their portfolios started and an understanding of the continuing process that will culminate in their senior seminar. We encourage them to look for assignments that can be placed in the portfolio as they move through the curriculum. We also suggest to transfer students that they save appropriate materials from their previous institution for inclusion in the portfolio.

MAINTAINING FOCUS AND MOMENTUM IN THE "BETWEEN" YEARS

There is a gap of 2 to 4 years between the time that we first introduce our students to the portfolio and the point at which they submit their completed collection in our Senior Seminar. For the portfolio to be an active and integrative element of the student's academic experience, its importance must remain prominent throughout the student's experience.

Low Maintenance Approaches to Maintaining a High Portfolio Profile

Our experience suggests that faculty commitment to maintaining focus on the portfolio process need not consume an unreasonable amount of time. Maintaining a high profile for the portfolio is integrated into three areas of our majors' regular academic experience: (a) academic advising, (b) "syllabus reminder language," and (c) paper grading.

Academic Advising

Academic advising is given a high priority in our department and represents an opportunity to use the portfolio. Because they need an online registration access personal identification number, students must meet with their advisor to discuss their academic progress. Faculty members have agreed not to advise students who fail to have their portfolio available for review. During the advising session faculty briefly review the evolving portfolio, which contains a student's goals and other artifacts, as well as graduate school and career plans and selection of appropriate courses for the upcoming semester.

Syllabus Reminder Language

Several sections of our student portfolio include papers or reports that demonstrate student learning outcomes (Table 10.1). As a faculty, we seek ways to remind students that their papers, if done well, will be acceptable for inclusion into one of these portfolio sections. One way of doing this is through "reminder language" in course syllabi, where course work appropriate for the portfolio is highlighted.

Paper Grading

A third approach used to maintain awareness of the portfolio by our students is the use of a "universal" paper evaluation summary grid that clearly indicates whether a paper is appropriate for inclusion in the portfolio. Students are made aware not only of a paper's strengths and weaknesses via a one-page summary grid, but also the status of this paper in relation to acceptability for the portfolio. This approach immediately reminds students of the portfolio's importance as a final receptacle for their best efforts. Additionally, at retreats and faculty meetings we remind ourselves about the commitment to note opportunities for portfolio contributions both on our syllabi and in announcements to our classes.

FACILITATING SUCCESSFUL PORTFOLIO COMPLETION IN A CAPSTONE COURSE

While we use various assessment methods, such as an objective exit examination and a Senior Seminar symposium where our graduating majors present their seminar papers publicly, the portfolio remains the primary focus of our assessment process. Below we describe an exercise that we currently use to bring the portfolio process to a smooth and successful finale during our Senior Seminar. We also address several additional issues, including grading and archiving of the portfolios.

Reorientation to Artifacts: The Personal Portfolio Review

As students begin their Senior Seminar, focus on the portfolio we have been emphasizing throughout their academic career becomes even more central. In the second class meeting, seniors perform a comprehensive assessment of their own portfolio for content and structure. Following a brief lecture reintroducing the sections of the portfolio and describing appropriate content for those sections, each student completes a simple exercise called a "personal portfolio review." In this exercise, students consider each section of the portfolio and note what is required for its completion and the action required to do this. This reorientation establishes a common baseline of understanding that compensates for variations in course scheduling and student advising that naturally accompany varying student academic paths and advising.

Updating Relevant Materials

During the Senior Seminar, students further revise materials first encountered during their orientation course. Specific areas of revision include:

1. *Prepare senior-year goal statements.* Each student not only states short-term post-graduation goals, but also describes idealized goals projecting up to 10 years in the future.
2. *Update resumés.* The resumé is revised to include recent research presentations and internship experiences.

3. *Draft sample cover letters.* Inquiries directed to potential employees or graduate schools are prepared and critiqued as part of a workshop-style presentation on letter preparation and interview skills.

4. *Complete paper revisions.* Students revise their papers in areas of critical thinking, research methods, and writing abilities. (As noted previously, papers frequently require revision before being placed in the final portfolio. More recently we have decided to require student revisions to papers within 2 weeks of starting the semester that follows a paper's return.)

Peer Evaluations of Draft Portfolios

One week prior to final portfolio submission and initiation of the departmental assessment, students bring in their "draft portfolio" for peer evaluation. It is a class requirement that this portfolio be in near-finished form. Classroom peers anonymously evaluate three portfolios randomly distributed to them. Each completes evaluation feedback using the same portfolio review form used later by the instructors, along with a second page that allows for detailed qualitative feedback (see Appendix 10.4).

We expect students to spend at least 15 minutes per portfolio compiling their ratings and comments. A discussion follows immediately to identify the "best and worst" portfolio practices. Students are encouraged to reflect on the contents, share appreciation for work well done, and note areas that could be improved. We have found that this collaborative and reflective learning process provides both motivation and clarification of learning. Thematic data from recent focus groups with graduating seniors suggest that these exercises have led to increased student investment in the portfolio process as well as recognition of its value in personal development. Faculty ratings have also indicated a marked improvement in portfolio appearance compared with previous years, in which the peer evaluation and reflection process was not used. In summary, the peer review process seems to provide a new dimension to our use of portfolios as a means for learning as well as assessment.

OTHER PRACTICAL PORTFOLIO CONSIDERATIONS

Departments considering the implementation of a portfolio-based assessment process are likely to uncover additional questions. These include:

1. *Should comprehensive portfolios be graded?* We presently grade our students' portfolios within the context of the Senior Seminar. Our experience suggests that grading their adherence to the assigned structure and attention to the presentation qual-

ity of the portfolio helps motivate students to build a better final product. We believe that this product moves them toward their occupational or graduate school goals. However, our grading is not based on quality of content, but on adherence to departmental guidelines for portfolio organization and appearance. Thus, papers from earlier courses are not re-graded via this process.

2. *Should portfolios be archived by the department?* At first, we planned to retain the portfolios as evidence for subsequent self-study processes. However, our opinions on this have changed for two reasons. First, archiving portfolios over several years consumes more space than we have available. Second, archiving the portfolios runs counter to the positive trend of students assuming more ownership of the portfolio as a product of their learning. As a consequence, we promptly review a sample of portfolios and return them to the students before they graduate. We occasionally ask student permission to duplicate portfolios so that we can have representative samples to share with others.

3. *Can portfolios be developed online?* Electronic portfolios (Cambridge, 2001; Carrier & Rosen, 2002) maintained on the Web on a commercial or university server represent a viable option for departments adopting this process. We have discussed the advantages and limitations of electronic portfolios and decided that the present process is more suited to our uses as faculty as well as the current needs of our students. The tangible links across our curricular, instructional, advising, and final assessment processes seem to fit our use of hard copy documents particularly well, but we will assuredly visit this question again in the future.

CONCLUSION

This chapter describes our experiences over a decade in using student portfolios to assess student learning in an undergraduate program within a small state university. Although we use other assessments—an objective exit examination, periodic surveys of majors and alumni, public presentations of student research, and focus groups—portfolios represent the core of our assessment process.

While portfolios provide us with useful quantitative and qualitative data about the effectiveness of our programs, they have just as importantly improved our culture of learning for both faculty and students. Put differently, the process of using portfolios has contributed to important changes in the ways we teach and the ways our students learn and assume responsibility for their learning. However, we believe the *process* of using portfolios as a means for assessment and improvement is as important as any formal ratings we might derive for required reports.

From a more technical perspective, we recognize that reliability and validity of ratings are important considerations in the adoption of portfolios as an assessment tool. We have briefly identified ways for improving both of these within this chapter. Our own data strongly suggest the need to improve the reliability of our portfolio ratings. Taking steps in this direction will be an important part of the evolution of our efforts to improve the assessment process.

In a sense we have embarked on a journey of discovery about teaching and learning that is mediated by portfolios. The process of assessing, reflecting, and improving will never be completed, but we gain considerable satisfaction from identifying ways to improve both our teaching and our students' learning as we move forward.

REFERENCES

Alverno College. (2002). *Digital diagnostic portfolio.* Retrieved December 13, 2003, from http://ddp.alverno.edu/faq.html

Baume, D., & Yorke, M. (2000). *Validity and reliability in the evaluation of portfolios for the accreditation of teachers in higher education.* American Association for Higher Education Assessment Forum. (ERIC Document Reproduction Service No. ED 446071)

Cambridge, B. L. (Ed.). (2001). *Electronic portfolios: Emerging practices in student, faculty, and institutional learning.* Washington, DC: American Association for Higher Education.

Carrier, L. M., & Rosen, L. (2002). An electronic portfolio project with graduating psychology majors. *Exchanges: The Online Journal of Teaching and Learning in the California State University.* Retrieved December 12, 2003, from http://www.exchangesjournal.org/classroom/1108_Carrier_Rosen_pg1.html

Cooledge, N., Cooledge, J., & Weihe, K. (2000, October). *Thorny issues of reliability, validity, and fairness when evaluating portfolio assessment.* Proceedings from the Annual Alliance/ACE Conference, Chicago, IL.

Halonen, J. S., Appleby, D. C., Brewer, C. L., Buskist, W., Gillem, A. R., Halpern, D., et al. (2002). *Undergraduate psychology major learning goals and outcomes.* Report of the Task Force on Undergraduate Psychology Major Competencies. American Psychological Association Board of Educational Affairs. Retrieved December 13, 2003, from http://www.apa.org/ed/pcue/taskforcereport2.pdf

Johnson, N. J., & Rose, L. M. (1997). *Portfolios: Clarifying, constructing, and enhancing.* Lancaster, PA: Technomic.

Kennesaw State University. (1999). *Congruence with institutional missions*. Retrieved December 13, 2003, from http://www.kennesaw.edu/psychology/goals.htm

Koretz, D. (1998). Large-scale portfolio assessments in the U.S.: Evidence pertaining to the quality of measurement. *Assessment in Education: Principles, Policy & Practice, 5*(3), 309–335.

Lucas, A. F. (1994). *Strengthening departmental leadership: A team-building guide for chairs in colleges and universities*. San Francisco: Jossey-Bass.

Lucas, A. F. (2000). A collaborative model for leading academic change. In A. F. Lucas (Ed.). *Leading academic change: Essential roles for department chairs* (pp. 33–54). San Francisco: Jossey-Bass.

McGovern, T., Furumoto, L., Halpern, D., Kimble, G., & McKeachie, W. (1991). Liberal education, study in depth, and the arts and science major—psychology. *American Psychologist, 46*(6), 598–605.

Meredith College Psychology Department. *Guidelines for psychology portfolio*. Retrieved December 13, 2003, from http://www.meredith.edu/psych/major/portfolio.htm

Moskal, B. M. (2000). Scoring rubrics: What, when, and how? *Practical Assessment, Research & Evaluation, 7*(3). Retrieved December 13, 2003, from http://ericae.net/pare/getvn.asp?v=7&n=3

Moskal, B. M., & Leydens, J. A. (2000). Scoring rubric development: Validity and reliability. *Practical Assessment, Research & Evaluation, 7*(10). Retrieved December 13, 2003, from http://ericae.net/pare/getvn.asp?v=7&n=10

Paris, S. G., & Ayres, L. R. (1994). *Becoming reflective students and teachers with portfolios and authentic assessment*. Washington, DC: American Psychological Association.

Shaklee, B. D., Barbour, N. E., Ambrose, R., & Hansford, S. (1997). *Designing and using portfolios*. Boston: Allyn & Bacon.

University of North Carolina Greensboro Psychology Department. *Psychology portfolio*. Retrieved December 13, 2003, from: http://www.uncg.edu/psy/undergraduateprogram/degreerequirements/psychologyportfolio.html

Wiggins, G. (1990). The case for authentic assessment. *Practical Assessment, Research & Evaluation, 2*(2). Retrieved December 13, 2003, from http://ericae.net/pare/getvn.asp?v=2&n=2

APPENDIX 10.1

MANSFIELD UNIVERSITY PSYCHOLOGY
DEPARTMENT PORTFOLIO GUIDE

The student portfolio is a record of each student's academic goals, objectives, and accomplishments. Students initiate their portfolios in PSY 151, Introduction to Applications of Psychology, and complete the final portfolio in PSY 490, Senior Seminar. The portfolio is designed to serve as a resource for students, advisors, professors, internship supervisors, prospective employers, and so forth. As a measure of our program's effectiveness, a sample of portfolios will be reviewed by the faculty at the completion of the Senior Seminar each semester. A well-done portfolio demonstrates the student's abilities, skills, and competencies across a variety of tasks and objectives. The portfolio contents are based on competencies identified by the American Psychological Association and the Psychology Department faculty. Each content or competency area should contain the **best** sample or demonstration of a student's ability in that area. The content areas for the portfolio are:

I. Goal Statements and Career Planning

    A. Your professional resumé or CV (PSY 151, 490)

    B. A copy of your Academic Record

    C. A neatly written or typed Senior-Year Goal Statement. This should identify your major post-graduation goals. (PSY 490)

    D. A neatly written or typed First-Year Goal Statement. This will reflect your original goals and objectives when you entered the Psychology department. (PSY 151)

    E. Ideal job description (PSY 490)

    F. A cover letter appropriate for sending to a prospective employer, graduate program, or both (PSY 151, 490)

    G. Professional Interview Write-up (PSY 490)

    H. Copy of Strong Vocational Interest Inventory Results (Administered in PSY 201 & PSY 490)

II. Writing Abilities: A topic paper or library research paper that represents your best writing and conceptualizing skills. You may include more than one if papers represent different skills or abilities. May come from any class but must include at least one paper from a psychology class.

III. Critical Thinking Abilities: Assignments or projects that demonstrate problem-solving abilities, critical thinking, analysis, etc. Examples include designed treatment plans, experimental designs, ethics case analyses, position paper, and so forth. May come from any course but must include at least one paper from a psychology course.

IV. Research Skills: A copy of a survey you developed, research proposal, experimental write-up, research symposium paper or poster presentation, etc. May come from any course but must include at least one paper from a psychology course.

V. Applied Experience: Internship experience (PSY 495), Research Apprenticeship (PSY 496), Independent Study (PSY 497) or Honors project: A copy of the final written report from your research or experience.

VI. University/Community Contributions: A summary of your contributions to the university and larger community, including organizations, clubs, social service projects, committees, and service to the department. Write a fairly detailed summary in reverse chronological order, expanding on your résumé information.

VII. Miscellaneous: Other academic accomplishments such as creative writing samples, telephone survey (*Public Mind Survey*), artistic projects, theater review, and so forth.

VIII. Awards and Honors: Certificates of *general knowledge* (PSY 490 Exit Exam), perfect attendance, outstanding scholarship, extra-curricular activities, athletic or social contributions, and so forth.

APPENDIX 10.2

PSYCHOLOGY PORTFOLIO REVIEW FORM

Portfolio ID: _____

Evaluator: _____

Circle the appropriate number for each area to be reviewed:

Presentation: How does the portfolio "look" at a cursory glance? Is it well organized, neatly typed, and professional in appearance? Would you feel comfortable having the student show this to a potential employer or graduate school evaluation committee?

1	2	3	4	5
Inadequate		*Adequate*		*Excellent*

General Knowledge: Does the student have an adequate knowledge base of the discipline? Do they understand the basic terms, theories, theorists, and concepts of the discipline?

1	2	3	4	5
Inadequate		*Adequate*		*Excellent*

Critical Thinking: To what extent does the material in the portfolio demonstrate the student's ability to analyze and evaluate a given topic or content area? Is there evidence of the ability to engage in adequate problem-solving? Could the student take a problem and develop a plan to complete the task or solve the problem?

1	2	3	4	5
Inadequate		*Adequate*		*Excellent*

Research Abilities: To what extent does the material in the portfolio demonstrate the student's ability to understand the basic concepts of research design and data analysis? Could the student correctly explain basic research designs to someone who knew nothing about the topic?

1	2	3	4	5
Inadequate		*Adequate*		*Excellent*

Writing Abilities: To what extent does the material in the portfolio demonstrate the student's writing ability? How well organized are the main concepts? How able is the student to use proper grammar, spelling, punctuation, and sentence structure? Are the written papers using vocabulary and style consistent with a college senior? Are they able to communicate effectively and clearly in the language of the discipline of psychology? Is there evidence of original thought and sufficient depth of coverage of the content? Have they used APA style appropriately? Would you feel comfortable having the student write independently for a professional audience?

1	2	3	4	5
Inadequate		Adequate		Excellent

Technology and Information Technology: Does the student appear to have a working knowledge of computer programs such as word processing and SPSS? Do they know how to utilize library resources, both on and off line? (e.g., evidence of http references)

1	2	3	4	5
Inadequate		Adequate		Excellent

Global Assessment of this Portfolio:

1	2	3	4	5
Inadequate		Adequate		Excellent

Comments on this Portfolio: _____

_____

_____

APPENDIX 10.3

PSYCHOLOGY WRITTEN ASSIGNMENT EVALUATION SUMMARY

Student: Date:

Area Evaluated	Rating				
Overall Format	*Excellent*	*Good*	*Fair*	*Poor*	*NA*
Paper conforms to guidelines given in class					
Double spacing (except for reference section)					
One-inch margins all around					
Page numbers in upper right corner					
Page headers					
Appropriate 12 pt font size use throughout					
Title page with identifying information					
Abstract					
Overall Format					
Technical Effectiveness					
Logical flow and organization of paper					
Use of section headings and subheadings					
Sentence structure and grammar					
Paragraph structure built around thesis sentence					
Spelling and punctuation					
Citation of references in the text					
Documentation of quotations					
Reference section following APA format					
Overall Technical Effectiveness					
Scholarship					
Content of paper addresses the assignment					
Conclusions and opinions backed by evidence					
Suitable coverage of the available literature					
Depth of analysis of topic area					
Other:					
Overall Scholarship					
Additional Comments:	Paper is suitable for Portfolio ? Paper is not suitable ? Paper is suitable with revisions ? Other recommendation: Overall Score _____				

APPENDIX 10.4

PSYCHOLOGY PORTFOLIO EVALUATION SHEET
(PAGE 1 OF 2. PAGE 2 CONTAINS COMMENTS.)

Student Name: _____ Date: _____

Reviewer: _____

Area Evaluated	Rating				
Basic Standards	Present (Yes)		Absent (No)		
All Psychology Papers Signed-Off					
Each Writing Section Has At Least 1 Signed-Off Psychology Paper					
Sign-off Page Clearly Displayed in Front Pocket					
All Assignments in Portfolio have been Revised					
Presentation and Appearance	Excellent	Good	Fair	Poor	Comment
Cover and Side Insertion					
Table of Contents- Clarity/Legibility					
Section Dividers Clearly Placed/Accessible					
Overall Neatness & Pleasing Display of Contents					
All Work Typed					
Overall Format					
Technical Presentation	Excellent	Good	Fair	Poor	Comment
Section 1: Effectiveness (Goals/Career Planning)					
Resume (Professional Display)					
ER / 1st Year and Senior Goal Statement (Present & Neatly Displayed)					
Sample Cover Letter & Ideal Job Description (Present & Neatly Displayed)					
Section 2: Writing Abilities:					
Appropriate Psychology Paper/Neatly Displayed/ Corrected/Signed-Off					
Section 3: Critical Thinking Abilities					
Appropriate Psychology Paper/Neatly Displayed/ Corrected/Signed-Off					
Section 4: Research Skills					
Appropriate Psychology Paper/Neatly Displayed/ Corrected/Signed-Off					

Section 5: Applied Experience Appropriate Materials /Neatly Displayed/ Corrected/Signed-Off (if a paper)					No Applied Experience Course Yet
Section 6: University/Community Service Appropriate Materials/Neatly Displayed/					
Section 7: Miscellaneous Appropriate Materials/Neatly Displayed					
Section 8: Awards & Honors Appropriate Materials / Neatly Displayed					
Overall Technical Presentation					

11

ASSESSING STUDENT LEARNING USING A LOCAL COMPREHENSIVE EXAM: INSIGHTS FROM EASTERN ILLINOIS UNIVERSITY

CARIDAD F. BRITO, ANUPAMA SHARMA, AND RONAN S. BERNAS

Could your department benefit from a comprehensive, cost-effective, curriculum-driven exam that would provide a direct assessment of student learning? This question is becoming increasingly important as colleges and universities feel pressure from accreditation boards to verify the quality of the educational programs they provide. Many state education boards either have launched or are considering launching comprehensive accountability efforts—a requirement that all public colleges and universities annually submit "performance indicators" (see chap. 1, this volume). In these uncertain economic times, there is great public pressure to demonstrate what students know and are able to do as a result of their college experiences. Student outcomes assessment allows both institutions of higher education and individual academic departments to quantify student learning.

There are a number of assessment measures that can be used in evaluating student learning. However, many of the more popular measures (e.g., student, alumni, and employer surveys; exit interviews of graduates; focus groups; graduation rates and length of time to degree) provide only indirect measures of student learning (Lopez, 1996). Indirect measures of student learning provide information about factors that contribute to or detract from student learning and can inform departments about how well they are meeting their missions. A problem with indirect measures is that they do not indicate what and how much students have actually learned. Consequently, direct measures of student learning (e.g., standardized tests, portfolio assessment, locally developed tests) should also be a part of departmental assessment programs—indeed, most departmental summative assessments consistently employ a combination of both indirect and direct measures (Lopez, 2000). Summative assessments generally provide an end-of-program overview of student learning, giving the department feedback about its curriculum and informing students about their own learning. Objective testing remains a sound and traditional type of direct summative assessment. Although commercially produced tests are available, departments often decide to develop their own local tests. Local tests allow for more budgetary flexibility and can provide more accurate information about student knowledge, abilities or skills, and values than the commercially produced tests.

Our chapter reviews the existing commercially available national tests, explores the advantages and disadvantages of both national and local comprehensive exams (LCEs), and presents important issues to consider when developing a local examination (see Table 11.1). Our goal is not to show that LCEs are superior to nationally developed tests, but to argue that they can be a viable alternative or complement to national tests. This will be especially useful for departments that cannot afford the national tests or want to make the test more congruent with curricular goals and objectives.

THE ASSESSMENT CHALLENGE AT EIU

Department Description

Eastern Illinois University (EIU) is a public, regional, masters-granting residential university of about 10,000 full-time students. The Psychology Department consists of 20 full-time tenure or tenure-track faculty members, all holding doctoral degrees, and two full-time annually contracted faculty. We graduate about 130 students each year, and average about 400 majors. Our curriculum emphasizes scientific psychology in the context of a liberal arts orientation. Students fulfill our departmental graduation requirements by taking required core courses (i.e., introductory psychology, statistics, and research methods), choosing courses within several content areas (cognitive/learning, abnormal/social, developmental, biopsychological), and selecting from a broad range of elective courses. We also encourage students to participate in supervised research with faculty and complete community-based internships.

TABLE 11.1
Major Steps Involved in Local Exam Development

Step	Questions to Ask
1)	**Knowledge Domains**
	▪ Which knowledge domains would be or are included in the comprehensive exam?
	▪ How would you weigh these domains?
	▪ What challenges or difficulties do you foresee?
2)	**Exam Items**
	▪ Who writes the items or where will they come from?
	▪ What types of items will be selected?
	▪ How many items on the exam (per domain)?
	▪ How much time will the students have to complete the exam?
3)	**Exam Administration**
	▪ Will pre- and posttests be used?
	▪ If used, how will pre- and posttest be used?
	▪ Who will take the exam (e.g., all graduating seniors, capstone course students)?
	▪ When and where will the exam be administered?
	▪ If no "capstone" course, will you try "carrots" or go for the stick?
4)	**Analysis and Reporting**
	▪ Who is going to analyze exam outcomes and prepare reports?
	▪ Who will receive the reports?
	▪ What types of group profiles will be reported?

Assessment History

Not unlike many other institutions and departments, our assessment efforts began slowly by sampling graduating seniors about the usefulness of advising and courses taken. Our efforts became more formative in the mid-1990s, and have evolved into a dynamic assessment program. These efforts basically parallel what has occurred at the university level, where the first assessment policy emerged in 1991. Initially, EIU's assessment efforts focused on evaluating programs, rather than individual student learning. A mandate by the Illinois Board of Higher Education led the Provost to form an Assessment Plan Task Force in 1999, resulting in the establishment of a Committee for the Assessment of Student Learning (CASL). CASL's efforts resulted in EIU's Plan for Assessment of Student Learning in 2000, which included provisions for assessing departmental majors. Each department must have an assessment plan with the goal of improving student learning. The plan should incorporate five basic elements: (a) student learning goals and objectives, (b) assessment measures, (c) assessment procedures, (d) analysis and reporting of assessment data, and (e) use of the assessment data to improve student learning. Currently, EIU's Office of Academic Assessment and Testing coordinates all university and departmental student outcomes assessment.

The psychology department's assessment program is led by a three-member Assessment Committee. Our approach in developing our assessment program has been multifaceted. We began developing direct measures of learning as soon as faculty consensus on some critical goals and objectives had been achieved. In our experience, delineation of goals and objectives is an ongoing process often modified by the outcomes of the assessment process itself. The first direct measure agreed upon by our faculty was to use a summative comprehensive exam. In 2000, we obtained limited funds to administer the Area Concentration Achievement Test in Psychology (ACAT-P) to a sample of graduating seniors. Our experience with this national test was somewhat unsatisfactory because the knowledge areas the exam assessed did not closely match our curriculum. We also did not have the financial resources to administer the test on a regular basis. Consequently, we have directed our efforts and resources toward developing a local comprehensive exam.

EVALUATING NATIONAL TESTS

Assessing student learning of content in psychology can be accomplished either by adopting a nationally developed test or by constructing an LCE. Both have advantages and disadvantages. Commercially available national tests come ready to administer and allow departments to "benchmark" their efforts against those of other institutions and programs. However, their financial costs can be prohibitive, and they may not reflect a department's curriculum. In psychology, two national tests are available: the Major Fields Test (MFT) and the Area Concentration Achievement Test (ACAT).

Major Fields Test

The MFT in Psychology is designed to be an end-of-program test that measures the development of knowledge in the discipline (Educational Testing Services, 2003). It consists of 140 multiple-choice items covering the most commonly offered courses in the field such as learning, cognition, perception, comparative, sensory processes, physiology, clinical/abnormal, developmental, personality, and social. Other areas assessed include psychological measurement and research methodology. The exam also tests the students' ability to analyze relationships, apply principles, make conclusions from data, and assess experiments. Four subscores are reported for each student and summarized for the group: (a) learning and cognition; (b) perception, sensory, physiology, comparative and ethology; (c) clinical, abnormal, and personality; and (d) developmental and social. The test can provide individual student reports as well as group reports on each subscore. The exam takes two hours to administer and costs about $24 per student. Results are scored by ETS once each month, except in September.

The MFT in Psychology is relatively new, and only a few studies have examined its usefulness. Norcross, Gerrity, and Hogan (1993) demonstrated that students who finished an undergraduate psychology program performed better on the MFT in Psychology than those who went through a management program.

Stoloff and Feeney (2002), on the other hand, raised some questions about the efficacy of the MFT in Psychology as an assessment measure for psychology majors at James Madison University. The authors found only a weak, although significant, correlation ($r = +.25$, $p < .05$) between scores on the MFT and the number of psychology courses completed by the students. Also, the MFT test scores were strongly related to only a few specific courses (abnormal, social, biopsychology, and counseling) from the department's curriculum. The MFT scores were correlated with measures of performance such as GPA and the Scholastic Aptitude Test (SAT), independent of the students' knowledge of psychology.

Area Concentration Achievement Tests

The second commercially available national test is the ACAT, which was originally developed in 1989 as the Project for Area Concentration Achievement (Golden, 1997). The Psychology ACAT (ACAT-P) offers twelve content areas (i.e., abnormal, animal learning and motivation, clinical and counseling, developmental, experimental design, history and systems, human learning and cognition, personality, physiology, sensation and perception, social, and statistics) (PACAT, 2003). A unique feature of the ACAT is that departments can select 4, 6, 8, or 10 content areas for inclusion in the test. This flexibility results in an exam that is more likely to be representative of the department's curriculum. Exam administration times vary between 48 and 120 minutes, depending upon the number of content areas selected. The exam costs about $12 per student, and results are processed once each month.

Research on the efficacy of the ACAT is limited. Noble and Stretch (2002) found that the Social Work ACAT is better than self-report measures for assessing domain knowledge and skills. Markus, Mukina, and Golden (1998) found that the ACAT-P is sensitive to gains in content area knowledge. They found significant ($p < .001$) gains in all content areas from pre- to posttest administration. One concern is potential gender differences. For example, Fleming and Golden (1997) reported that men who had taken research methods and planned to attend graduate school performed better than women on the research methods subtests of the ACAT-P.

Advantages of Using National Tests

A major advantage of adopting a national test for assessing student learning is that the tests do not require much work from a psychology department. These tests have already undergone rigorous statistical analysis for item difficulty, reliability, and validity. Furthermore, individual and group report summaries and ready-made professional-looking report graphs are readily available. The ACAT-P allows tailoring the test to a department's curriculum by providing flexibility in the content areas tested; the MFT has the added advantage of allowing up to 50 locally written multiple-choice items to be added to the exam. Finally, exam scores aggregated across many institutions provide opportunities for psychology departments to assess how their students fare compared with students from other institutions taking the same exam.

Disadvantages of Using National Tests

The costs associated with procuring and scoring the national test instruments can be prohibitive, especially for large departments and when pre- and posttesting is desired. Some flexibility is also needed with respect to when the test is administered as a department has to keep track of and plan around the scoring schedule set by the national testing company. These tests also have lengthy and detailed instructions for administering the exam and handling exam materials (e.g., the MFT's Test Administration Manual is 26 pages long); they allow only multiple-choice questions; and administration times can be long. The MFT takes two hours to administer, and the administration of the ACAT-P ranges from 48 to 120 minutes. However, the shorter ACAT-P administration time results in fewer content areas (e.g., only four in 48 minutes) being assessed. More importantly, although these national tests have been designed to test basic psychology knowledge on content areas typically found in undergraduate psychology programs, the test may not be an especially good fit for the local curriculum. The national test can either omit a specific area that a local curriculum emphasizes or may include a sub-area that the local curriculum does not cover. Consequently, the results can underestimate student achievement. Although the psychology department can disregard the exam results from the sub-area not deemed relevant, an ill-fitting assessment wastes student time and department resources.

DEVELOPING A LOCAL COMPREHENSIVE ASSESSMENT

Faculty in many departments have collaborated to produce their own exams as a way of generating an assessment well-tailored to their curriculum. As we have learned all too well, LCEs demand a large investment of time from faculty, may take years to develop, and do not allow comparisons with other institutions. Item selection, exam administration, performance expectations, and psychometric properties must be considered. However, because LCEs are customized to the curriculum and student learning goals of a specific department, they can provide information on outcomes particularly relevant to student learning experiences. As such, the test provides outcomes that allow for detailed local curriculum review and evaluation. These local tests are also much less financially costly (though *not* cost free) than adopting a nationally developed exam because local resources are being tapped. For instance, test items can come from the instructors themselves or from members of a department's assessment committee.

Identifying Relevant Domains

A general issue to consider when developing a local test is its compatibility with local university standards (e.g., writing across the curriculum) and national standards in the discipline. Relevant national guidelines have been established by the American Psychological Association (APA; 2002a, 2002b) and are reflected in national comprehensive exams such as the MFT and the ACAT-P discussed above, as well as the Advanced Placement (AP) examination in psychology (College Board, 1999, 2002). These standards can serve as useful guides when developing local tests. Individual psychology departments vary in the knowledge areas emphasized in their curriculum, and the content of an LCE should reflect this distinction. The test can assess not only learning of content material, but also abilities such as critical thinking and practical application of knowledge. Compatibility between standards and local tests is important because the goal of the comprehensive exam is not solely to assess individual student learning, but also to evaluate how well the department is meeting its stated goals and objectives in educating psychology majors. However, the comprehensive exam is typically not the only assessment measure of student learning (e.g., portfolio assessments); thus it is not necessary that every stated objective be measured.

Prior to the development of our LCE, we identified three general learning goals and specific learning objectives that correspond with guidelines outlined by APA: (a) *psychology knowledge*: students will have a clear understanding of psychological theories, methodologies and empirical findings for studying behavior, and socio-emotional, cognitive, and physiological processes; (b) *computer skills*: students will acquire analytic skills in the use of current computer technology for the collection, statistical analysis, and interpretation of research data; and (c) *research and communication skills*: student will acquire research and oral communication skills appropriate for the discipline. We use our LCE primarily to assess our first student learning goal, psychology knowledge; therefore it was critical for us to identify the domains to be assessed before the actual construction of our LCE.

Several sources are available for identifying domain areas to be assessed (see Table 11.2). The APA (2002a) national goals and outcomes for undergraduate psychology curricula are categorized into two broad areas: (a) knowl-

TABLE 11.2
Knowledge Domains in Psychology

Domain	APA[a]	MFT[b]	ACAT-P[c]	AP Exam[d]	EIU Exam[e]
History & systems			X	X	
Methods					
Research methods	X	X		X	X
Experimental design			X		
Statistics			X		X
Measurement		X			
Biopsychological					
Biological bases of behavior	X		X		X
Physiological					
Animal learning			X		
Sensation & perception	X	X		X	X
Motivation & emotion	X			X	
Stress, coping, & health	X				
Cognition	X		X	X	X
Learning	X		X	X	X
Memory	X	X			
Thinking & knowledge	X	X			
States of consciousness				X	
Developmental	X	X	X	X	X
Lifespan development	X				X
Sociocultural					
Individual differences	X			X	
Personality & assessment	X		X	X	X
Psychological disorders/ abnormal	X	X	X	X	X
Treatment of psychological disorders	X			X	
Clinical/counseling		X	X		
Social psychology			X	X	X
Social and cultural dimensions of behavior	X				

[a]Domains identified by APA for high school standards.
[b]Major Fields Test in psychology.
[c]Area Concentration Achievement Test in psychology.
[d]ETS Advanced Placement Exam in psychology.
[e]The local comprehensive exam developed by the Psychology Department at Eastern Illinois University.

edge, skills, and values consistent with the science and application of psychology and (b) knowledge, skills, and values consistent with liberal arts education that are further developed in psychology. For the first broad area, more specific guidelines include knowledge of theory and content, research methods, critical thinking skills, application, and values. The APA standards also indicate the importance of non-content-specific information for students to learn how "to reject simplistic explanations of behavior in favor of richer, more complex approaches." Another source to which psychology departments may refer are the five broad content areas identified by APA that serve as guidelines for high school psychology courses (APA, 2002b; see Table 11.2). These general areas are Methods, Biopsychological, Cognitive, Developmental, and Sociocultural, which, in turn, contain more specific areas such as research methods, learning, and personality development.

Although general domains have been identified by APA, individual departments may differ in the specific content areas they adopt. For example, the California State University Psychology faculty (Allen, Noel, & Deegan, 2000) emphasize the importance of students demonstrating knowledge in multiple areas including: research methodology, learning, perception and cognition, personality and social processes, biological and physiological bases of behavior, lifespan development, the history and systems of psychology, individual differences, psychological tests and measurements, abnormal behavior, and at least one applied area of psychology (e.g., industrial/organizational). In addition, students should be able to distinguish between major theoretical approaches (biological, psychoanalytic, cognitive, behavioral, humanistic, social, and developmental).

In our department, all psychology majors are required to complete introductory psychology, statistics, and research methods; they also have to select one or two courses from each of 4 required "groups": (a) a cognitive/learning group (learning and cognitive), (b) a biopsychological group (physiological, sensation and perception), (c) an abnormal/social group (personality, abnormal, and social psychology), and (d) a developmental group (child psychology, adolescence, and adult development). Students also have to complete a variety of elective courses. However, the decision of the assessment committee and department was that the comprehensive test should only assess the domains all students are required to take and not the elective courses. We also strongly focused our efforts on the domains themselves rather than on individual courses.

After determining what the domains are at the national or local level, several questions remain before beginning exam construction. For one, will the choice of domains to be covered on the LCE be decided by the entire faculty, the departmental assessment committee, or the department chair? Faculty may have differing opinions as to which domains should be included as well as the weighting of the content areas. Although the degree of individual faculty input may vary depending on the size of the department, it is important to have faculty input on the content areas to be assessed prior to construction of the exam. Our department decided by faculty consensus to use the domains that had been established by the department curriculum committee (see Table 11.2) as the starting place for constructing an initial comprehensive exam. The issue of domain weighting, or how many questions to devote to each domain, can be more problematic and will be discussed in greater detail below.

Developing Exam Items

Exam item construction can be an intimidating process for some of us. In fact, a major hesitancy for developing LCEs may be the belief that we cannot achieve the same level of quality as the national tests. It should be kept in mind, however, that the exam items on the national exams are often derived from questions contributed by faculty members. When it comes to selecting items for an LCE, questions can come from faculty members themselves, textbook test banks, released AP exams (College Board, 1999), and even published Psychology GRE items. These questions may be used either in their entirety or as a starting point for later editing.

In the process of developing exam items, several issues will arise that require consideration. For instance, maintaining consistent levels of difficulty among exam items will be important; this is especially true when individual faculty are asked to contribute exam items. Individual faculty may have different views of how hard items should be, and they will most certainly write items in different voices. We have anecdotal evidence of students reporting that they could tell which faculty had written particular exam items because of the wording used, which would have given some students an advantage over others. The overall difficulty of the items should be determined based on the level of proficiency required for each learning objective the exam is designed to address. Items should be constructed at a level of difficulty that distinguishes students who have not achieved learning objectives from those who have (Nitko, 2001).

How many items will represent each of the learning objectives and/or knowledge domains being tested? One approach could be an even distribution of items per objective or knowledge domain; another approach is to have different numbers of items for the various domains assessed by the exam. The critical factor is that the domain weights appropriately reflect the curriculum, distinguishing required courses from electives. The latter approach was more applicable in our situation, in which only a small number of courses (i.e., statistics and research methods) are taken by *all* of our majors; consequently, our exam includes twice as many statistics and research methods items (20) as any other content area (10 items).

The department must decide whether the exam will be composed of open-ended (e.g., essays) or close-ended (e.g., multiple-choice, true/false, fill-in-the-blank, matching) items, as well as proportions of applied/conceptual and factual items. Which item types are selected should primarily be determined by the learning objectives targeted to be assessed by the exam. Practical considerations, such as the time allotted to students to complete the exam, will also play a major role in shaping the total number and types of items on the exam. For instance, if the exam will be administered during a regular 50-minute class session, a 20- or 30-item essay exam will be impossible for students to complete. We have limited our exam to multiple-choice items, and have found 70 items to be a maximum number for students to complete during a 50-minute class session.

Administering the Exam

In most cases, graduating seniors will be selected to take the exam toward the end of their final semester in the department. Administering the exam in a pre- and posttest design, where beginning students (e.g., Introductory Psychology) take the pretest and then take it again as seniors just before they graduate should also be considered. This approach will generate data that will give a clearer picture of student learning as a consequence of going through the department's curriculum—the so called "value added" approach (see chap. 1, this volume). A pre- and posttest administration is particularly recommended with LCEs because national norms are not available. Unfortunately, such administration raises a number of practical concerns that need to be addressed, such as record keeping and how to deal with transfer students who may have taken psychology courses elsewhere. Time and money constraints will also play a role in determining whether all students or only a random sample will take the exam. Currently, we are administering the exam to most introductory psychology students as a pretest, and to graduating seniors as a posttest.

If a "capstone" course taken by all seniors is available in your department, it will probably be explored as the primary avenue for administering the exam. We have found it very difficult to entice students to take the exam when it is neither a course or graduation requirement—pizza, prizes, and promises of enduring gratitude have not been sufficient. In discussions with our seniors about their reluctance to take the exam, one comment recurs: "What if I don't do well?" Even after repeatedly assuring them that the exam assesses the department, *not* individual student performance, some students continue to be especially concerned about embarrassing themselves with a poor performance. In our experience, anonymity was not possible because of our implementation of a longitudinal pre- and posttest design. Consequently, we highly recommend that taking the exam be made a graduation requirement in such cases. Administration of a pretest, of course, has its own challenges. Students may not take the test seriously and faculty may be reluctant to give up class time for exam administration.

Establishing specific performance standards is another issue. A primary reason for the reluctance of many departments to use nationally developed tests is that performance requirements vary dramatically among those employing the exams. Presumably, students will be more motivated to perform well on the exam if they must achieve a certain score to graduate. Unfortunately, such requirements are sure to also generate hostility on the part of students. Provisions also need to be put in place if students must perform at a specific level to pass or graduate—what happens to those students who "fail" the test? In such instances, the exam will have to be administered with sufficient time for re-takes or other compensatory measures to be completed. Rather than employ performance standards, we address motivation issues by limiting test duration, providing individual score reports to students, and offering to mention good exam performance in letters of recommendation.

USING THE EXAM RESULTS

Exam analysis and reporting typically revolve around a number of issues. Decisions will have to be made about who will analyze and report the outcomes, as well as establishing the audience for the report. Additional thought also needs to be given to the kinds of scores generated and how those scores will be interpreted.

Analyzing the Exam

It is often those who have been given the task of putting together the LCE who are also responsible for analyzing and reporting the exam results. In many cases, including our own, these may be the members of the psychology department's assessment committee. Nonetheless, it may also be fruitful to consult other faculty members and the department chair as to what kinds of information they would like to receive.

There are three potential recipients of the exam outcomes: the students, the faculty, and institutional administrators (including the department chairperson). Knowing whom the audience will be matters because it determines the kinds of reports that should be generated. For instance, administrators are particularly interested in trends and are less knowledgeable about the intricacies of statistical significance testing. When administrators are the intended audience, therefore, reports of the percentages of students who perform at certain levels will be more useful than statistical analyses. In the next section, we outline some of the various kinds of reports that can be delivered.

Another important issue is whether individual reports will be provided for the students. When this option is available and students expect a report of their exam performance, then extra effort will have to be made to acquaint the students with the meaning of the results. In most cases, students can be apprised about their strengths and areas for improvement during their scheduled advising sessions. Providing feedback to individual students increases motivation for and interest in the LCE.

A primary goal of any locally developed psychology comprehensive exam is to provide an instrument that measures basic factual knowledge in psychology that a student is expected to have mastered by completing the department's undergraduate psychology program. As such, it is important to make sure that the instrument is doing what it is supposed to do. Can the developed exam really measure knowledge that was gained from completing an undergraduate psychology program? A comparison of scores between those who had and who had not completed the coursework in psychology can be performed. When feasible, a comparison of scores obtained at pretest with those from the posttest can also be conducted, especially if the same people have taken both pretest and posttest. This longitudinal pre- and posttest approach is what we have adopted in our department; we believe that it will yield the kinds of data about student learning we are trying to assess. It is important to recognize that the process will take several years to complete, and it is critical that both faculty and administrators understand the process and are willing to be patient with this part of the department's assessment program.

Reliability estimates can also be obtained by standard reliability testing approaches such as test–retests, alternative-forms, and split-halves (Carmines & Zeller, 1979). However, one has to be aware of the strengths and weaknesses of these estimates. Test–retest methods are problematic because first testing experiences often influence performance in the second testing. With the split-halves approach, the obtained correlation between halves is often different and it depends on how the halves were created. There is also the difficulty of constructing an alternative form of the locally developed exam. Nonetheless, we have carried out split-halves reliability estimates for each domain tested on our LCE because the ordering of questions within each domain was not systematic. The average split-half correlation for the domains tested on our first LCE was a disappointing .23; subsequent exam item revisions have shown steadily rising correlations across domains, and have been as high as .91 in one domain.

Communicating the Results

Total, as well as sub-area, scores for individual students and for the entire group can be obtained from LCEs. For descriptive purposes, the means and standard deviations of these scores can be reported. Another option is to present the total percent correct as well as the sub-area percent correct. The latter is often easier for nonscientific audiences to understand, especially if they are not well acquainted with statistical reporting. For comparative purposes, pretest and posttest differences on the total and each of the sub-area scores can be presented. This is a measure of knowledge gain. How the students performed in one sub-area relative to another can also be examined by looking at sub-area performance differences. In both comparison assessments, statistical significance testing can be conducted.

Refining the Curriculum

We previously discussed the importance of relating the comprehensive exam to the learning goals and objectives of the department. Review of the comprehensive exam results should enable departments to identify goals and objectives that may have to be modified or, perhaps more importantly, those that are not being adequately met. Analysis of how exam results relate to the stated goals and objectives will also allow for reexamination of the local curriculum itself. For example, the exam results showing that students are not demonstrating adequate knowledge of information in a particular domain or content area may suggest weaknesses in the curriculum. Identifying deficits in student learning may result in conflict or defensiveness on the part of colleagues, especially if only certain faculty teach courses in these domain areas. Therefore, it is critical that this examination of the LCE results be done with full faculty involvement. We suggest that, whenever possible, the focus of assessment be directed toward learning of domain knowledge and not learning of individual course content. The fact is that in most departments domain topics are covered in a variety of courses (e.g., physiological processes are presented not only in biopsychology courses, but also in abnormal and developmental psychology). Additionally, low student scores in a domain area may reflect poor exam items rather than curricular problems with instruction in that domain.

IMPROVING THE EXAM

Postadministration uses of the comprehensive exam should not be overlooked. One important use of the data will be to identify potential ways to improve the LCE for future administrations. Based on our experiences, we would expect that the initial exam will have to undergo modifications after analysis of the results, and a final comprehensive exam will likely take several semesters to develop. In this development process, decisions will have to be made as to which items to omit or to add. Before doing so, it is important that some thought be put into the criteria upon which these decisions are based. Additionally, as with other decision points (see Table 11.1), the department will need to determine whether these changes will be made with the input of all faculty members, only by the assessment committee members, or by some previously established objective criteria (e.g., an item might be deleted from the exam if more than 90% of all respondents, seniors and beginning students, answered the item correctly or incorrectly). Those items that did not discriminate between the best and worst performers on the exam and items that, on second perusal, were poorly worded may also be re-evaluated.

As discussed above, it is also important to consider the general properties of the exam, such as validity and reliability (Nunnally, 1967). This information will further assist in improving the usefulness of the comprehensive exam as an assessment tool. For example, further analyses could be conducted to assess the concurrent or predictive validity of the test. The latter is especially important if the test is, over time, given to first-year students and all psychology department graduating seniors. This would allow departments to compare not only a student's performance from prepsychology to graduation, but to also assess whether test results correlate with variables such as students' performance in psychology courses, overall university courses (GPA), college completion, or admission to graduate schools.

CONCLUSIONS

It is our hope that sharing the experiences we have had in developing the local comprehensive exam at EIU will motivate other departments to do the same. The actual steps we have outlined above in developing, administering, and using the results from our locally developed test (see also Table 11.1) have yielded several unintended benefits. For one thing, developing our own LCE has afforded us greater flexibility in budgeting our assessment expenditures. Furthermore, because the LCE is more directly linked to our curriculum and made use of input from all faculty, it generated more interest among faculty than did our trial use of the ACAT-P. Specifically, faculty were less dismissive of the results due to having had input in the construction of the LCE. Another unintended advantage of developing our own LCE was that it required the assessment committee and faculty as a whole to critically address more global assessment areas in the department. For example, prior to developing the LCE itself, the learning goals and objectives of our department first had to be revisited and the curriculum had to be reviewed to aid in identifying relevant domains. As mentioned earlier, examining the LCE results necessitated a "hard look" at other curricular issues such as areas of deficiency in student learning. At each decision point (see Table 11.1) the faculty as a whole was consulted and, due primarily to the local nature of the test, an intrinsic interest and motivation in participating in the process arose. Such interest and cooperation from faculty facilitated the development of other direct and indirect assessment measures. Finally, given the importance of faculty input at multiple levels in the process of developing and using a local comprehensive exam, it is our strong recommendation that departments consider holding an assessment retreat in which more thoughtful consideration can be given to the issues outlined above (at EIU, we are in the process of developing such a retreat). Although development of a local comprehensive exam can be a lengthy and difficult process, there are multiple benefits that make the effort worthwhile.

REFERENCES

Allen, M. J., Noel, R., & Deegan, J. (2000). *Goals and objectives for the undergraduate psychology major: Recommendations from a meeting of California State University psychology faculty.* Retrieved December 15, 2003, from Office of Teaching Resources in Psychology Web site: http://www.lemoyne.edu/OTRP/teachingresources.html#outcomes

American Psychological Association. (2002a). *National guidelines and suggested learning outcomes for the undergraduate psychology major.* Retrieved December 15, 2003, from http://www.apa.org/ed/ resources.html

American Psychological Association. (2002b). *National standards for the teaching of high school psychology.* Retrieved December 15, 2003, from http://www.apa.org/ ed/hsstructure.html

Carmines, E. G., & Zeller, R. A. (1979). *Reliability and validity assessment.* London: Sage Publications.

College Board. (1999). *Released exam: AP psychology.* New York: College Entrance Examination Board.

College Board. (2002). *Course description: Psychology advanced placement exam.* New York: College Entrance Examination Board.

Educational Testing Services. (2003). *Major Field Tests.* Retrieved December 15, 2003, from www.ets.org/hea/mft/index.html

Fleming, S., & Golden, A. (1997, May). *Gender differences in research methods across disciplines.* Poster session presented at the meeting of the American Psychological Society, Washington, DC.

Golden, A. (1997). *Project for Area Concentration Achievement Testing.* Washington, DC: Fund for the Improvement of Postsecondary Education. (ERIC Document Reproduction Service No. ED 416212)

Lopez, C. L. (1996). *Opportunities for improvement: Advice from consultant-evaluators on programs to assess student learning.* Presented at the 102nd Annual Meeting of the North Central Association of Colleges and Schools, Commission on Institutions of Higher Education. [Reprint April, 1997] Retrieved December 30, 2003, from http://www.ncacihe.org/resources/assessment/97ASSESS.pdf

Lopez, C. L. (2000). *Measures, methods, results, and national initiatives.* Presented at the 2nd Annual Consortium for Assessment and Planning Support Conference, Terre Haute, IN. April 2000. Retrieved December 30, 2003, from http:// web.indstate.edu/oirt/caps/pdf/lopezwhp.pdf

Markus, T., Mukina, S., & Golden, A. (1998, June). *Significant psychology score increases from pretest to posttest across the major.* Poster session presented at the meeting of the American Psychological Society, Washington, DC.

Nitko, A. J. (2001). *Educational assessment of students* (3rd ed.). Upper Saddle River, NJ: Prentice Hall.

Noble, J. H., & Stretch, J. J. (2002). Grade-induced beliefs about undergraduate generalist social work practice competency. *Evaluation Review, 26,* 213–236.

Norcross, J. C., Gerrity, D. M., & Hogan, E. M. (1993). Some outcomes and lessons from a cross-sectional evaluation of psychology undergraduates. *Teaching of Psychology, 20,* 93–96.

Nunnally, J. C. (1967). *Psychometric theory.* New York: McGraw-Hill.

PACAT, Inc. (2003). *The ACATs.* Retrieved December 30, 2003, from http:// www.collegeoutcomes.com/ACATS/psych.htm

Stoloff, M. L., & Feeney, K. J. (2002). The Major Field Test as an assessment tool for an undergraduate psychology program. *Teaching of Psychology, 29,* 92–98.

12

ASSESSING DISTANCE-LEARNING STUDENTS AND COURSES

CHANDRA M. MEHROTRA, KENNETH A. WEAVER, AND PAUL NELSON

Distance learning means different things to different people and organizations. Fundamentally, distance learning is education delivered over a distance to one or more individuals located in one or more venues. Distance learning is not new, but advances in information technology, and particularly the Internet, have profoundly altered its character and have stimulated the development of new and richer models of providing instruction. Sensing an opportunity to use technology to reach geographically dispersed adult learners and supplement flagging tuition revenues, many educational institutions have expanded their missions to include distance education. Indeed, distance learning has undergone dramatic growth in the past five years. According to one estimate, more than 50,000 distance courses served more than 1.5 million students in the academic year 1997–1998 (Lewis, Snow, & Farris, 1999). Indications are that these numbers will continue to increase (Phipps, 2002).

Distance learning has also created new challenges and opportunities in the area of assessment. Accrediting agencies, employers, legislators, prospective students, the public, and the educators themselves are all asking assessment-related questions such as:

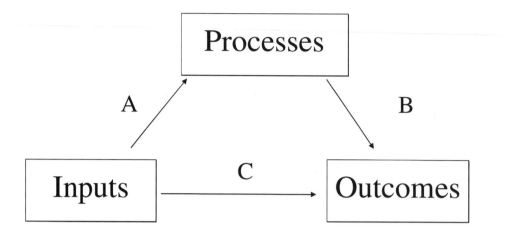

Figure 12.1. The I-P-O Model.

1. How can an institution ensure the quality of its distance courses?
2. What safeguards should be employed to sustain integrity and deter potential abuses?
3. How can institutions document the extent to which students achieve the expected outcomes?

Within the framework of these questions, this chapter addresses the assessment of distance-learning outcomes for students and individual courses. Our strategy is guided by Astin's (1991) Input–Process–Outcome (I-P-0) Model. Throughout the discussion, we address the three questions outlined above. Astin proposed that, regardless of the mode of instructional delivery, evaluation of students and courses is incomplete unless it includes data on inputs, learning processes, and expected outcomes (see Figure 12.1).

1. *Inputs* refer to characteristics of learners, course design, and instructional resources.

2. *Processes* represent what the learners actually do; their interaction with the instructor, with each other, and with the course content.

3. *Outcomes* refer to the changes in students' knowledge and skills the course aims to foster.

Although assessment has traditionally focused on the relationship between processes and outcomes, Astin indicates that this relationship cannot be understood without taking into account the inputs, which may be related to both outcomes (see Arrow C in Figure 12.1) and processes (see Arrow A in Figure 12.1). In other words, inputs affect the observed relationships between the processes and the outcomes and should be integral to the assess-

EXHIBIT 12.1
Inputs: Student Characteristics

1. What are students' learning styles?
2. What is their experience with technology?
3. What is their level of self-motivation?
4. What is their work experience?
5. What are their attitudes toward distance learning?
6. How did they perform on the pretest?
7. What are their grade point averages?

Assessment Methods: Application forms; application essays; attitude scales; measures of learning styles; and achievement tests.

---

ment efforts. Including an examination of inputs and processes better enables us to: (a) interpret outcome data; (b) help understand for whom the given mode of delivery works and for whom it does not; and (c) make needed improvements. In addition, assessment of inputs and processes provides useful information for dissemination of an effective design, thereby facilitating its use by others (Phipps & Merisotis, 1999).

Principles underlying useful evaluations of distance courses are not fundamentally different from those used in assessing on-campus offerings. However, the mode of delivery affects how instructors operationalize these principles, what aspects of the I-P-O model they evaluate, and how and when they collect the needed information.

In the following sections we focus on what methods may be used in assessing each component of the model, what is distinctive about assessment of distance learning, and how to address the questions outlined earlier. For each component we present the rationale, outline key questions, and provide examples of assessment methods useful in the context of distance learning.

INPUTS

Examination of inputs focuses on two key areas: characteristics of students and features of course design and resources. We have outlined key questions in Exhibit 12.1. In addition, we have also included examples of methods that may be used to collect the needed information in distance courses.

Student Characteristics

Since distance learning attempts to make post-secondary education accessible, it is reasonable to expect that distance-learning students come from geographically dispersed communities and represent a broad spectrum of backgrounds (Weaver, 2001). Our experience indicates that distance students are predominantly adult learners who bring a wide range of life experiences to the course. They appreciate opportunities to relate course content to their personal experiences and prior knowledge. Although this diversity of perspectives enriches the understanding and application of material, it may necessitate using a variety of instructional strategies and assessment approaches to facilitate and demonstrate student learning. Indeed, successful distance courses center around the student who is considered a client of the organization (Phipps, Wellman, & Merisotis, 1998; Simonson, Smaldino, Albright, & Zvacek, 2000). According to Simonson et al. (2000) "the more the distance education teacher knows about individual students, the more elegant the application of education tools to the learning situation" (p. 131). This means that before beginning the course an effective instructor collects information about student characteristics such as work experience, attitudes towards distance learning, grade-point average in relevant courses, performance on a pretest, experience with technology, learning styles, and level of motivation (see Exhibit 12.1). Sharing this information with students in the class (consistent with relevant privacy guidelines) helps familiarize them with one another and facilitates creating a learning community (Palloff & Pratt, 1999).

Course Characteristics

Distance courses vary considerably. Therefore, a detailed description of their characteristics, such as intended outcomes, learning design, technology delivery mode, learner support, and assessment procedures can clarify these differences. Exhibit 12.2 includes examples of questions useful in evaluating course or program characteristics. Describing course characteristics in some detail is useful both for current and prospective students. For example, before distance students enroll in a course, they presumably would like to have detailed information about the course outcomes, the delivery mode, the computer equipment, and the expectations regarding the level of interaction with classmates and instructors. In addition, they would appreciate knowing what assessment procedures will be used, and what support services will be available. In keeping with the self-directed and self-paced nature of distance learning, it is also useful to include due dates for assignments, projects, examinations, and other course responsibilities.

What approaches do we recommend for assessing these characteristics for distance courses? One possible approach is to institute a peer review process using the *Distance Learning Evaluation Guide* developed by the American Council on Education (1996). This *Guide* provides the reviewers with a checklist of questions in seven categories: learning design, learning objectives and learning outcomes, learning materials, technology, learner support, and the course content and outcomes. The reviewers examine the course materials and conduct interviews with students and those responsible for designing and offering the course. Based upon this information, they rate a given

EXHIBIT 12.2
Inputs: Course Characteristics

1. What are the expected outcomes?
2. Is the learning design shaped to achieve the intended outcomes?
3. Are instructional materials appropriate for distance study?
4. What delivery modes will be used?
5. What are the expectations regarding levels of participation?
6. Is the reading level keyed to the reading competence of the average participant?
7. Is the study guide easy to understand?
8. Is the learning experience organized to increase learner control over time, place, and pace of instruction?
9. What learning resources will be available?
10. Are resources accessible?
11. Do the resources accommodate different cognitive styles?
12. Are the students instructed in the proper methods of effective research?
13. What methods of assessment will be used?
14. How frequently will assessment be conducted?
15. To what extent does the course syllabus provide students with needed information?

Assessment Methods: Review by external evaluators who examine course syllabus, study guide, and instructional materials and conduct interviews with students, program designers, and instructors.

---

course in each of the seven categories as "meets the evaluation criteria," "partially meets the evaluation criteria," or "does not meet the evaluation criteria." In addition, the reviewers may provide friendly suggestions for course improvement.

Another possibility is to use the benchmarks considered essential to the quality of distance education courses (Phipps & Merisotis, 2000). These benchmarks represent the following categories: institutional support, course development, teaching–learning process, course structure, student support, faculty support, and evaluation and assessment. Some examples of benchmarks include: course design includes a variety of methods to facilitate student interaction with faculty; each module or segment requires students to engage themselves in analysis, synthesis, and evaluation as part of their course assignments; sufficient library resources are available to the students; students can get help in using electronically accessed data successfully; and faculty provide feedback to students in a constructive and nonthreatening manner. Phipps & Merisotis suggest that the reviewers use a seven-point Likert scale to rate each benchmark on two criteria: First, to what extent is the benchmark true for the course (rated from 1 = *completely absent* to 7 = *completely present*)? Second, how important is the benchmark to ensuring quality (rated from 1 = *not important* to 7 = *very important*)? The readers may adapt the above approaches and design a review process that would be helpful in making reasonable and informed judgments about their own distance courses.

When the goal is to contrast the effects of different formats of distance-learning and on-campus courses, reviewers should collect data on both student characteristics and course characteristics for the formats under consideration. Thus, data collection methods should have the sensitivity to capture the key features of all formats under consideration and the specific characteristics of the students they serve. This information is useful in interpreting outcome data and in identifying similarities and differences across courses.

PROCESSES

Learning Processes

The assessment of teaching–learning processes aims to ascertain implementation of practices and activities the instructor has outlined in the syllabus. Exhibit 12.3 presents examples of questions that should be addressed in conducting assessment of the processes. The emphasis in this phase is on what the instructors and the learners actually do, how often they do it, and how well they do it. Monitoring such interactions provides an indication of the effectiveness of the course in creating a community of learners and keeping the students moving forward and staying productive (Grubb & Hines, 2000).

An important way of monitoring the processes through time is to develop a management information system (MIS). This approach provides continuing data in areas such as frequency of students' participation in each of the activities, their use of library or other support services, and their interaction with each other and with the instructor via chat rooms and electronic mailing lists. Another approach is to use software such as WebCT and Blackboard to track students' participation in the activities the instructor has included in the syllabus. For assessment purposes, instructor may also use frequency of student participation as the basis for the grade.

Instructors of distance courses often ask students to keep a log or journal with the goal of stimulating them to note their reactions, questions, comments, criticisms and insights. Given the personal nature of the writing and the variability in the content that students focus on, many instructors do not grade journals. Instead they allocate a specific number of points for writing in the journal. Examining student journals for the course can provide unique insights into learning processes of students from different segments of the population.

Conducting a content analysis of e-mail messages students send to the instructors and support staff also provides valuable information on what the students are experiencing and what changes and adjustments would make the course more effective. When the analysis includes using messages from the Help Desk or other support personnel, the instructor needs to obtain prior permission from the students. As Harasim, Hiltz, Turoff, and Teles (1995) suggest, meaningful categories should be devised in advance to separate po-

EXHIBIT 12.3
Processes

1. What activities did the students actually undertake?
2. How does the nature and frequency of participation compare with what was expected?
3. How often did the students interact with each other and with the instructor?
4. What is the total number of messages the instructor answered in the course under review?
5. How often did the instructor respond to messages he/she receives from individual students?
6. Was access to technical support readily available? How often was the support actually used?
7. How do the students experience and perceive the program?
8. What methods were used to provide feedback to students?
9. Was feedback provided in a timely manner?
10. Were the library and other learning resources used appropriately by the students?
11. What strategies were used to promote the development of a community of learners?
12. How effective were these strategies?
13. What methods were used to ensure the integrity of student work?
14. What approaches were used to communicate assessment results to students?

Assessment Methods: Review of students' assignments, records of students' participation in online discussion, student journals, correspondence between students and the instructor, examples of checks regarding plagiarism, and documentation regarding use of support services.

---

tentially relevant communications as they arrive. This allows data classification and filing on a continuing basis.

Ensuring Integrity

Distance learning also influences how instructors promote integrity. Is the student actually doing the work? Is the work being done under the conditions specified by the instructor? One possible solution to academic dishonesty is to reduce the need and desire to cheat. When the instructor gets to know the student better through continuing communication and creates a desirable, exciting learning environment, students want to achieve the course outcomes without cheating (Hudspeth, 1999). Furthermore, having communicated with the students throughout the course, the instructor can easily recognize when the voice in a paper or an essay examination is markedly different from the e-mail correspondence. Under some circumstances, however, it may still be necessary to ensure integrity by incorporating appropriate safeguards for monitoring participation, protecting assessment instruments, and proctoring the exams.[1]

---

[1] Harris (2002) provides a variety of excellent strategies for preventing and detecting plagiarism. In addition, a number of useful online sites are available to support the instructor's attempt to detect plagiarism. Examples include: www.plagiarism.phys.virginia.edu, www.turnitin.com, www.plagiarism.com, and www.wordchecksystems.com

The widespread availability of class notes and course-related material on the World Wide Web suggests that instructors should pay special attention to plagiarism, as well (Gibelman, Gelman, & Fast, 1999). We have found it useful to include in the course syllabus a policy regarding cheating and plagiarism. Explaining what plagiarism is and emphasizing that it is a serious offense may not only prevent students from committing unintentional plagiarism but also deter the intentional plagiarists. Furthermore, advising students that the instructor routinely checks for plagiarism also serves as an important deterrent; its goal is to ensure that students do their work, not to trap them.

In summary, multiple assessment methods create a developmental picture of how the course engages students in the learning process, whether they act with integrity, how frequently they interact with each other and with the instructor, and what difficulties they encounter and how they resolve them. Preparing a detailed explanation of the processes helps in making course modifications and adjustments and in understanding students' progress in achieving the learning outcomes. In the next section, we devote our attention to a discussion of assessing learning outcomes.

STUDENT OUTCOMES

Outcomes refer to those aspects of students' development that the course does influence or attempts to influence. Examples of outcomes include student learning, student retention, and student satisfaction. Exhibit 12.4 presents key questions for each of the three areas and provides examples of assessment methods that may be used to collect data for each outcome. Additional comments about each of these areas follow.

Student Learning

Given limited face-to-face interactions in many distance programs, conducting ongoing assessment of student learning serves valuable purposes for both instructors and students. For instructors, it provides information on student progress and allows them to determine the degree to which students are achieving the intended outcomes. For students, ongoing assessment of learning provides benchmarks for monitoring their progress and adjusting their learning strategies. This perspective implies that instructors design and use assessment methods that are embedded in the curriculum and are, therefore, administered on a continuing basis. These methods may include (a) self-check quizzes presented online, in print materials, and in videotaped presentations; (b) comprehension tests included at the end of sections within a topic area; and (c) application exercises, case studies, or simulations that are embedded at various points in the instructional materials and invite the students to apply their newly acquired knowledge and understanding. In-

EXHIBIT 12.4
Outcomes

Student Learning
To what extent has the student achieved intended learning outcomes such as:
1. Knowledge
2. Comprehension
3. Application
4. Analysis
5. Synthesis
6. Evaluation

Assessment Methods: Achievement tests, student portfolios, and participation in online discussions.

Student Retention
1. What percentage of students drop out of the course?
2. How do these students differ from those who complete the course?

Assessment Methods: Course records and follow-up surveys of dropouts.

Student Evaluation
1. What do learners say about the course?
2. What is their level of satisfaction with the course?
3. What do they cite as major strengths and weaknesses?

Assessment Methods: Course evaluation forms and follow-up surveys.

---

structors may creatively use available software to administer assessment measures and to provide immediate feedback, thus creating milestones of accomplishment that help the distance students grow toward the expected outcomes. Providing students with continuing opportunities to monitor their learning and to assess whether the assigned activity is working has the potential to stimulate student-to-student and student-to-teacher interactions (Mehrotra & Fried, 2002).

Another option is to divide the distance course into learning modules and to include self-administered tests with each module. Students take these tests immediately after completing a given module to assess their mastery of the material. Available technology such as WebCT then evaluates students' responses and determines which module they should take next. In a way, this design of instruction and assessment is similar to what has been traditionally used in branched approaches to programmed learning and takes into account individual differences in students' ability to learn (Mehrotra, Hollister, & McGahey, 2001). It allows students to advance to a more difficult section of the material, skipping some modules if they demonstrate mastery of the essentials of the topic at hand. If the students' mistakes indicate poor progress in learning the material, they can be directed to a different presentation of the same material for remedial assistance. Available technology records and analyzes students' responses automatically, provides immediate feedback on their progress, offers relevant suggestions, and guides them to the next module.

Instructors in distance courses should consider a variety of technologies and media to administer assessment instruments, to obtain students' responses, and to provide feedback. For example, they may use (a) a course bulletin board to post course assignments and discussion questions; (b) electronic mail and fax to receive student assignments, to communicate grades, and to provide personalized feedback; and (c) videotapes to assess students' oral presentations and counseling skills.

Methods of assessing learning outcomes in distance programs include achievement tests, student portfolios, and participation in online discussions. Although it is beneficial to use multiple methods of assessing student learning outcomes and to administer them throughout the course, this ideal must be balanced against the instructor's workload and available time. Instructors need to plan carefully the number and the schedule of assessment strategies they will use. There may be an advantage in combining some of them or deleting others. As Mehrotra, Hollister, and McGahey (2001) have suggested, distance education instructors must plan ahead, be highly creative and organized, and communicate with students in new ways. Because many useful resources are available regarding assessment methods, the discussion presented below focuses on aspects especially relevant for distance courses.

Achievement Tests

If the institution requires end-of-course exams to determine the extent to which distance students have achieved the outcomes envisioned for the course, we recommend designing several forms of the test and randomly selecting the form for a given student. Another approach is to develop a large pool of questions from which an automated testing program randomly selects the questions for each student. If the students need to complete the test within a specified amount of time, the instructor may use automated testing programs that include this feature.

To ensure integrity, many distance courses require students to take a monitored exam. Consequently, each student is responsible for identifying a qualified person to supervise his or her exam—a staff person in the human resources department, a supervisor, a librarian, a minister, or a rabbi. Instructors send the exam to the proctor with instructions for the maximum time allowed, the period in which the exam is to be given, and any special considerations, such as whether a student may have a calculator or any notes. The proctor signs the exam to certify that it was taken under supervision, puts it in the envelope, and returns it to the instructor or to the distance education office. Our experience indicates that proctors take their responsibilities very seriously and this method in combination with the use equivalent forms of the same test helps ensure integrity.[2]

---

[2]See the Dallas TeleCollege's Web site for an example of proctor protocol at http://ollie.dcccd.edu/Admissions/TestingInfo/sub/proctorInfo.htm

As we have noted earlier, distance courses attract students from diverse backgrounds. Many of them hold day jobs in a variety of settings. Assessment measures can incorporate their work experiences, allowing them to use their personal situations as the basis for demonstrating what they have learned. This approach not only allows them to apply their newly acquired knowledge but also reduces the probability of cheating.

Another possibility is to use computer-adaptive testing (CAT), an approach that has been successfully used by the Educational Testing Service (ETS) to administer admission tests such as the Graduate Record Examination (GRE) and the Graduate Management Admissions Test (GMAT). Typically, a CAT begins with medium difficulty questions but then tailors itself to each student's achievement level. Students who give correct answers automatically receive more difficult questions; conversely, incorrect answers beget easier questions. Because CAT individualizes the test items for each student, this approach minimizes the possibility of cheating. Although this approach has strong potential for use in distance courses, it requires considerable technical support in creating test questions that cover the broad range of skills and knowledge and then establishing their level of difficulty. If a number of institutions are working together to make distance courses available to a large number of students, computer-adaptive tests may be cost-effective for them.

Student Portfolios

Because distance education has the potential to accommodate the special needs, characteristics, and situations of each student, portfolios present a useful assessment technique to document a student's development throughout the course (see chap. 10, this volume). Using computer technology, students develop their electronic folders or portfolios where they store their initial draft, a revision, and the final form of various assignments; their reflection about the work they did; and a discussion of how well their work on each assignment demonstrates progress towards or achievement of course outcomes. During the process of developing their portfolios, students may work together, exchange their drafts electronically, and provide constructive feedback to each other. At several points during the course they may submit their work-in-progress to the instructor, seeking answers to their questions and suggestions for improvement. This continuing interaction among geographically dispersed students reduces the isolation many of them experience and promotes the development of a learning community.

Distance-learning courses may also use portfolios in conjunction with a learning contract defining what the instructor has proposed and what the student has agreed to do. Although the written agreement clearly describes the learning outcomes, it provides considerable flexibility regarding the measures and methods that the student may use to achieve them. Distance students may use a large variety of the learning resources available in their places of employment, in their communities, and via the Internet to achieve the expected outcomes. They then develop portfolios in which they explain how the pieces they have included document the achievement of outcomes stated in the learning contract. This approach to assessment allows the distance students to use local resources, makes learning relevant, and engages them in self-evaluation and reflection.

Class Participation

Many distance courses expect participation in discussion as an important outcome and allocate a portion of the grade for such participation (Stevens-Long & Crowell, 2002). Engaging students in discussing the key topics or issues on a weekly basis helps to develop a group bond and makes each student motivated to do the required work.

In one Web-based course on aging and diversity, the instructor requires that students participate in asynchronous discussion each week (Mehrotra & Fried, 2002). Of the total course grade, 30% depends on students' contribution to the questions or the activity the instructor posts in the course conference area each week. The instructor posts a case study or an issue that challenges students to (a) describe what they have understood and absorbed from the course; (b) apply whatever decision rules seem relevant; (c) analyze the facts; (d) synthesize what has been learned; and (e) evaluate the data for action and implementation (Bloom, 1956). The instructor then monitors the group discussion, reviews the themes that surface, and notes the misconceptions and the difficulties that students may have shown with regard to a given case. Available software allows the instructor to track students' participation in the discussion and keeps records for grading purposes. At the end of the week, the instructor brings closure to the discussion by synthesizing the key points from the discussions and by providing clarification or explanation in areas in which students may have experienced difficulty. Hodges and Saba (2002) describe a similar approach in teaching an online statistics course to graduate students. Brown (2002) describes a course on leadership for mid-career professionals in which she used the case method in online networked classrooms at a distance.

Completion Rate

Concern about the drop-out rate in distance education has prompted an increasing number of programs to use completion rate as an outcome measure (Merisotis, 1999). Because many distance courses provide students with flexibility regarding when they can enter and when they can graduate, completion rate may not be a useful measure. If completion rates are central to the assessment of course outcomes, instructors should consistently report these data in a context that reflects realistic baseline expectations. We recommend that they give careful thought to determine how they will calculate the numbers and rates, how they will use them, and how they will communicate them to potential users.

Instructors may gain some valuable information by comparing the characteristics of students who complete the distance-learning course with those of students who drop out. They may make such comparisons by using archival data from sources such as application materials, records of prior work, the notes and comments they wrote on students' work, records regarding students' interactions with others enrolled in the program, and patterns of resource use. In addition, they may design a short questionnaire and administer it electronically to all or a random sample of students. Software available at www.zoomerang.com ensures respondents' anonymity and also compiles responses. Given the concerns about low return rates for mailed questionnaires, instructors may also conduct phone interviews with a sample of students. We have found that such interviews provide a deeper understanding of selected questions or issues and provide valuable information for course improvement.

Student Satisfaction

Obtaining learners' reactions to and satisfaction with various aspects of the distance course through a survey can improve course design. What course characteristics should the survey include? Biner (2003) has designed a Web course evaluation questionnaire to administer at the end of the course. Available on the Web site (http://www.distance-educator.com/portals/webcourse_eval.html) the survey asks the distance students to rate instruction and instructor characteristics, technology, and course management and coordination. Examples of items include: the clarity with which class assignments were communicated, the timeliness with which papers, tests, and written assignments were graded and returned, the extent to which the instructor made the students feel they were part of the class, the in-person or telephone accessibility of the instructor, the quality of the streaming sound and video when applicable, access to library resources when needed, and the degree to which support was available to help troubleshoot system problems. Instructors may collect such data electronically or via regular mail halfway through the course, at the end of the course, and at the end of the program as a whole. Mehrotra (1996) and Mehrotra and Fried (2002) provide examples of evaluation conducted at the end of distance courses in statistics and adult development, aging, and diversity. Evaluation surveys conducted during the course provide valuable information for midcourse corrections; collecting data at the end of the course allows the learners to reflect upon the course as a whole, to make comparisons with other courses, and to examine the extent to which the course helped them to achieve the intended outcomes.

Assessing students' satisfaction six months to one year after they have graduated from the program can also be beneficial. Such follow-up surveys allow the alumni to reflect on their experience in the program, to make comparisons with graduates of other programs, and to examine the extent to which the program helped them develop knowledge, attitudes, and skills they need to succeed in their work settings (Mehrotra, 1999).

When instructors collect satisfaction data at several points during and after learners' participation in a program, they need to identify when they collected such data, which component was or was not included, and what combination of technologies students experienced. Such identification is critical in light of the evolving nature of many distance education programs and the large number of changes they continue to experience. If the intent is also to track developmental changes in the same participants through time, it is important to include participants' identification information in the satisfaction measures they complete. Tracking such information allows a comparison of the satisfaction level of those who drop out with that of those who graduate (Mehrotra et al., 2001).

Data Interpretation

Interpreting outcome data always involves making some comparisons. Numbers in isolation do not make sense without a frame of reference or basis of comparison (Patton, 1997). What are some possible bases for making useful comparison? The outcomes of a distance-learning course can be compared with the following:

1. The outcomes of similar courses offered on campus and via distance learning.
2. The outcomes of similar courses using different delivery modes.
3. The outcomes of distance courses offered by another institution.
4. The outcomes of the same course offered during the previous year or cycle.
5. The stated goals of the distance course.
6. Standards of minimum acceptability (e.g., basic licensing or accreditation standards).

Regardless of which comparison is made, it is important to conduct data analysis separately for each outcome. Such analysis may reveal significant differences in some outcomes and not in others. For example, in comparing achievement and completion outcomes of a distance course with an on-campus course in statistics, the investigator reported that the grade distributions for the two modes of delivery were similar but the completion rate for an on-campus course was significantly higher than that for the distance course (Mehrotra, 1996).

CONCLUSION

We believe that, given their knowledge of measurement and evaluation and their skills in the use of technology, psychologists have the potential to make valuable contributions by exploring creative approaches to assessment in distance-learning courses. These approaches may focus on unique ways in which distance learning affects students in areas such as (a) communicating in writing; (b) giving and receiving feedback sensitively and effectively; (c) managing time; (d) collaborating effectively; and (e) developing metaskills such as higher order thinking and taking the perspective of others (Lapadat, 2000; Rudestam & Schoenholtz-Read, 2002). In addition, using the three components of the I-P-O model, psychologists may investigate what method of instructional delivery is best for what types of students under what circumstances. This information would be highly useful to institutions interested in using a blend of teaching modalities and methods in ways that match student needs and capacities, thereby creating optimal learning outcomes. Thus, we view assessment not as an academic exercise but as a means of making improvements in pedagogy for distance learning, instructional resources, and student services.

REFERENCES

American Council on Education. (1996). *Distance learning evaluation guide*. Washington, DC: Author.

Astin, A. W. (1991). *Assessment for excellence: The philosophy and practice of assessment and evaluation in higher education*. New York: Macmillan.

Biner, P. (2003). *Distance-Educator.com*. Retrieved March 4, 2003, from http://www.distance-educator.com/portals/webcourse_eval.html

Bloom, B. S. (Ed.). (1956). *Taxonomy of educational objectives: The classification of educational goals: Handbook I: Cognitive domain*. New York: Longmans, Green.

Brown, B. M. (2002). Teaching virtual leadership: Using the case method online. In K. E. Rudestam & J. Schoenholtz-Read (Eds.), *Handbook of online learning: Innovations in higher education and corporate training* (pp. 375–387). Thousand Oaks, CA: Sage.

Dallas TeleCollege. (n.d.). *Proctor info*. Retrieved December 16, 2003, from http://ollie.dcccd.edu/Admissions/TestingInfo/sub/proctorInfo.htm

Gibelman, M., Gelman, S., & Fast, J. (1999, Fall). The downside of cyberspace: Cheating made easy. *Journal of Social Work Education, 35*(3), 367–376.

Grubb, A., & Hines, M. (2000). Tearing down barriers and building communities: Pedagogical strategies for the Web-based environment. In R. A. Cole (Ed.), *Issues in Web-based pedagogy: A critical primer* (pp. 365–380). Westport, CT: Greenwood Press.

Harasim, L. M., Hiltz, R., Turoff, M., & Teles, L. (1995). *Learning networks: A field guide to teaching and learning online*. Cambridge, MA: MIT Press.

Harris, R. (2002, March). Anti-plagiarism strategies for research papers. *Virtual Salt*. Retrieved December 16, 2003, from http://www.virtualsalt.com/antiplag.htm

Hodges, P., & Saba, L. (2002). Teaching statistics online. In K. E. Rudestam & J. Schoenholtz-Read (Eds.), *Handbook of online learning: Innovations in higher education and corporate training* (pp. 389–404). Thousand Oaks, CA: Sage.

Hudspeth, D. (1999). Testing learner outcomes in Web-based instruction. In B. H. Khan (Ed.), *Web-based instruction* (pp. 353–356). Englewood Cliffs, NJ: Educational Technology.

Lapadat, J. C. (2000, May). *Teaching online: Breaking new ground in collaborative thinking.* Paper presented at the annual conference of the Canadian Society for the Study of Education Congress of the Social Sciences and Humanities, Edmonton, Alberta.

Lewis, L., Snow, K., & Farris, E. (1999). Distance education at postsecondary education institutions: 1997–98. U.S. Department of Education, National Center for Education Statistics, *Statistical Analysis Report, NCES 2000-013.*

Mehrotra, C. M. (1996, August). *Providing distance instruction in introductory statistics.* Paper presented at the 104th Annual Convention of the American Psychological Association, Toronto, Canada.

Mehrotra, C. M. (1999, April). Using assessment to strengthen distance learning programs. In S. E. Van Kollenburg (Ed.), *A collection of papers on self-study and institutional improvement* (pp. 64–76). Chicago: North Central Association of Colleges and Schools, Commission on Institutions of Higher Education.

Mehrotra, C. M., & Fried, S. B. (2002). Assessment of an on-line course on adult development, aging, and diversity. *Gerontology and Geriatrics Education, 23*(1), 49–57.

Mehrotra, C. M., Hollister, C. D., & McGahey, L. (2001). *Distance learning: Principles for effective design, delivery, and evaluation.* Thousand Oaks, CA: Sage.

Merisotis, J. P. (1999, September–October). The "what is the difference" debate. *Academe, 85*(5), 47–51.

Palloff, R. M., & Pratt, K. (1999). *Building learning communities in cyberspace: Effective strategies for the online classroom.* San Francisco: Jossey-Bass.

Patton, M. Q. (1997). *Utilization-focused evaluation.* Thousand Oaks, CA: Sage.

Phipps, R. A. (2002, March). *Access to postsecondary education: What is the role of technology?* Washington, DC: Institute for Higher Education Policy.

Phipps, R. A., & Merisotis, J. P. (1999). *What's the difference? A review of contemporary research on the effectiveness of distance learning in higher education.* Retrieved December 16, 2003, from http://www.ihep.com/Pubs/PDF/Difference.pdf

Phipps, R. A., & Merisotis, J. P. (2000). *Quality on the line: Benchmarks for success in Internet-based distance education.* Retrieved December 16, 2003, from http://www.ihep.com/Pubs/PDF/Quality.pdf

Phipps, R. A., Wellman, J. V., & Merisotis, J. P. (1998, April). *Assuring quality in distance learning: A preliminary review.* Washington, DC: Council for Higher Education Accreditation.

Rudestam, K. E., & Schoenholtz-Read, J. (2002). *Handbook of online learning: Innovations in higher education and corporate training.* Thousand Oaks, CA: Sage.

Simonson, M., Smaldino, S., Albright, M., & Zvacek, S. (2000). *Teaching and learning at a distance: Foundations of distance education*. Upper Saddle River, NJ: Merrill.

Stevens-Long, J., & Crowell C. (2002). The design and delivery of interactive online graduate education. In K. E. Rudestam & J. Schoenholtz-Read (Eds.), *Handbook of online learning* (pp.151–169). Thousand Oaks, CA: Sage.

Weaver, K. A. (2001). The challenges of distance education. In S. F. Davis & W. S. Buskist (Eds.), *Teaching of psychology: Essays in honor of Wilbert J. McKeachie and Charles L. Brewer* (pp. 323–333). Mahwah, NJ: Erlbaum.

13

SERVICE LEARNING, RESILIENCE, AND COMMUNITY: THE CHALLENGES OF AUTHENTIC ASSESSMENT

DONNA KILLIAN DUFFY

This story begins by going back in time to the fall of 1993 to a therapeutic riding farm called Challenge Unlimited in Andover, Massachusetts. Students Joanne and Mark from my abnormal psychology course spent two hours each week for eleven weeks at the farm assisting clients who had a variety of diagnoses such as attention-deficit/hyperactivity disorder (ADHD) or autism. The students helped clients prepare horses for riding, assisted them as they rode horses, and then reviewed their progress for the day. The course assignment required students to connect their observations and reflections from the horse farm to course material in specific, detailed ways. Supervisors at the farm completed written evaluations of the students on the basis of their ability to work with clients, contribution to the program, and general level of responsibility at the site. I collected the supervisor evaluations but did not consider them appropriate to include as part of the students' final grades.

THE DILEMMA

Joanne wrote a well-organized paper but received poor evaluations from the supervisor: "does not relate well to individuals, difficult to work with, has a negative attitude toward clients." Mark wrote a marginal paper yet received stunning comments from the supervisor: "incredible in connecting to clients, anticipates problems in the setting, would hire him tomorrow." What to do? The marked disparity between the paper grades and the supervisor's evaluation was problematic but reflects an ongoing assessment challenge involved in working in the community. How do you incorporate multifaceted aspects of a student's work to create an accurate assessment? This question is one that I have been exploring in various ways since my experiences with Joanne and Mark back in the fall of 1993.

In this chapter I discuss the pedagogy of service learning and how it presents unique features for creating a permeable classroom—a place where insights gained from community experiences flow easily into the content of the course and where course content is applied in concrete settings outside the classroom walls. Students in such a classroom learn that knowledge can be constructed in a variety of settings, not only within the rigid walls of a classroom. Venturing into the community presents new opportunities and challenges for assessing students. I would like to share how I have redesigned my abnormal psychology course to meet the challenges of authentic assessment. Finally, I would like to explore how the redesigned course fits with the *Undergraduate Psychology Learning Goals and Outcomes* recently published by the American Psychological Association (APA, 2002).

SERVICE LEARNING DEFINITION

First, what is service learning? Service learning is defined as a "course-based, credit-bearing educational experience in which students (a) participate in an organized service activity that meets identified community needs and (b) reflect on the service activity in such a way as to gain further understanding of course content, a broader appreciation of the discipline, and an enhanced sense of civic responsibility" (Bringle & Hatcher, 1995, p. 112). As a form of experiential education, service learning shares similarities with internships, field education, practica, and voluntary service. Furco (1996) places these forms of education on a continuum. At one end are internships and practica, with their primary focus on student learning. At the other end are volunteer activities with an emphasis on service to recipients in the community. Service learning is in the middle of the continuum with an equal focus on student learning and service to the community. Some students have seen the value of this approach as evidenced in the following quotes: "Working in a service learning situation can bring what you learn in the text to life. You can learn three dimensionally," "The best way to describe it would be the difference in reading a screenplay and actually acting it out."[1]

---

[1]For more detailed information on service learning and psychology courses see the APA service learning and civic engagement Web site, http://www.apa.org/ed/slce/home.html, or Bringle and Duffy (1998).

BENEFITS FOR STUDENTS

Working in the community can present unique opportunities for students. This was most evident in the fall of 1998 when John,[2] a student in my abnormal psychology class, spent the semester working at the Bedford Veterans' Administration Hospital with Sam, a veteran who turned 105 that fall. John, who was in his late 20s, was a veteran himself and formed a strong bond with Sam. I designed the course focus on the generative topic of resilience, and Sam was a perfect model. John shared Sam's experiences during three wars, and topics such as post-traumatic stress disorder, depression, and coping strategies were woven throughout the stories. As the semester progressed, students asked what Sam thought about a variety of issues and John's weekly visits with Sam were amplified with the questions of twenty other students in the class. At the end of the semester I wondered how I could generate such sharing and enthusiasm among students in other classes.

Creating a permeable classroom through service learning is an especially powerful approach for community college students. Often students who enter community colleges have had negative experiences in the educational system. Katz (1997) suggests that entering community colleges as well as military service can create turning points and second-chance opportunities for students who have experienced earlier failure. In a similar way, Astin (1998) states that an important problem in higher education is that "we value *being* smart much more than we do *developing* smartness" (p. 22). For students who have struggled, it is important for them to recognize that they can develop their strengths in a variety of ways in higher education. Service learning encourages different ways of obtaining knowledge and can help students to gain more confidence in their capabilities.

Work in the community generates several important questions for practitioners. How can we assess authentic settings in the most effective way? How can we share community learning to capture levels of meaning? How can we help students solve complicated problems in the community without becoming overwhelmed by them? What are ways to harvest the maximum learning from the experience?

REDESIGN OF COURSE

In 1998 as part of my work as a Carnegie Scholar, I redesigned my abnormal psychology course to try to address these challenges and to realign my materials with the discipline's emerging focus on positive psychology. In his introduction to the American Psychological Association's 106th Annual Convention, Martin Seligman explained how psychology "has evolved since

---

[2]The student stories used in this paper are disguised and the names used are pseudonyms.

World War II from a discipline with three fundamental missions—curing mental illness, making the lives of all people more fulfilling, and identifying high talent—to one devoted almost exclusively to treatment of and research on mental illness" (1998, p. xxv). He encouraged psychologists to move from a deficit model to a model that focuses on building human strengths and civic virtues for the 21st century. Seligman's call for a more strength-based model is reflected in recent publications (Aspinwall & Staudinger, 2003; Keyes & Haidt, 2003; Snyder & Lopez, 2002).

As a practicing therapist in the community I use a strength-based focus in my work, but as a professor of abnormal psychology I recognize that abnormal psychology texts do not yet reflect this trend. A traditional course in abnormal psychology presents a wide range of disorders, focuses on deficits rather than strengths, and often defines problems in neat categories that do not reflect the complexity of the world beyond the classroom. Two of the main objectives in my abnormal psychology course are to help students interpret situations from multiple perspectives and to confront the social implications of mental disorders. Working in the community can help students to meet these objectives, but the community experiences usually add ambiguity and frustration. When students use their experiences as "text," they have less control over the content of the information yet they can play a more active role in solving actual problems.

I redesigned the course around the generative topic of resilience and had two questions weaving throughout the semester. First, why are some people resilient in the face of difficult life situations while others develop maladaptive behaviors? Second, what kinds of approaches will promote greater resilience in individuals and communities? Students often explained that they felt overwhelmed by the complex problems they saw in the community; these questions helped to decrease feelings of being overwhelmed and helped to increase problem solving. An added benefit was that the questions encouraged students to recognize their own resilience. Since 1998, I have incorporated articles on resiliency, woven the topic throughout assignments during the semester, and designed a group project in which service learning students analyze a critical incident with students who are not working in the community.

Typically, approximately half of the students in my abnormal psychology class elect to do service and half do not. Class sizes each semester range from 15 to 40 with an average of about 20. Given the nature of our student population—about 85% of our students are employed and about 27% are parents of dependent children—it is important to provide course options that will accommodate a variety of needs. The service learning students perform 22 hours of service in a community setting, write four reflection papers, complete a critical incident group project as a team, and receive evaluations from site supervisors. Other students in the class complete a series of written projects as well as the critical incident group project. Examples of course materials can be found on the CD-ROM that accompanies the case study, "Resilient Students, Resilient Communities," in *Opening Lines: Approaches to the Scholarship of Teaching and Learning* (Hutchings, 2000).

The course design has evolved over several semesters. I began with overly ambitious expectations about what would be reasonable for students and have developed a more workable and integrated design in recent semesters, as demonstrated in Table 13.1. Students can earn up to 400 points. In the course design used since Fall 2000, the individual project is worth 100 points, the average of two exams is worth 100 points, and the total of group projects is 100 points. There are about ten weekly quizzes worth ten points each; the highest six scores are selected and are worth 60 points. The resiliency essay at the beginning of the course is worth 20 points and the essay at the end of the course is worth 20 points for a total of 40 points. As part of a sabbatical project in 1999 I created a short guide for students that aims to integrate the various assignments in the course. Introducing the topic of resiliency into the course seemed rather disjointed in the early semesters; the course guide helped students to see how their individual projects (service learning or alternative assignments) and other activities in the course could connect around the topic of resilience.

Individual Project

For the individual project, students can select the service learning option or other individual project options. These other project options are varied, for example, critique of research articles, Internet investigations, or book reviews. A challenge is to create reasonable equity across different types of assignments. Since 2000, I have been trying to create more choices for students who want to work in the community but are not able to manage the two-hour per week commitment. I have also tried to create more places for intersections among students pursuing different types of projects in class. In one of the new assignments, students translate concepts into applications by designing a program to promote resilience in a certain population. They create a pilot project for one segment of the population (preschool, school age, high school, college, young adults, middle-aged adults, or elderly adults) and target one area of concentration. Possibilities include wellness programs, dropout prevention, violence prevention, prevention of drug abuse, programs for the chronically mentally ill, depression prevention, or a similar topic selected by students. Students then have to create two or three key questions they will try to answer and describe five key resources available on the Internet or through readings to answer the questions. They then must interview at least three people in the target population and visit one program in the community that attempts to deal with the issue selected. Students may join one of their classmates involved in service learning at a community site to accomplish this part of the assignment. The final task is to create a program design

TABLE 13.1
Evolution of Course Design

Fall 1998	Spring 1999	Spring 2000	Fall 2000, Spring and Fall 2001, Spring and Fall 2002
Pre- & post-course resiliency descriptions Articles on resilience Site visits in early weeks	Pre- & post-course essays on resilience article	Pre- & post-course essays on resilience article	Pre- & post-course essays on resilience article
2 critical incident group projects and 2 other group projects	1 critical incident group project and 3 other group projects	1 critical incident group project and 5 other group projects	1 critical incident group project and about 6 other group projects
Service learning or alternative assignment	Service learning or alternative assignment	Course guide coordinating individual project assignments	Course guide coordinating individual project assignments
Quizzes	Quizzes	Quizzes	Quizzes
Exams	Exams		Exams

for the pilot project and to obtain comments from two other students in class regarding the design.

In another assignment students can develop presentations for the community related to reducing the stigma associated with mental illness. The National Alliance for the Mentally Ill, a nonprofit support and advocacy organization for people with severe mental illness, has a wide range of materials for confronting the stigma of mental illness. Students working alone or in teams have organized materials dealing with stigma and have presented lessons to a class or an after-school program. This assignment allows students to participate in the community and to learn more about national programs focused on prevention. Students often share materials and questions with the class as they prepare their presentations; this practice allows for more exchanges and "comparing notes" between students involved in different forms of inquiry.

Critical Incident Group Project

The critical incident group project has been a useful approach for integrating the learning gained by students working in the community with that of students involved in more traditional projects. Students work in teams of two to four with one of the students in each team participating in service learning. The service learning student writes about a critical incident that occurred at the site. This could be a situation that presented a problem of some type or an incident that left a lasting impression. The event might be dramatic or it might be a simple exchange during a daily routine. The other students then try to connect the incident to material from the course and then all students attempt to describe any new understandings they have gained through this process. A short example may be helpful. One student described an incident relating to a second-grade student named Denise whom he was helping with reading. She was quiet, fearful, and did not relate to other children. The student described an incident in which she arrived at the tutoring session with bruises on her cheekbone. He was concerned and wondered what he should do. The other students in the group explored the situation and suggested that the child may be depressed, may have anxiety, and may have problems in coordination relating to her learning problem. They wondered whether she was being bullied at school or whether she was possibly being abused at home. They connected different theoretical perspectives to the incident and considered legal issues. In the new understanding section, students discussed the importance of not having biases in dealing with the multifaceted possibilities inherent in actual community settings. They expressed the need to find general clues to understand the complexity. One student wrote:

> On a more personal level, this particular project has taught me that there is certainly no room for biases and prejudices when looking at an individual; that one must resist the urge to hastily classify an individual's problems or disorders. In addition, it is essential to remember that when looking at an individual's problems, we look for general clues that will help us understand and treat individuals as we attempted to do with Denise in the *Connections* portion of this project. When doing so, it became apparent that each of the connections made did not fully address Denise's problem on their own, however, provided considerable clues to answer whether *together* they point to a more accurate explanation.

The critical incident group projects have provided a collaborative way for students to share their different experiences and to develop deeper levels of understanding of course material. The connections section of the project encourages students to look beyond the text material and to consider how a particular dilemma might be viewed by other agents in the community. The course material on resilience has helped students to reframe situations in new ways. For example, they consider the ways that communities foster resiliency in people with Alzheimer's disease, leading to lively discussions about local programs as well as societal views of aging. These group reflections often help students to begin to develop the "enhanced sense of civic responsibility" that is central to the pedagogy of service learning.

Student work in the community typically brings new issues and questions into the classroom. This past semester a student who worked in the

Alzheimer's Day Care Center came into class and discussed the turmoil that had occurred at the center that morning because a visitor had forgotten to take off her winter coat. Other students were curious about why keeping a coat on should cause a problem. We discussed a variety of issues and the student stated that several of the clients at the center thought the person with the coat meant that it was time for them to go home. They thought the visitor was there to take them home. The student reported that one of the first guidelines she learned was always to leave her coat in the closet before entering the center. This simple example illustrates how learning about a guideline at the center helped students to translate the symptoms of Alzheimer's disease into a daily living situation. This translating aligns with work on teaching for understanding (Wiske, 1998) and supports Perkins' (1998) definition:

> Understanding is the ability to think and act flexibly with what one knows . . . .an understanding of a topic is a "flexible performance capability" with emphasis on the flexibility. In keeping with this, learning for understanding is like learning a flexible performance—more like learning to improvise jazz or hold a good conversation or rock climb than learning the multiplication table or the dates of the presidents or that F = MA. Learning facts can be a crucial backdrop to learning for understanding, but learning facts is not learning for understanding. (p. 40)

Resiliency Essays

In recent semesters I have observed that students have made more comments about their role in creating change in their essays about resiliency at the end of the semester. In the first week of class students read the article, "Finding Strengths" (Blum, 1998). They use a highlighter to note the ideas, concepts, or stories that they find most interesting. In the essay they select three items from the article, explain why they are interesting, and connect ideas to other courses or experiences. At the end of the semester students reread the article and use a different color highlighter to note ideas or concepts that have new meaning for them at the end of the course. They select three ideas or concepts and explain how or why they view them differently. They discuss how their experiences over the past semester have influenced the way that they now read the article. A theme that has emerged in the final essays of many students is a focus on their role in creating change. A student wrote:

> Over the past semester my experiences in class were definitely helped by my partner working out in the community as well as others in the class that have shared their stories. I have been able to see that there are many different types of problems in people's lives stemming from anxiety and stretching all the way to schizophrenia. The best thing that I have learned

TABLE 13.2

Question 3: How much has this class added to your skills
in each of the following?

	Spring 1999 (N = 10)	Spring 2000 (N = 19)	Fall 2000 (N = 18)	Fall 2001 (N = 21)	Spring 2002 (N = 37)	Fall 2002 (N = 14)
1. Interpreting situations from multiple perspectives	4.1	4.2	4.1	4.1	3.9	4.6
2. Developing strategies to confront the social implications of mental disorders	3.7	3.8	4.0	3.9	3.9	4.5

Note. All ratings in this chapter are reported on a five-point scale where 1 = *not at all* and 5 = *a great deal*.

is that I want to be one of the people that gives them help and the ability to not only cope, but perhaps face their problems.

QUESTIONNAIRE RESULTS

At the end of the semester, I distribute a questionnaire to assess gains in student learning. Students rank a series of statements on a scale of 1 (*not at all*) to 5 (*a great deal*). Tables 13.2, 13.3, and 13.4 display results of the questionnaires from Spring 1999 to Fall 2002. The total number of students completing the survey has ranged from 10 to 37. The ratings have been quite consistent over several semesters and suggest that the generative topic of resilience and the accompanying activities helped to strengthen student learning. The narrative comments of students indicate that the critical incident group project helps in sharing learning and in solving complex problems even though students find the exercise difficult to do.

CONNECTION TO GOALS

Work in the community provides a more multifaceted way to assess student learning, but does it help students in achieving the benchmarks suggested in the new *Undergraduate Psychology Learning Goals and Outcomes* (APA, 2002)? I would like to use data from student materials to show how they fit with the *Undergraduate Psychology Learning Goals and Outcomes*.

There are ten suggested goals for the undergraduate psychology major: knowledge base, research methods, critical thinking skills, application, values, information and technological literacy, communication skills, sociocultural and international awareness, personal development, and career plan-

TABLE 13.3
Question 4. To what extent did you make gains in any of the following as a result of what you did in this class?

	Spring 1999 (N = 10)	Spring 2000 (N = 19)	Fall 2000 (N = 18)	Fall 2001 (N = 21)	Spring 2002 (N = 37)	Fall 2002 (N = 14)
1. Understanding how concepts in class can be applied to deal with real-world problems	4.2	4.4	4.3	4.3	4.2	4.6
2. Using a framework of resiliency when thinking about situations	4.0	4.4	3.9	4.0	3.7	4.5

ning and development. I have selected examples from pre- and post-course resiliency essays, reflection assignments, and group projects of students in classes from 1998 to the present. The following examples begin to show how a permeable classroom can generate multifaceted student learning and can meet at least nine of the ten suggested goals:

Knowledge Base (Reflection Assignment 4)

I especially enjoyed learning the different models because as I worked with each child I was able to explain to myself why one therapy might be better than another. For example, Derek, an 11-year-old boy who has ADHD, depression, and post-traumatic stress disorder is seeing a psychiatrist for his medications, a psychologist to deal with his emotional problems from his abuse, losses and bad thoughts about himself, and a speech therapist for his speech disorder. Once I learned about all the various models, I was able to understand why these three types of treatments had been chosen for Derek. If he had been seeing a humanistic or sociocultural psychologist, I would have thought this to be inappropriate for Derek. He needs someone to help him learn to think better and deal with past traumas so he can learn to function and deal with problems better.

Critical Thinking Skills (Group Project)

When trying to assess the problem I realized that for this case, it wasn't black and white, like in the book. The child I wrote about didn't have the symptoms of one disorder. He had a few of many. But how could this be? If he doesn't completely fit into one category, where does he go? This was a problem I thought about all semester.

TABLE 13.4

Question 5: How much of what you learned in this class (i.e., knowledge, skills, and other gains) do you think you will remember, and carry with you into other classes or other aspects of your life?

	Spring 1999 (N = 10)	Spring 2000 (N = 19)	Fall 2000 (N = 18)	Fall 2001 (N = 21)	Spring 2002 (N = 37)	Fall 2002 (N = 14)
Understanding ways to promote resiliency in individuals and communities	3.9	4.5	4.2	4.0	3.9	4.5

Application (Reflection Assignment 4)

The handout on Functional Assessment enabled me to track certain behaviors and think of different ways to approach him. I normally did this in my head by watching him and how people react. I remembered what approaches worked and which ones did not. For behaviors that are more difficult to control, such as running out of the classroom, I made a chart like the one in the handout. I have not solved this problem, but I learned that becoming angry just makes him do it even more.

Values (Resiliency Essay 2)

A student wrote about taking three men from a community residence to help paint the home of an elderly woman in a Habitat for Humanity program: "I was able to help three of the individuals with disabilities participate in this program and that was a great milestone for these guys. *They* were able to give to the community."

Communication Skills (Reflection Assignment 4)

Knowing that my subject cannot communicate much I still talk to him. I noticed he was fidgeting with his hand so I went over and gave him a puzzle to do. First I showed him and then I asked him if he understood me, he looked at me and in a low voice and said "ya." I sat there and watched him and he did exactly what I asked of him. This situation is one of the reasons I believe that patients suffering from Alzheimer's have an idea what's going on around them.

Sociocultural Awareness (Reflection 3)

Students created concept maps to illustrate the complexity of connections present in one individual's life and to link life events with course material. In one concept map the student describes Juan, who is a bilingual student in a classroom for students with emotional and behavioral problems. The student suggests a diagnosis for Juan, shows how he connects to his neighborhood, city, and country, and lists ways that sociocultural factors may play a role in his difficulties. The concept maps help students to see the importance of viewing a diagnosis in the context of an individual's life situation. Juan's father was in prison and his mother had limited funds to care for Juan and his three siblings. Students reflected on how this fact influenced Juan's present diagnosis and how it might relate to his prognosis in future years.

Personal Development (Reflection 4)

> To get to and from school I use the bus that picks me up in front of the V.A. Hospital. While I wait there I see how a lot of people act and most of them are patients from the hospital with mental problems. I used to avoid them and try to shut them out with my Walkman but now I have a better understanding of their problems and I try to have more compassion for them. I take off my Walkman and try to listen.

Career Planning (Reflection Assignment 4)

> Another thing this course has taught me is the fact that I now know what I want to do after I graduate. I've switched from major to major like every semester and I knew I wanted to work with kids but I didn't know what. Before I took this course I wanted to be some type of child counselor like an elementary school guidance counselor but I wasn't too sure about that. After this experience with having a relationship with these three kids on a one to one basis really helped me figure out what I want to do with my life. I know I have what it takes to be a counselor especially with children and that's what I'm pursuing.

Although these examples are brief, they demonstrate how students can apply information and can learn in meaningful ways in the context of complicated settings. A criticism often leveled against higher education is that students have difficulty translating information from courses when faced with the complexity of a work setting. Service learning helps to alleviate this problem and supports the importance of contextual learning.

Huba and Freed (2000) suggest that "an exemplary assessment task is one that involves college students in addressing enduring and emerging issues and problems that are ill-defined and of current relevance in their disciplines" (p. 224). They further state that an exemplary assessment task demonstrates eight characteristics. It is valid, coherent, authentic, rigorous, engaging, challenging, respectful, and responsive. The service learning approach demonstrates each of these characteristics, but it is especially effective in engaging and challenging students. There are few "right" answers in responding to community settings; students have to make inquiries, try multiple solutions, and persevere.

As I reflect on the Fall 1993 assessment dilemma of Joanne and Mark described at the beginning of this paper, I realize that it is a clear example of respectful and responsive characteristics. Huba and Freed (2000) define a respectful task as one that "allows students to reveal their uniqueness as learners" (p. 224). Joanne's effective written communication and her more limited interpersonal skills contrasted with Mark's marginal writing proficiency and impressive interpersonal talent in work at the therapeutic riding farm. The authentic setting was responsive to these students by giving them feedback that could lead to improvement. Mark's success on the job may motivate him to develop better writing skills, while Joanne may begin to realize that writing well is only one component to being successful in work settings. A traditional classroom setting would acknowledge Joanne's writing effectiveness but probably would not illuminate the mismatch with her interpersonal skills. Similarly, Mark's aptitude for interacting with others may never have been seen in a classroom while his limited writing performance may have been a source of discouragement and negative feelings. The service learning assignment provided different ways both to assess and to enhance each student's unique approach to learning.

Community settings do not place ideas in neat categories with clear-cut answers but rather challenge students to navigate complexity and make sense of their observations using the resources provided through course content. As the English proverb states: "A smooth sea never made a skilled mariner."

REFERENCES

American Psychological Association Task Force on Undergraduate Psychology Major Competencies. (2002). *Undergraduate psychology major learning goals and outcomes: A report.* Retrieved December 16, 2003, from http://www.apa.org/ed/pcue/reports.html

Aspinwall, L. G., & Staudinger, U. M. (Eds.). (2003). *A psychology of human strengths: Fundamental questions and future directions for a positive psychology.* Washington, DC: American Psychological Association.

Astin, A. (1998, Winter). Higher education and civic responsibility. *National Society for Experiential Education Quarterly,* 18–26.

Blum, D. (1998, May/June). Finding strength: How to overcome anything. *Psychology Today,* 32–73.

Bringle, R. G., & Duffy, D. K. (1998). *With service in mind: Concepts and models for service-learning in psychology.* Washington, DC: American Association for Higher Education.

Bringle, R. G., & Hatcher, J. A. (1995). A service-learning curriculum for faculty. *Michigan Journal of Community Service Learning, 2*, 112–122.

Duffy, D. K., Velasquez, J., & Wholeben, B. (2002). *Service-learning and civic engagement.* Retrieved December 16, 2003, from http://www.apa.org/ed/slce/home.html

Furco, A. (1996). Service-learning: A balanced approach to experiential education. In Corporation for National Service (Ed.), *Expanding boundaries: Serving and learning* (pp. 2–6). Colombia, MD: Cooperative Education Association.

Huba, M. E., & Freed, J. E. (2000). *Learner-centered assessment on college campuses.* Boston: Allyn & Bacon.

Hutchings, P. (Ed.). (2000). *Opening lines: Approaches to the scholarship of teaching and learning.* Menlo Park, CA: The Carnegie Foundation for the Advancement of Teaching.

Katz, M. (1997). *On playing a poor hand well.* New York: W. W. Norton.

Keyes, C. L., & Haidt, J. (Eds.). (2003). *Flourishing: Positive psychology and the life well-lived.* Washington, DC: American Psychological Association.

Perkins, D. (1998). What is understanding? In M. S. Wiske (Ed.), *Teaching for understanding* (pp. 39–57). San Francisco: Jossey-Bass.

Seligman, M. (1998, August). Message from the president of APA. *Convention Program,* 106th Annual Convention of the American Psychological Association, San Francisco, CA.

Snyder, C. R., & Lopez, S. J. (Eds.). (2002). *Handbook of positive psychology.* New York: Oxford University Press.

Wiske, M. S. (Ed.). (1998). *Teaching for understanding.* San Francisco: Jossey-Bass.

IV

ASSESSING ASSESSMENT
IN PSYCHOLOGY

14

LIBERAL ARTS, DIVERSE LIVES, AND ASSESSING PSYCHOLOGY

THOMAS V. McGOVERN

This book is aptly titled: *Measuring Up: Educational Assessment Challenges and Practices for Psychology*, a handbook of strategies to be applied directly to campus-specific needs. Measuring is one of the things that psychologists do best; *measuring up* reflects our hope of doing this task effectively in a time when almost all departments must do so.

Measurements remain a challenge. Changes in student population characteristics, new delivery systems (e.g., asynchronous, distance learning), and shifts in faculty priorities and institutional missions require continual fine-tuning of our practices. This book demonstrates why psychology faculty can be seen as reflective practitioners. A seasoned or neophyte reader on this topic could conclude that a standard portfolio of assessment methods has been developed very well. The material in this book, coupled with the Web sites on assessment that many of the authors have developed in conjunction with the Education Directorate of the American Psychological Association (APA), answer the following question, in splendid detail and with sensitivity to faculty time, intellectual rigor, and varying delivery systems: How do you know that your students know what you want them to know—after every class session, course completion, and degree awarded?

But other questions need to be addressed. In "Transforming Under-graduate Psychology for the Next Century" (McGovern, 1993), I proposed the following:

> What kind of *outcomes* can be achieved with
> What kind of *students* taught by
> What kind of *faculty* using
> What kind of *teaching methods* as part of
> What kind of *curriculum?* (p. 218)

I propose in this chapter that faculty work in assessment must be challenged by the complexity of this query and how it relates to the complexity of the world and its information and problems. Liberal arts education has regained its cachet among even the most specialized employers. The outcomes of liberal arts education deserve a fresh look, and we must determine how psychology fits into this broader context. How does higher education produce citizens of a global and diverse world—inspired by the possibilities of a reflected life and shamed by the perpetuation of ignorance? Psychologists and what we think, write, and argue about offer students rich methods and insightful perspectives from the pervasive introductory course to the selective capstone.

First, I consider how the assessment movement came about and why higher education was perceived as *not* measuring up. Second, I offer a brief history (via a content analysis of the journal, *Teaching of Psychology*) of how psychologists constructed their scholarship and practice of assessment before and after this movement was upon us. Third, I evaluate the fine chapters that comprise this book. Fourth, and finally, I suggest a postdisciplinary liberal arts future for psychology and the diverse lives we meet in our classes and communities.

MEASURING UP

Innovations in higher education come and go. McGovern and Brewer (2003) described the tensions between continuity and change in undergraduate education in psychology. The roots of faculty work derived from the social constructions of disciplines and professional associations; continuity required slow and cumulative reflection. The fruits of faculty work are the demonstrable effects in their students' lives and how public audiences valued those effects. After examining the conscientiously developed programs described in the chapters of this book, I asked myself the question: Why did the movement for assessment of student learning outcomes come and stay? I reread the research texts that shaped my own responses to this phenomenon.

Feldman and Newcomb's (1969) *The Impact of College on Students* synthesized the research findings of approximately 1,500 published and unpublished studies from the mid-1920s to the middle sixties. Pascarella and Terenzini's (1991) *How College Affects Students* brought this evaluation another twenty years and another 2,600 studies forward. They synthesized evidence for: (a) individual change during college, (b) whether college attendance produces that change, (c) different effects on change by kinds of institutions, (d) different effects of differing experiences in the same institution, (e) individual differences that mediate the effects of the college experience, and (f) the long-lasting effects of college.

Pascarella and Terenzini (1991) concluded that the greatest effects can be seen on cognitive change dimensions. Students from first year to senior year showed modest increases in general verbal and quantitative skills, but the largest magnitude of change was in (a) knowledge in a major field of study, (b) critical thinking skills, (c) use of reason and evidence to solve problems, (d) a capacity to deal with conceptual complexity and (e) a decline in authoritarian thinking. Positive, but more modest, changes were found in an increased respect and valuing of the liberal arts and of diverse ideas. College graduates revealed attitudinal shifts toward the intrinsic value and rewards of learning. Modest changes took place in their use of principled reasoning to judge moral issues and in reported psychological well-being and self-esteem.

> Our synthesis of the evidence suggests that college has a rather broad range of enduring or long-term impacts. These include not only the more obvious impacts on occupation and earning but also influences on cognitive, moral, and psychosocial characteristics, as well as on values and attitudes and various quality of life indexes. . . . Moreover, it would also appear that the impacts extend beyond the individuals who attend college to the kinds of lives their sons and daughters can expect. (p. 573)

These same scholars found that "similarities in between-college effects would appear to vastly outweigh the differences" (p. 590), and that "within-college effects, like between college effects, tend to be smaller in magnitude than the overall net effect of college attendance" (p. 610). This synthesis evaluation was so positive and significant. What happened? Who was (not) listening? What led the public to demand more report cards? I reread more.

Astin's (1977) *Four Critical Years* and *What Matters in College: Four Critical Years Revisited* (1993) were based on national studies with large samples of students and faculty. Reading his lucid analyses about changes during college, I was struck by a methodological feature of this data and by a conclusion that he drew at the end of the second book. Like my very first venture into evaluating our undergraduate curriculum in psychology at Virginia Commonwealth University, the measures were primarily self-report surveys by the faculty and students. Self-report measures were both a methodological and a public relations limitation; this became more clear to me with a fresh reading of Astin's (1993) final thoughts.

Institutions espouse high-sounding values, of course, in their mission statements, college catalogues, and public pronouncements by institutional leaders. The problem is that these explicitly stated values—which always include a strong commitment to undergraduate education—are often at variance with the actual values that drive our decisions and policies. The real issue in reforming undergraduate education, it seems to me, is to effect a better rapprochement between our explicitly stated values and the values that really drive our institutional policies and decisions. (pp. 435–436)

Higher education scholars had been measuring the effects of undergraduate education for a long time. Our measurements and statistical analyses grew in methodological sophistication, but they were still indirect. More importantly, outside of our institutional walls and academic journal discourse, in the mid-1980s a variety of publics began to judge that we had not been *measuring up*. Many constituencies felt free to challenge how faculty spent their time, what we taught in our courses, and whether we knew that our students knew what we claimed to want them to know. Assessment, post-tenure review, and "scholarship reconsidered" were the mandated consequences.

In "An Emerging Scholarship: A Brief History of Assessment," Ewell (2002) proposed that the "birth of a movement" was the 1985 First National Conference on Assessment in Higher Education. Ewell believes that now, twenty years later, external stakeholders (e.g., state legislatures, regional accrediting groups) are adamant about its continuance, institutions are data hungry, and technological changes and new pedagogies require an evaluative component beyond cost effectiveness—assessment processes and products fill some of these needs.

ASSESSMENT AND PSYCHOLOGY BEFORE THE "MOVEMENT"

In the first volume of the journal, *Teaching of Psychology*, McGuigan (1974) examined "Amount Learned: An Empirical Basis for Grading Teachers and Students." McGahie and Menges (1975) used the term "learning outcomes" to assess self-directed learning in a behaviorally oriented psychology course. Matthews (1982), in a special issue on the future of undergraduate education, saw evaluation as the major challenge for the 1980s and urged the use of "standardized outcome measures so that replication at several institutions would be feasible" (p. 52). However, scholarly teachers publishing in this journal were interested primarily in course pedagogy and not program-level evaluation questions.

Empirical descriptions of innovative instructional activities were complemented first by research on alumni satisfaction and then on departmental goals. Cates' (1973) survey of baccalaureates in psychology was the first of many early contributions to this literature. McGovern and Carr (1989) reviewed studies on alumni surveys, recommending that departments should construe such programs as long-term projects, designing more sophisticated assessments for each administration and linking them to curricular and program changes over time. Ware's (1986) and Lunneborg's (1986) small and large university approaches were excellent examples of an increasing sophistication in using survey data to improve programs. The alumni survey literature addressed questions about the employability of our graduates and a longstanding concern about how best to balance the goals of a liberal arts education with the vocational aspirations of students (Kulik, 1973; McKeachie & Milholland, 1961). Boltuck, Peterson, and Murphy (1980) reported data from 1,811 human service agencies on psychology majors' employability. McKeachie (1982) summarized undergraduate education from the 1950s to the 1990s as responding to the "continuing tensions among cognitive, subject-matter-oriented goals, personal development or affective goals, and applied, career relevant goals" (p. 63).

Malin and Timreck (1979) linked their survey of student goals to their department's curriculum. McGovern and Hawks (1984, 1986) evaluated student and faculty goals to renew overall undergraduate program activities. Walker, Newcomb, and Hopkins (1987) added employers' and alumni perspectives to internal constituents' expectations for their curriculum evaluation and revision model. Rajecki and Metzner (1991) used university-wide data to map students' decisions to major in psychology. Metzner, Rajecki, and Lauer (1994) extended their archival approach to test the "feminization of the major."

From approximately 1974 to 1990, psychologists developed a portfolio of campus-specific strategies to evaluate student characteristics, expectations, and levels of satisfaction during the degree, at graduation, and as alumni. Direct assessment of student learning using standardized measures, however, emerged during the "movement." McCallum (1983) was the first report I found in *Teaching of Psychology* that used a comprehensive examination to evaluate psychology students' learning; the author did not list a single reference.

Assessing Psychology and Learning Directly

Halpern's (1988) article, "Assessing Student Outcomes for Psychology Majors" first used all the words and became a touchstone for psychologists' subsequent campus and national efforts on assessment. Sheehan's (1994) "multimethod assessment" was designed in the context of the 1987 Colorado Higher Education Accountability Bill as a campus-based case study using a local test, senior and alumni surveys, a capstone course, and non-intrusive measures.

Assessment moved to center stage during the 1990s, and a number of projects contributed rich conceptual material. The joint Association of

American College's (AAC) and American Psychological Association reports on the arts and sciences major required a section on outcomes and their assessment (McGovern, Furumoto, Halpern, Kimble, & McKeachie, 1991). The steering committee of the Saint Mary's National Conference on Enhancing the Quality Undergraduate Education in Psychology placed assessment at the top of the list of its agenda items as well as in the first chapter of its handbook (Halpern et al., 1993). Assessment was woven into the *Principles for Quality Undergraduate Psychology Programs* approved by the Council of Representatives as Association policy (McGovern & Reich, 1996). It took time for national recommendations to make their way into campus practices.

Korn, Sweetman, and Nodine's (1996) analyses of consultants' reports suggested that the evaluators' recommendations about assessment were still ahead of actual departmental practice: "a rubric for evaluating undergraduate programs does not exist either formally through the APA or informally in the networks of department chairs or teaching consultants" (p. 14). Jackson and Griggs' (1995) national survey of departmental assessment activities suggested a similar disconnect between externally mandated expectations and actual practice. They concluded that the higher the prestige of the institution (especially among national universities and liberal arts colleges), the lower the probability of any formal assessment program in psychology. Moreover, 59% of the surveyed institutions that reported doing assessment said that it led to no changes in either their baccalaureate requirements or individual courses!

This situation changed in the second half of the decade. The methodological literature in psychology grew as accrediting associations, state legislatures, and institutional academic program review mandates demanded data and not just plans. The campus case studies reported in *Teaching of Psychology* drew on the conceptual material from various conference reports and measurement strategies used by other departments; a synergy of efforts began to be apparent (Pusateri, 2002). The senior seminar could embed a department's assessment requirements (Morgan & Johnson, 1997). Psychologists working in university institutional research offices continued to refine the use of archives and larger sampling capacities (Borden & Rajecki, 2000). Comparative studies of psychology and various other majors (Kruger & Zechmeister, 2001) and examining course-taking patterns and standardized test performance (Stoloff & Feeney, 2002) enhanced our understanding of what kinds of outcomes are accomplished by what kind of curriculum.

One of the most fruitful avenues of scholarship on student learning outcomes and their assessment has been focused on critical thinking skills. Halpern and Nummedal (1995) made the case for this particular outcome, tracing its historical roots from John Dewey to contemporary higher education reports on what was lacking in its graduates (across the curriculum), and to public policy initiatives. Halonen's (1995) "Demystifying Critical Thinking" was an example of one scholar–teacher's almost 15-year effort to make sense of the concept in her courses, in the curricular programs she developed, and in her truly significant work with the American Psychological Association's undergraduate initiatives. This book should be seen as a direct result of psychologists' efforts over the past quarter century. In the following section, I offer synoptic evaluations of the chapters.

ASSESSING ASSESSMENT IN 2004

Halpern (chap. 1) is among the movement's most influential scholars and a battle-scarred veteran of its debates and program development efforts at the campus, state, and national levels. Her seven guidelines for good practice are empirically sound and strategically shrewd. Departments should post them on their chairs' and deans' walls:

1. Student outcomes assessment improves teaching and learning.
2. There is no single indicator of educational effectiveness.
3. Successful assessment programs are owned by the faculty.
4. Faculty expertise and hard work doing assessment must be recognized and rewarded.
5. Assessment programs create links with other segments of higher education.
6. Care must be taken so that data are not misused.
7. American higher education's greatest strength is in its diversity.

Her nine categories of student learning outcomes and seven measurement strategies effectively summarize this literature. By reading this chapter first, new practitioners and jaded veterans will arrive at a common vocabulary and set of assumptions to orient their subsequent efforts.

James Madison University (JMU) became a "public Alverno College" in the 1990s through its campus-wide commitment to building an assessment culture. It is very important to learn from Stoloff, Apple, Barron, Reis-Bergan, and Sundre (chap. 2) that this departmental program began in 1989; sophisticated and meaningful assessment, like good teaching and scholarship, is an iterative process. Even more important is that, with approximately 1,000 declared majors, the rigorous JMU methodology could potentially generalize to every large university institutional setting. Their seven goals of program assessment are sophisticated, pragmatic, and make demonstrable differences in students' learning and the quality of their educational experiences. Absent university support, the JMU Campus Assessment Day could be a "departmental assessment day" with comparable results, especially on residential campuses.

The *sine qua non* of assessment, demonstrated by the JMU program and by Firment, Devine, and Whittlesey (chap. 3) at Kennesaw State University, is a significant number of the "right faculty" who find assessment scholarly, intellectually stimulating, and directly applicable to their teaching and learning. This chapter illuminates how faculty analyzed recommendations from national groups to arrive at ten learning outcomes and five assessment methods. The KSU group clearly demonstrates how to use data to reform a curriculum, co-curricular programs, and subsequent assessment strategies. Their model will be helpful for commuter populations and diverse student demographics. The recruitment and retention of students who differ in gender, ethnicity, class, age, and enrollment characteristics can be significantly enhanced by assessment strategies that manifest a department's commitment to attend to all students' learning.

Pusateri, Poe, Addison, and Goedel (chap. 4) extract from their experiences as administrators, program consultants, and evaluators to describe a prototypical self-study report. Since 1996, when Korn, Sweetman, and Nodine lamented the absence of models, institutions have now developed common expectations for Academic Program Reviews. These authors list 20 different online resources for guidelines; institutional types vary from the liberal arts college to research universities. They begin their chapter with a pragmatic admonition: "We believe that chairs may be more successful in obtaining needed program resources if their requests are data driven." Weaver (chap. 5) sketches a "psychology chair portfolio." Here is a truly reflective practitioner at work. His "flashlight" versus "spotlight" approach to articulating one's philosophy, stating objectives, gathering quantitative and qualitative data, considering results, and implementing change should be a metaphor for renewal beyond the individual case.

The eight chapters on *Best Practices in Assessment* offer a cornucopia of strategies for adaptation to specific institutional missions, departmental goals, and course objectives. Sternberg (chap. 6) captures course-based classroom assessment at its best with his approach to "teaching for successful intelligence." I found his arguments particularly persuasive in their emphasis on respecting student differences across multiple levels of education and experiences. I promptly revised my syllabus for Introductory Psychology based on what I read. Osborne and Wagor (chap. 7) articulate a "formative assessment" approach that includes: defining learning outcomes, deciding on assessment methods, detailing outcomes and methods to students, discovering levels of learning and providing feedback, and deciding what to modify.

Bosack, McCarthy, Halonen, and Clay's "Developing Scientific Inquiry Skills in Psychology: Using Authentic Assessment Strategies" (chap. 8) could be used as a blueprint for major external funding, national reputation, and local pride on and off campus. This collaborative effort was begun with the APA Psychology Partnerships Project and was influential in the Board of Educational Affairs endorsement of the National Learning Goals and Outcomes for the Undergraduate Psychology Major in 2000. The authors describe eight skill sets (description, conceptualization, problem solving, ethical reasoning, scientific values and attitudes, communication, collaboration, and self-assessment) across five levels of students' academic programs (before training, after introductory psychology, during the major, at the capstone level, and after graduate or professional training). The authors include three different assignments with assessment rubrics and grading criteria that illustrate the depth of their commitment to scientific inquiry and the complexity of its application. Dunn, McEntarffer, and Halonen (chap. 9) amplify the capstone skill set of this model in their descriptions of formative self-assessment and summative self-evaluation. These authors' students are from a high school, a liberal arts college, and a comprehensive university. Their chapter reflects a deep appreciation for cognitive development in the second decade of life. They operationalize and directly measure what the Pascarella and Terenzini findings suggested. Students learn the content of a major to varying degrees, but more importantly they change their epistemologies.

The iterative requirement of continuous quality improvement and building excellent assessment programs should be recalled often when reading chapter 8. The power of assessment to affect individual student lives over the course of an academic program and beyond should motivate a careful reading of chapter 9. Both chapters speak volumes about the importance of making the time to do this task well. It is a testament to the power of faculty to transform assessment from sound-bite satisfactions to a scholarly reflection on teaching and learning.

As someone interested in writing across the curriculum and its assessment, I particularly appreciated Keller, Craig, Launius, Loher, and Cooledge's (chap. 10) commentary on student portfolios. Beginning with departmental discussions as far back as 1985, and implementing an assessment strategy in 1993, these authors understood that assessment was as much about faculty development as about the measurement of student learning. They took advantage of their smaller number of majors ($n = 150$) at a public university and systematically developed their portfolio process. I read this thought-provoking and pragmatic chapter after my department had just concluded its annual portfolio review workshop as an interdisciplinary faculty.

Brito, Sharma, and Bernas (chap. 11) give readers a cost–benefit appraisal of off-the-shelf measures versus locally developed tests. Their arguments for the locally developed instrument include budgetary constraints and direct application of obtained results to curriculum development, as well as broader and deeper faculty motivation to establish the validity of their assessment practices. Evaluating the psychometrics of such an instrument could become an effective case study for any department's students as critical consumers of their own scientific education.

In 1981, my university appointed a new chairperson to elevate the status of undergraduate education in a department with APA-accredited programs in clinical and counseling psychology. As Director of Undergraduate Studies, it was my first venture into program evaluation and curriculum renewal. In 1985, the provost sent me to the first American Association of Higher Education (AAHE) assessment conference as a pathfinder for our institution. As Director of Assessment, I used resources from the state's newly initiated funds for excellence to launch a campus-wide assessment program and a significant reform of general education across the university. In 1997, another provost, this time in Arizona, sent me to AAHE to hear Sir John Daniel, Chancellor of Great Britain's Open University, wax eloquent about distance learning. I was harangued immediately by faculty colleagues about "closeness learning." Several years later, after staving off the Board of Regents' desire to eliminate tenure in Arizona universities due to a perceived lack of attention to undergraduate education, the universities used distance-learning initiatives to upgrade technology at campuses throughout the state. The regents subsequently approved a "learner-centered environment" agenda and grant funding to implement innovative programs on behalf of undergraduates. Thus, I was taught again and again to discern the problems external agendas were trying to solve and to transform such impulses into scholarly activity across the campus.

Mehrotra, Weaver, and Nelson's commentary on distance learning (chap. 12) reminded me of this important lesson. Using Astin's Input–Process–Outcome model, their approach to assessment includes all the variables articulated in the complex question I posed at the beginning of this chapter. Demands for change in how we deliver instruction ought to be a catalyst for renewed reflection on the possible outcomes that derive from changing student characteristics, types of courses, types of curricula, innovative teaching strategies, and the faculty styles best suited to orchestrate this complex interaction. If we construe teaching as mediated learning and truly believe that the value of our efforts derives from students' lifelong learning, then distance learning models and their assessment can be rich stimuli for our future scholarship.

The service-learning activities and their assessment described by Duffy (chap. 13) foster similar scholarly and pedagogical diversity in our undergraduate curricula. After graduation, our students will be more apt to volunteer at a local clinic or battered women and children's shelter, to vote to appropriate funds for local K–12 school programs, or to benefit from the volunteer services of a Center on Aging or American Cancer Society than to compose another research paper in APA style or to demonstrate their memory skills on a multiple-choice examination. Blue-ribbon task forces have talked about experiential learning in the undergraduate curriculum for 50 years. Duffy makes the connection between these activities and the Undergraduate Psychology Major Learning Goals and Outcomes (Table 13.4). As one faculty member's case study, she reminds us how we started to measure cognitive goals a quarter century ago. The past is prologue.

A POSTDISCIPLINARY LIBERAL ARTS

Veysey (1973) examined three forces that have shaped American higher education since the innovative Progressive Era from 1880 to 1910: the utilitarian urges of American society to educate a democracy of peoples for a democracy of vocations; advances in science and the expectation of empirical evidence in the constructions and applications of knowledge; and public belief in liberal arts learning for an educated citizenry. In the 1800s, America's higher education institutions wove its pragmatic character into the general education patterns of the European medieval university. The 1900s could be understood as the century of the "major."

Psychology is among the most reflective disciplines in the arts, humanities, social sciences, and sciences in constructing its undergraduate major programs. We have topographical maps of curricula (Perlman & McCann, 1999a, 1999b) and a tradition of reviewing undergraduate education (Brewer et al., 1993). We now have a rich portfolio to evaluate the efficacy of the discipline and its benefits to students' learning.

We can continue down the path of measuring how undergraduate education in psychology fosters the utilitarian needs of students and society while maintaining the traditional goals of scientific methods and knowledge (Nummedal, Benson, & Chew, 2002). To do so will require more attention to three critical variables in my original equation: What students benefit most from what programs delivered in what ways?

The Morrill Land-Grant Act deconstructed the *artium baccalaureatum* and broadened its homogeneous consumers. The post-World War II GI Bill brought different ages and socioeconomic demographics onto our campuses. The Civil Rights movement, the women's movement, and open admissions policies created a rainbow palette and balanced the gender composition in our classrooms. Distance learning can be seen as the fourth stage of America's adventure with enfranchising all peoples. Technology has enabled higher education to overcome its final boundary—geographical distance.

We can build on the assessment models in this handbook to measure directly: a psychology of variance (Puente et al., 1993), efforts to engender psychology (Denmark, 1994), the diversification of psychology (Sue, Bingham, Porche-Burke, & Vasquez, 1999), and the interaction between diversity variables and student learning (Kowalski, 2000; O'Campo et al., 2003; Simoni, Sexton-Radek, Yescavage, Richard, & Lundquist, 1999).

There is an alternative path to follow but it requires a challenge, not just to our methodologies, but to how psychology constructs itself as one of the liberal arts. In a postdisciplinary liberal arts future, another question needs to be raised to measure up: What outcomes?

Ratcliff (1997) described the dominant form of the 20th century academic major:

> A *discipline* is literally what the term implies. . . . Disciplines can provide a conceptual framework for understanding what knowledge is and how it is acquired. Disciplinary learning provides a logical structure to relationships between concepts, propositions, common paradigms, and organizing principles. Disciplines develop themes, canons, and grand narratives to join different streams of research in the field and to provide meaningful conceptualizations and frameworks for further analysis. (p. 14)

The authors of this volume are articulate spokespersons for the modernist's faith in disciplines and science as the heart of undergraduate education in psychology. If psychology departments were to follow the examples from this book and adapted these assessment strategies for their institutional settings, our discipline would be judged as measuring up by many current national, regional, and local constituencies.

Alas, the rainbow demographics of American society, its complex problems, and the interconnectivity that persons create and technology enables all suggest the need for a 21st-century, postdisciplinary liberal arts in higher education. The Association of American Colleges and Universities launched its American Commitments Project (1995) and made the same critical connections that John Dewey did between formal learning, service that builds democratic communities, and an active citizenship grounded in working out a diverse pluralism.

> We have reached the limits of an earlier conception of American society: monocultural, monochromatic, individualistic. As an older era ends and we struggle with alternative conceptions of the future, leadership is needed, at the level of principle, at the level of knowledge, at the level of building human capacities for associated living. The academy, which has already become a gathering place for American pluralisms, does not have the answer to all of these questions. But it is our mission to raise fundamental questions. (p. 7)

Schneider and Schoenberg (1998) identified five emerging goals of liberal learning to blur the intersections between what has been traditionally assigned to "general education" courses and to "majors": (a) acquiring intellectual skills or capacities; (b) understanding multiple modes of inquiry and approaches to knowledge; (c) developing societal, civic, and global knowledge; (d) gaining self-knowledge and grounded values; and (e) concentration and integration of learning.

What is new is the *a priori* assumption that institutions and society now blur differences between major field specialization and general education. The writing-across-the-curriculum movement was an early antidote to the compartmentalization of learning spawned by departmental specializations; in psychology, we grounded our writing activities in cognitive theory (Nodine, 1990), thereby enhancing their potential generalizability. The contemporary emphasis on critical thinking skills, amply and creatively described by authors in this book, builds on this potential for one discipline to yield general education outcomes. The challenge is to add broader and deeper dimensions to the matrix of psychology outcomes.

Psychology already has much diversity in its student populations, intellectual breadth in its scholar–teachers, and quantitative and qualitative methodologies to define and assess the integration of general education goals and major field outcomes. Consider that every year, psychology departments across the country award over 75,000 baccalaureates. The market for Introductory Psychology textbooks exceeds one million students every academic year; a significant subset of those students who major in other academic disciplines and professional fields also enroll in social, developmental, and abnormal psychology courses. How do we synergize and then measure the effects of the different life experiences, aspirations, and academic preparation in these forums? How do we help students to connect with one another and become autonomous individuals; to understand that all knowledge, even science, is contextualized; to learn the power of empathy; and to practice pluralism and not just analyze its antecedents and consequences? I do not think that disciplinary architectures were constructed to accomplish such integrated outcomes. To maintain its assertion of being one of the liberal arts, psychology must fashion a postdisciplinary future for the 21st century.

Klein (1999), a scholar of the philosophy and practice of interdisciplinarity, proposed the following desired outcomes for such programs: (a) greater tolerance of ambiguity and paradox; (b) sensitivity to ethical dimensions of issues; (c) ability to synthesize or integrate; (d) ability to demythologize experts; (e) humility and sensitivity to bias; (f) enlarged perspectives or horizons; (g) critical thinking and unconventional thinking; (h) empowerment; (i) creativity and original insights; and (j) ability to balance subjective and objective thinking (p. 19). To accomplish such outcomes requires a postdisciplinary perspective coupled with a continuing commitment to quantitative and qualitative assessment measures and innovative pedagogy.

The Psychology Partnerships Project brought together faculty from various types of institutions and levels of education. I propose that a postdisciplinary liberal arts strategy for teaching, learning, and assessing undergraduate psychology education will require building partnerships among scholar–teachers among many former disciplines. Our research activities have become increasingly multi-disciplinary in their players and methodologies. Our service activities are most often accomplished as members of cross-disciplinary teams and task forces. Teaching, as always, inspires our most creative energies; measuring up can be intrinsically rewarding. The challenge of lifelong learning will come from the liberal arts as we learn more from diverse lives and do so via the rich tradition that psychology offers.

REFERENCES

Association of American Colleges and Universities American Commitments Project Panel. (1995). *The drama and diversity of democracy*. Washington, DC: Author.

Astin, A. (1977). *Four critical years*. San Francisco: Jossey-Bass.

Astin, A. (1993). *What matters in college? Four critical years revisited*. San Francisco: Jossey-Bass.

Boltuck, M. A., Peterson, T. L., & Murphy, R. J. (1980). Preparing undergraduate psychology majors for employment in the human services delivery system. *Teaching of Psychology, 7*, 75–78.

Borden, V. M. H., & Rajecki, D. W. (2000). First-year employment outcomes of psychology baccalaureates: Relatedness, preparedness, and prospects. *Teaching of Psychology, 27*, 164–168.

Brewer, C. L., Hopkins, J. R., Kimble, G. A., Matlin, M. W., McCann, L. I., McNeil, O., et al. (1993). Curriculum. In T. V. McGovern (Ed.), *Handbook for enhancing undergraduate education in psychology* (pp. 161–182). Washington, DC: American Psychological Association.

Cates, J. (1973). Baccalaureates in psychology: 1969 & 1970. *American Psychologist, 28*, 262–264.

Denmark, F. L. (1994). Engendering psychology. *American Psychologist, 49*, 329–334.

Ewell, P. (2002). An emerging scholarship: A brief history of assessment. In T. Banta & Associates (Eds.), *Building a scholarship of assessment* (pp. 3–25). San Francisco: Jossey-Bass.

Feldman, K. A., & Newcomb, T. M. (1969). An analysis of four decades of research. In *The impact of college on students: Vol. 1*. San Francisco: Jossey-Bass.

Halonen, J. S. (1995). Demystifying critical thinking. *Teaching of Psychology, 22*, 75–81.

Halpern, D. F. (1988). Assessing student outcomes for psychology majors. *Teaching of Psychology, 15*, 181–186.

Halpern, D. F., Appleby, D. C., Beers, S. E., Cowan, C. L. Furedy, J. J., Halonen, J. S., et al. (1993). Targeting outcomes: Covering your assessment concerns and needs. In T. V. McGovern (Ed.), *Handbook for enhancing undergraduate education in psychology* (pp. 23–46). Washington, DC: American Psychological Association.

Halpern, D. F., & Nummedal, S. G. (Eds.). (1995). Psychologists teach critical thinking [Special issue]. *Teaching of Psychology, 22*(1).

Jackson, S. L., & Griggs, R. A. (1995). Assessing the psychology major: A national survey of undergraduate programs. *Teaching of Psychology, 22*, 241–243.

Klein, J. T. (1999). *Mapping interdisciplinary studies*. Washington, DC: Association of American Colleges and Universities.

Korn, J. H., Sweetman, M. B., & Nodine, B. F. (1996). An analysis of and commentary on consultants' reports on undergraduate psychology programs. *Teaching of Psychology, 23*, 14–19.

Kowalski, R. M. (2000). Including gender, race, and ethnicity in psychology content courses. *Teaching of Psychology, 27*, 18–24.

Kruger, D. J., & Zechmeister, E. B. (2001). A skills-experience inventory for the undergraduate psychology major. *Teaching of Psychology, 28*, 249–253.

Kulik, J. (1973). *Undergraduate education in psychology*. Washington, DC: American Psychological Association.

Lunneborg, P. W. (1986). Assessing students' career needs at a large state university. *Teaching of Psychology, 13*, 189–192.

Malin, J. T., & Timreck, C. (1979). Student goals and the undergraduate curriculum. *Teaching of Psychology, 6*, 136–139.

Matthews, J. R. (1982). Evaluation: A major challenge for the 1980s. *Teaching of Psychology, 9*, 49–52.

McCallum, L. W. (1983). Use of a senior comprehensive exam in evaluation of the psychology major. *Teaching of Psychology, 10*, 67–69.

McGahie, W. C., & Menges, R. J. (1975). Assessing self-directed learning. *Teaching of Psychology, 2*, 56–59.

McGovern, T. V. (1993) Transforming undergraduate psychology for the next century. In T. V. McGovern (Ed.), *Handbook for enhancing undergraduate education in psychology* (pp. 217–238). Washington, DC: American Psychological Association.

McGovern, T. V., & Brewer, C. L. (2003). Undergraduate education. In D. K. Freedheim (Ed.), *History of psychology* (pp. 465–481). Volume 1 in I. B. Weiner (Editor-in-Chief), *Handbook of psychology*. New York: Wiley.

McGovern, T. V., & Carr, K. F. (1989). Carving out the niche: A review of alumni surveys on undergraduate psychology majors. *Teaching of Psychology, 16*, 52–57.

McGovern, T. V., Furumoto, L., Halpern, D. F., Kimble, G. A., & McKeachie, W. J. (1991). Liberal education, study in depth, and the arts and sciences major— psychology. *American Psychologist, 46*, 598–605.

McGovern, T. V., & Hawks, B. K. (1984). Transitions and renewal of an undergraduate psychology program. *Teaching of Psychology, 11*, 70–75.

McGovern, T. V., & Hawks, B. K. (1986). The varieties of undergraduate experience. *Teaching of Psychology, 13*, 174–181.

McGovern, T. V., & Reich, J. N. (1996). A comment on the quality principles. *American Psychologist, 51*, 252–255.

McGuigan, F. J. (1974). Amount learned: An empirical basis for grading teachers and students. *Teaching of Psychology, 1*, 10–15.

McKeachie, W. J. (1982). Undergraduate education in psychology from the 1950s to the 1990s. *Teaching of Psychology, 9*, 62–63.

McKeachie, W. J., & Milholland, J. E. (1961). *Undergraduate curricula in psychology*. Glenview, IL: Scott, Foresman.

Metzner, B. S., Rajecki, D. W., & Lauer, J. B. (1994). New majors and the feminization of psychology: Testing and extending the Rajecki-Metzner model. *Teaching of Psychology, 21*, 5–11.

Morgan, B. L., & Johnson, E. J. (1997). Using a senior seminar for assessing the psychology major. *Teaching of Psychology, 24*, 156–159.

Nodine, B. F. (Ed.). (1990). Psychologists teach writing [Special issue]. *Teaching of Psychology, 17*(1).

Nowaczyk, R. H., & Frey, J. D. (1982). Factors related to performance on the GRE Advanced Psychology test. *Teaching of Psychology, 9*, 163–165.

Nummedal, S. G., Benson, J. B., & Chew, S. L. (2002). Disciplinary styles in the scholarship of teaching and learning: A view from psychology. In M. T. Huber & S. P. Morreale (Eds.), *Disciplinary styles in the scholarship of teaching and learning: Exploring common ground* (pp. 163–179). Washington, DC: American Association for Higher Education.

O'Campo, C., Prieto, L. R., Whittlesey, V., Connor, J., Janco-Gidley, J., Mannix, S., & Sare, K. (2003). Diversity research in *Teaching of Psychology*: Summary and recommendations. *Teaching of Psychology, 30*, 5–18.

Pascarella, E. T., & Terenzini, P. T. (1991). *How college affects students: Findings and insight from twenty years of research*. San Francisco: Jossey-Bass.

Perlman, B., & McCann, L. I. (1999a). The most frequently listed courses in the undergraduate psychology curriculum. *Teaching of Psychology, 26*, 177–182.

Perlman, B., & McCann, L. I. (1999b). The structure of the undergraduate psychology curriculum. *Teaching of Psychology, 26*, 171–176.

Puente, A. E., Blanch, E., Candland, D. K., Denmark, F. L., Laman, C., Lutsky, N., et al. (1993). Toward a psychology of variance: Increasing the presence and understanding of ethnic minorities in psychology. In T. V. McGovern (Ed.), *Handbook for enhancing undergraduate education in psychology* (pp. 71–82). Washington, DC: American Psychological Association.

Pusateri, T. P. (2002). A decade of changes since the St. Mary's Conference: An interview with Thomas V. McGovern. *Teaching of Psychology, 29*, 76–82.

Rajecki, D. W., & Metzner, B. S. (1991). Declaring the psychology major: An archival, general model from an urban university. *Teaching of Psychology, 16*, 4–8.

Ratcliff, J. L. (1997). What is a curriculum and what should it be? In J. G. Gaff, J. L. Ratcliff, and Associates (Eds.), *Handbook of the undergraduate curriculum: A comprehensive guide to purposes, structures, practices, and change* (pp. 5–29). San Francisco: Jossey-Bass.

Schneider, C. G., & Schoenberg, R. (1998). *Contemporary understandings of liberal education*. Washington, DC: Association of American Colleges.

Sheehan, E. P. (1994). A multimethod assessment of the psychology major. *Teaching of Psychology, 21*, 74–78.

Simoni, J. M., Sexton-Radek, K., Yescavage, K., Richard, H., & Lundquist, A. (1999). Teaching diversity: Experiences and recommendations of American Psychological Association Division 2 members. *Teaching of Psychology, 26*, 89–95.

Stoloff, M. L., & Feeney, K. J. (2002). The Major Field Test as an assessment tool for an undergraduate psychology program. *Teaching of Psychology, 29*, 92–98.

Sue, D. W., Bingham, R. P., Porche-Burke, L., & Vasquez, M. (1999). The diversification of psychology: A multicultural revolution. *American Psychologist, 54,* 1061–1069.

Veysey, L. (1973). Stability and experiment in the American undergraduate curriculum. In C. Kaysen (Ed.), *Content and context: Essays on college education* (pp. 1–63). New York: McGraw-Hill.

Walker, W. E., Newcomb, A. F., & Hopkins, W. P. (1987). A model for curriculum evaluation and revision in undergraduate psychology programs. *Teaching of Psychology, 14,* 198–202.

Ware, M. E. (1986). Assessing students' career needs at a small private university. *Teaching of Psychology, 13,* 185–187.

AUTHOR INDEX

Carrier, L. M., 198, *199*
Cates, J., 262, *272*
Chew, S. L., 269, *274*
Chickering, G. A., *162*
Chickering, A. W., 125, *140*
Christopher, A. N., 142, *162*
Clay, S., 9, 142, 143, 145, 147–149, 151, 153, 155, 156, *162*, 172, 174, 175, 182, *186*
Clinkenbeard, P., 120, *124*
College Board, 215, 217, *224*
Connor, J., 269, *274*
Connor-Greene, P. A., 142, *162*
Cooledge, J., 193, *199*
Cooledge, N., 193, *199*
Council for Higher Education Accreditation, 12, *26*
Covington, M. V., 128, *140*
Cowan, C. L., 9, *26*, *272*
Cowie, B., 129, 130, *140*
Crawford, C., 9, 19, 22, *25*
Crawford, M., 34, *46*
Cromwell, L., *10*
Cross, K., *61*
Cross, P. K., 183, *186*
Crowell, C., 236, *241*
Curry, W., 25, *26*

Dallas TeleCollege, *239*
Davis, S., 59, *62*
Deegan, J., 9, 19, 22, *25*, 217, *223*
Denmark, F. L., 269, *272*, *274*
Diez, M., *10*
Dillinger, R., 59, *62*
Doherty, A., *10*, 22, *26*, *162*
Doyle, D. P., 15, *26*
Dressel, P., 160, *162*
Duffy, D. K., 244n1, *255*, *256*
Dunn, D. S., 9, *186*

Easterbrook, J. A., 98, *103*
Educational Testing Services, *224*
Eison, J. A., 160, *162*
El-Khawas, E., *61*
Englehart, M. B., 128, *140*
Erwin, T. D., 42, *45*
Ewell, P., *61*, 262, *272*

Farris, E., 225, *240*
Fast, J., 232, *239*
Feeney, K. J., 33, 39, *46*, 73, 80, 213, *224*, 264, *274*

Feinburg, S., 93, *103*
Feldman, K. A., 260, *272*
Ferrari, M., 120, *124*
Figuli, D. J., 95, *103*
Finley, M. L., 185, *186*
Fleming, S., 213, *224*
Fonzi, G. L., 37, *46*
Forsythe, G. B., 114, *124*
Freed, J. E., 254, 255, 256
Frey, J. D., *274*
Fried, S. B., 233, 237, *240*
Friedlich, J., *84*
Furco, A., 244, *256*
Furedy, J. J., 9, *26*, *272*
Furomoto, L.,
Furst, E. J., 128, *140*
Furumoto, L., 19, *26*, 32, *46*, 48, *62*, *84*, 189, 194, 200, 264, *273*

Gamson, Z. F., 125, *140*
Gardner, H., 113, *123*, *124*
Garhart, C., 50, *62*
Gelman, S., 232, *239*
Gerrity, D. M., 212, *224*
Gibelman, M., 232, *239*
Gillem, A., 47, *62*
Gillem, A. R., *45*, *104*, 191, *199*
Gillese, E., 139, *140*
Golden, A., 213, *224*
Graham, S. E., 4, 9, 72, *79*
Granrud, C. E., 4, *10*
Griggs, R. A., 72, *79*, *84*, 264, *272*
Grigorenko, E. L., 113, 114, 120, *124*
Grubb, A., 230, *239*

Hacker, D. J., 51, *62*
Hager, E., 25, *26*
Haidt, J., 246, *256*
Halonen, J., 47, *62*
Halonen, J. S., 7, 9, *26*, 32, *45*, 95, *104*, 142, 143, 145, 147–149, 151, 153, 155–157, *162*, 172, 174, 175, 182, *186*, 191, 194, *199*, 264, *272*
Halpern, D., 9, *45*, 47–48, *104*, 171, 189, 191, 194, *199*, 200
Halpern, D. F., 4, 9, 14, 16–17, 19–20, 22, 25, *26*, 32, *46*, 65, 69, *79*, *84*, *162*, 263, 264, *272*, *273*
Hannafin, M., 51, *62*
Hansford, S., 188, *200*
Harasim, L. M., 230, *239*, *240*
Hardy, M. S., 142, *162*

SUBJECT INDEX

ABOUT THE EDITORS

Dana S. Dunn, PhD, is a social psychologist and professor of psychology at Moravian College in Bethlehem, Pennsylvania. He received his PhD from the University of Virginia in 1987. A Fellow of the American Psychological Association (APA), Dunn is active in the Society for the Teaching of Psychology and a participant in the 1999 APA-sponsored Psychology Partnerships Project (P3). His research and writing interests include the teaching of psychology, social psychology, and rehabilitation psychology. He is the author of three previous books: *The Practical Researcher, Statistics and Data Analysis for the Behavioral Sciences*, and *A Short Guide to Writing About Psychology*.

Chandra, M. Mehrotra, PhD, is professor of psychology and dean of special projects at The College of St. Scholastica in Duluth, MN. He received his PhD from The Ohio State University in 1968. He is a Fellow of the Division 2 and Division 20 of the APA. Dr. Mehrotra received his College's Distinguished Teaching Award in 1979 and the APA Division 20 Mentor Award in 2003. Since 1998 he has directed a research training program for college teachers in the psychology of aging. In 2003 he co-founded the Institute on Aging and Social Work. He has received major support from the National Science Foundation, and the National Institute on Aging, National Institutes of Health. His research and writing interests include program evaluation, faculty development, and the psychology of aging. He is co-author of the books *Distance Learning* and *Aging and Diversity* and editor of *Teaching and Aging*.

Jane S. Halonen, PhD, is dean of the College of Arts and Sciences at the University of West Florida in Pensacola. She was formerly a professor and director of the school of psychology at James Madison University in Harrisonburg, Virginia, and professor at Alverno College in Milwaukee,

Wisconsin. She received her PhD from the University of Wisconsin—Milwaukee in 1980. A Fellow of the APA, she is former president of the Society for Teaching of Psychology and the Council of Teachers of Undergraduate Psychology. Halonen is the author of five previous books, including *Teaching Critical Thinking in Psychology* and *Teaching Social Interaction at Alverno*. She received the American Psychological Foundation's Distinguished Teaching Award in 2000 and was named an Eminent Woman in Psychology by the APA in 2003.